I Too Have Some Dreams

SOUTH ASIA ACROSS THE DISCIPLINES

Edited by Muzaffar Alam, Robert Goldman, and Gauri Viswanathan

Dipesh Chakrabarty, Sheldon Pollock, and Sanjay Subrahmanyam, Founding Editors

Funded by a grant from the Andrew W. Mellon Foundation and jointly published by the University of California Press, the University of Chicago Press, and Columbia University Press

For a list of books in the series, see page 271.

I Too Have Some Dreams

N. M. RASHED AND MODERNISM IN URDU POETRY

A. Sean Pue

UNIVERSITY OF CALIFORNIA PRESS

University of California Press, one of the most distinguished university presses in the United States, enriches lives around the world by advancing scholarship in the humanities, social sciences, and natural sciences. Its activities are supported by the UC Press Foundation and by philanthropic contributions from individuals and institutions. For more information, visit www.ucpress.edu.

University of California Press
Oakland, California

Library of Congress Cataloging-in-Publication Data

Pue, A. Sean, 1975–.
I too have some dreams : N.M. Rashed and modernism in Urdu poetry / A. Sean Pue.
pages cm. — (South Asia across the disciplines)
Includes bibliographical references and index.
ISBN 978-0-520-28310-7
1. Rashid, N.M., 1910–1975—Criticism and interpretation. I. Title.
PK2200.R333Z83 2014
891.4'3916—dc23

2014002560

23 22 21 20 19 18 17 16 15 14
10 9 8 7 6 5 4 3 2 1

CONTENTS

ACKNOWLEDGMENTS

One of the subjects of this book is the transnational Urdu literary community, which has endured nearly constant strain. Nevertheless, I remain in awe of its vibrancy, hospitality, scholarship, creativity, and passion. And I am very grateful for the incredible generosity of many people and institutions that have aided me. Completing this book has been a challenging but very rewarding experience, and I must thank the friends, colleagues, and acquaintances who have made it so worthwhile.

I decided to work on N. M. Rashed while reading the poem "*Dil, mire ṣaḥrā-navard-e pīr dil*" (Heart, My Old Desert-Wandering Heart, §18) as a second-year graduate student while studying with my PhD advisor, Frances W. Pritchett, now Professor Emerita of Columbia University. At that time, I was deeply engaged in the study of Persian, and my other graduate advisor, Hamid Dabashi, was sitting with me every week to read Rumi's *Mas̤navī*. I had a very strong aesthetic reaction to Rashed's desert poetry, and it also seemed to unify my interests in the twentieth century, Urdu poetry, Persian, and critical theory. I followed Rashed's poem to my dissertation project, which came to focus on his entire oeuvre. I am indebted to Frances Pritchett for her kindness and generosity, and I thank her for reading so many drafts of this work. Her love of literature, especially Urdu poetry, is always rejuvenating. Hamid Dabashi, Janaki Bakhle, and Jack Hawley also generously shared their insights and time with me. This book is written in memory of Aditya Behl, who was my first Hindi and Urdu teacher, my undergraduate advisor at UC Berkeley, and who guided me through the dissertation process as well. I blame him entirely for luring me to the study of Urdu poetry, as well as to the academic life, through his extraordinary erudition and contagious passion for literature.

As a graduate student, I spent a year researching in India on a Fulbright Hays-DDRA fellowship. I was affiliated with the Department of Urdu at Jamia Millia Islamia in New Delhi. Qazi O. Rehman Hashmi, Mohammad Zakir, the staff of the Zakir Husain library, and especially Shamim Hanfi were very helpful while I was there. The Anjuman-e Taraqqī-e Urdū also provided me with great hospitality and the use of their library. In Hyderabad, I am thankful to have received access to the Urdu Research Centre collection at Sundarayya Vignana Kendram. I must also express my deep gratitude to Shamsur Rahman Faruqi and to the late Mughanni Tabassum for their assistance.

The American Institute of Pakistan Studies funded my presentation of portions of this work in Philadelphia and Heidelberg and later provided me with a Short Term Lecturing and Research fellowship to work in Lahore and Islamabad in 2011. I arrived at a salutary time, and was able to attend several events commemorating the centennial birth anniversary of poet Faiz Ahmad Faiz and collect materials from N. M. Rashed's birth centenary that had been published the previous year. I thank the Lahore University of Management Sciences' School of Humanities and Social Sciences, where I was affiliated, as well as the indefatigable staff of AIPS. I am very grateful to my host and old friend Nomanul Haq, as well as to my new friend and guide to the fabulous Lahore literary scene, Ahmed Atta. Salimur Rahman kindly read through my translations and let me join in his group discussions of world literature. I must also thank Ziya-ul-Hassan, Tehsin Firaqi, Saadat Saeed, Yasmeen Hameed, Ghulam Hussain Sajid, and Fakhr-ul-Haq Noori. In Islamabad, I am grateful to Iftikhar Arif, Kishwar Naheed, Fateh Muhammad Malik, and Haris Khalique for their insights into Rashed's poetry.

Rashed's daughter Yasmin Hassan kindly met with me in Montreal to discuss her father. She also allowed me access to his papers; Pasha Muhammad Khan helped facilitate this, and I thank him for that. I am grateful to Nurjahan Akhlaq for permission to reproduce her father's beautiful work on the book's cover, and to Hammad Nassar and Anita Dawood for introducing us and providing a publication-quality image.

C. M. Naim, Kamran Asdar Ali, Geeta Patel, Jeff Gatrall, Carla Petievich, Nosheen Ali, and Sara Mirza Bano all made invaluable comments on my project, and I thank them for their insights and support.

Michigan State University has generously supported my research travel and, even more importantly, given me time to write. For their assistance, I thank the College of Arts and Letters as well as the Muslim Studies Program, one of the most vibrant parts of our academic community.

Earlier versions of sections of the introduction and chapters 2, 3, and 4 appeared in the following articles: "Time is God: Temporality in Pakistani Modernism," *Journal of Commonwealth and Postcolonial Studies* (2009); "In the Mirror of Ghalib: Postcolonial Reflections on Indo-Muslim Selfhood," *Indian Economic and Social History Review* (2011); "N. M. Rashed and Faiz Ahmed Faiz: A Comparative Analysis," *Bunyaad* (2011); "Ephemeral Asia: N. M. Rashed's *A Stranger in Iran*," *Comparative Literature* (2012); and "Rethinking Modernism and Progressivism in Urdu Poetry," *Pakistaniaat* (2013).

I am thankful that the editors of the South Asia Across the Disciplines series saw the value of this project and efficiently shepherded it through the review process. I thank the two anonymous reviewers for their excellent comments and correctives on the manuscript, though of course all remaining faults are my own. The acquisition editor at UC Press, Reed Malcolm, and his assistant, Stacy Eisenstark, have been flawless in their support. I also thank the production team, Francisco Reinking, Brian Ostrander, and Susan Campbell.

I am very grateful to my family and friends who have made the long journey of finishing this book more than bearable. My parents and sister, as well as my extended family and families-in-law, have offered their unending support.

Finally, I thank my brilliant wife and best friend, Karin Zitzewitz, who has offered innumerable insights, always insisted on clarity of argument, and saved many translations from falling into the interlingual abyss. This book is dedicated to her and our daughter, Clara, who shows great promise as a scholar of Braj Bhasha, among other things.

NOTE ON TRANSLITERATION

The transliteration system used in this book attempts to convey both the orthography and the pronunciation of the Urdu and Persian texts.

The transliteration of vowel sounds and letters is standard—*a*, *i*, *u*, *ā*, *ī*, *e*, *ai*, *ū*, *o*, and *au*. The letter *alif maqṣūrah,* pronounced "ā," is indicated as *â*. Cases where a long vowel is pronounced but not written are sometimes indicated as *ĕ* or *ŏ*. The *iẓāfat* is indicated as *-e* at the end of a word.

The transliteration used for consonants is fairly standard for Urdu texts. A consonant's aspiration, represented by *do-chashmī he* in Urdu, is indicated by a following *h*, as in *k*, *kh*, *g*, *gh*, *ch*, *chh*, *j*, *jh*; retroflex *ṭ*, *ṭh*, *ḍ*, *ḍh*; dental *t*, *th*, *d*, *dh*; and *p*, *ph*, *b*, *bh*. The retroflex flap is *ṛ*, differentiated from *r*, and its aspirated form is *ṛh*. Otherwise, *h* represents the letter *he*, which is often silent at the end of words. The letter *baṛī ḥe*, also pronounced "h," is *ḥ*. Other consonants include *f*, *q*, *y*, and *l*. The three "s"-sound letters are: *sīn* as *s*, *ṡe* as *ṡ*, and *ṣvād* as *ṣ*. *Shīn* is *sh*. For the "z"-sound letters, *ze* is *z*, *żāl* is *ż*, *ẓuʾād* is *ẓ*, and *z̤oʾe* is *z̤*. The rare letter *zhe* is indicated as *zh*. The letter *ʿain*, which in Urdu is not usually pronounced, is indicated as ʿ. The letter *hamzah*, which indicates the presence of a vowel, is ʾ. When necessary, a straight quotation mark signals a break between consonants, as in *ib'hām*. The fricatives *k͟he* and *ġhain* are indicated as *k͟h* and *ġh*. The letter *nūn* is transliterated as *n*, and the letter *nūn-e ġhunnā* as *ñ*. It indicates either a nasal consonant or the nasalization of the previous vowel, working much like the *bindī* in *devanāgarī*. The consonant form of the letter *vāʾo* is indicated as *v*, and it is usually silent in words like *k͟hvāb* and *k͟hvāhish*.

Proper names usually follow preferred English-language spellings in the text, but are transliterated in the references.

Introduction

ai ʿishq-e azal-gīr-o-abad-tāb, mere bhī haiñ kuchh ḳhvāb
mere bhī haiñ kuchh ḳhvāb!
is daur se, is daur ke sūkhe hu'e daryā'oñ se,
phaile hu'e ṣaḥrā'oñ se, aur shahroñ ke vīrānoñ se
vīrānah-garoñ se maiñ ḥazīñ aur udās!
ai ʿishq-e azal-gīr-o-abad-tāb
mere bhī haiñ kuchh ḳhvāb!

O love, embracing the Beginning and illuminating the End,
I too have some dreams
I too have some dreams!
This age, the dried-out rivers of this age,
the outspread deserts, the ruins of cities,
their destroyers leave me sad and forlorn!
O love, embracing the Beginning and illuminating the End,
I too have some dreams!

THE LINES ABOVE, from the free-verse poem "I Too Have Some Dreams" (Mere bhī haiñ kuchh ḳhvāb) by N. M. Rashed (Nażr-e Muḥammad Rāshid, 1910–1975), introduce the central concerns of a crucial figure in the history of poetic modernism in Urdu. The passage describes the forces of ruination in an age in which the rivers have run dry and cities have returned to desert or been ravaged by human destruction. Against these forces of desolation, the narrator calls out to "love," asserting that he still has his own dreams. In the remainder of the poem, the narrator notes the mutability of the present and the future, and the possibility, if not the certainty, of newness and change in the world. The dreams he describes relate to beauty, to place, to language, to tradition, to the new, to community, and to being "human." This poem articulates the ambitions of the author for his poetry.

The poem further illustrates the manner in which Urdu poetry is enmeshed in a politics of language. Its opening line is divided into two phrases, the first of which *(ai ʿishq-e azal-gīr-o-abad-tāb)* is entirely comprehensible in Persian, while the second *(mere bhī haiñ kuchh ḳhvāb)* is in a *bolchāl* (spoken language) idiom. Sometimes referred to as Hindustani, this spoken language is shared by both Urdu and what is now Modern Standard, or *khaṛī bolī,* Hindi. The poem demonstrates how Hindi and Urdu are, for all intents and purposes, spectrums of one language written in two scripts.[1] Subject to language reform movements for much of their modern history, the two languages became attached to religious communities across the nineteenth century. Urdu, shot through by Persian vocabulary and poetics, transformed into the language of a Muslim minority, and Hindi, studded with Sanskrit words, became a national language of a Hindu majority. Urdu would become the national language of Pakistan following the violent Partition of British India in 1947, while Hindi was adopted by the postcolonial Indian state.

In this poem and throughout his larger oeuvre, N. M. Rashed emphasized the composite nature of Urdu and asserted the indigeneity, not the foreignness, of "Persian" aesthetics, as this poem makes clear both in terms of meter and lexicon. Though not confined by rhyme or a fixed number of metrical feet, the poem maintains the basic outlines of Urdu and Persian meter, derived from the prosody of Arabic and distinct from the Sanskrit and Braj Bhāshā metrics adopted and transformed in modern Hindi poetry from the early twentieth century on.[2] Rashed's poem maintains these links despite being an example of what is called *āzād naẓm*, or "free verse" in Urdu, which Rashed pioneered and popularized at the end of the 1930s. While breaking with classical forms, such as the ghazal,[3] Rashed's poetry mines the histories of language.

The composite nature of the language of Urdu makes it impossible to read this literature in isolation from other languages. Rashed's poetry demands a comparative and multilingual methodology. The genealogy of thought this poetry participates in is similarly rich.[4] Take, for instance, the opening line of this poem, "O love, embracing the Beginning and illuminating the End, I too have some dreams." The words *azal* and *abad*, translated as "Beginning" and "End," refer to the eternities on either side of time. Both terms most probably derive from the Middle Persian language of Pahlavi, signaling an encounter with the temporal understandings of Zoroastrianism. Also, the term used for "love" *(ʿishq)* in this poem brings to mind a worldview often associated with *taṣavvuf* (Sufism) according to which the universe is created out of and sustained by divine love. While Sufism is certainly a polyvocal phenomenon, frequently more worldly and collective than transcendent and individual, its "mystical" conventions feature quite prominently in classical Persian and Urdu poetry, especially the ghazal.[5] For readers familiar with modern texts, *ʿishq* also invokes the poetry of Muḥammad Iqbāl (1877–1938), an Islamic modernist and Persian and Urdu poet credited as the spiritual father of Pakistan. Iqbal, a critic of many of the worldly and mystical practices of Sufism, repurposed love as an active force of creation, writing in dialogue with the vitalism of Henri Bergson. Finally, the line invokes a wide set of possible ideas about dreams, including, for readers familiar with Rashed's poetry, Freudian ideas of the unconscious. The poetry is dense with intertextual and linguistic references.

Rashed's poetry therefore demands a very sophisticated form of close reading that is grounded in text and in context. It also demands attention to his formal experimentation. Rashed's modernism was guided by a vision of the purpose of literature that was unique in the history of Urdu writing in the twentieth century, but that also challenges a number of contemporary modes of understanding the significance of non-Western literature. Rashed's writing decisively opposes the reading of literature as representative of communities or contributing to identitarian politics. This aspect of Rashed's poetry also sits uneasily within Urdu- and Hindi-language criticism and histories of literature.

Rashed's poems use both markedly Persian elements and the common speech associated with Hindustani, resisting the naturalized association of languages to peoples. His poetry recasts the formal conventions and traditional worldview of Urdu poetry from within, infusing them with other modes of analysis, often taken from Western modes of thought. Aspects of Muslim thought and Islamicate references are found throughout Rashed's poetry, but they are typically reworked in creative ways. In his own modernist self-presentation, whether in critical writings or in the manifesto-esque introductions to his own works, Rashed rejected the conservative forms of traditionalism that were prevalent in Pakistani Urdu letters and instead projected himself as an avant-garde modernist rupturing with tradition.

Rashed's modernism was defined by his profound distrust of collective forms of identity. He instead celebrated poetry as a site for articulating individual dreams. In critical writings and in his poems he argues for individual experience over collective belonging, whether in the form of the nation-state, religious identity, or restrictive ideological commitments, including traditionalism and socialism. In their place, as in "I Too Have Some Dreams," he emphasized the value of individual perception and critical insight. A focus on individual experience over ideological determination is a defining feature of modernism in South Asia, as elsewhere. Yet it should be noted that there is no lack of collectivity in his poetry. In the quotation with which I began, as in his later work especially, he visualizes collective life in the form of a city or cities, or a shared secular space, rather than as a national, ideological, or religious community.

Rashed's focus on individualism and criticism of identitarianism is best understood as emerging from the trenchant criticism of empire and domination that pervades his poetry in various forms throughout his oeuvre. While his criticism of British colonialism in his earlier work is obvious to all but the most contrary of readers, his inhabitance of an anti-identitarian position is most thoroughly developed in his poems about World War II and the devastation of the Partition of British India, which highlight the terror and violence of modern forms of identity. After the formation of Pakistan, *vaṭ̤an* (homeland) largely disappears from his published work. Instead, he turns, as in this poem, to "the outspread deserts, the ruins of cities / their destroyers." He offers the possibility of new dreams, the mutability of the present and future, and of the "new celebration of Man's birth."

In post-Partition works, Rashed's earlier focus on embodiment transforms into a criticism of forms of belonging grounded in ideas of religious transcendence. This is particularly the case in poems opposing national teleology, especially the promise of Pakistan as in line with a divine mission. As in the poem excerpt above, Rashed's poetry maintains a proximity to religious discourse, even as it refutes the Islamic modernism of thinkers like Iqbal from a secular position. The final chapters of this book examine Rashed's turn to a modernist form of allegory as a means to imagine an ideal form of collectivity, addressing a transnational Urdu literary community. They chart the adjustments in the address of Rashed's poetry to take into account the changing status of religious and national identity in the Pakistan of the 1960s.

Although this study is divided both chronologically and thematically, Rashed's poetry holds together as a body of work, and it is rewarding to see how his aesthetic project was shaped by a changing historical and cultural context. One of the challenges of writing about a single author, especially a poet like Rashed who kept reforming his work in style and content, is to chart how modernism changes dynamically over several decades. This book is about the history of the possibility of modernism in Urdu poetry, and in South Asia more broadly, across the twentieth century, as particular avenues closed and opened.

WHAT IS MODERNISM IN URDU POETRY?

The assertion that Urdu modernism developed in ways both meaningful and innovative, rather than artificial and derivative of European models, should no longer be surprising to contemporary Anglophone readers. Over the last two decades, works in the field of (New) Modernist Studies have expanded the study and definition of the ever-elusive term "modernism" in temporal, spatial, social, lingual, textual, and disciplinary directions.[6] These works have challenged the standard time frame of modernism, expanded its canon, emphasized the significance of multilingualism and translation, and moved modernism's study out of an exclusive domain of the aesthetic and into a "sociocultural matrix."[7] Yet academic studies of South Asian modernist literature have continued to lag behind studies of postmodern—and often diasporic—Anglophone literature. Modernist literature had distinctly different aesthetics, however. This study traces the emergence of a modernist aesthetic across the late colonial and early postcolonial eras.[8]

This book considers the definition of modernism in South Asia through an analysis of Rashed's richly intertextual poetic work. Modernism for Rashed involved establishing a new relationship with an Urdu poetic tradition that had come to be viewed both as a site of moral corruption in need of reform and as a source of authenticity and of difference. Through literary experimentation, Rashed sought to develop an aesthetic that would be open to contemporary experience and modern thought while also remaining intelligible and recognizable as Urdu poetry. His literary experimentation involved a notion of individualism, the promotion of new reading practices, and the universalism of modern experience in ways that anticipate theorizations of the "global" or "planetary" in what has been called "geomodernism" in modernist studies.

Rashed became a standard-bearer of modernism in Urdu, and his work was judged, sometimes in large part, as a representation of a modernist approach to literature. In the chapters that follow, I detail the critical reception of Rashed's work at particular historical moments. But Rashed's critical presentations of his own volumes of poetry provide a good sense of what was at stake overall for the author in promoting a modernist aesthetic. The introductions to his volumes read as defensive and arrogant; in one text, he condemns those who dislike the "melody" of modern poetry as simply stuck in the past.[9] But the introductions also accurately anticipate the major criticisms of his work: characterizations of his poetry as insufficiently social, as unsuitable for performance, as unconnected with political or religious projects, and as distant from his literary or national community.

In the introduction to his first volume, Rashed justifies his literary experimentation by emphasizing its place in the life of the community, preempting the critique that his poetry is insufficiently social. He argues there that the advancement of a "community/nation" *(qaum)* cannot happen "when literature is deprived of new experiences/experiments *(tajribāt)*."[10] Experimentation and individualism are united here, and he stresses the need in literature, as in the community, for action and for individualism over languor and religious otherworldliness or identification. The goal of modern poetry for Rashed is to find a style that can reveal an author's individuality with the heroic aim of revitalizing the community and its literature, not of destroying the old just for the sake of destruction. Describing and justifying his own style at length, he argues that poetry should continue to be affective while also breaking with literary convention.

Rashed also anticipated the criticism of his work, both as free verse and as written abroad, for its distance from the *mushāʿirah*, or poetic gathering, at which Urdu poetry is often debuted. In the introduction to his second work, published while he was living in New York, he declared that the modern poet was no longer a part of society, as he was in the premodern period. The individuality of the modern writer is linked to what Rashed describes as the breakdown of the *mushāʿirah*, which leaves the contemporary writer to reflect more on the depths of the human psyche than did the writers of the past.[11] Establishing writing as a solitary enterprise also permitted Rashed, who spent most of the latter half of his life abroad, to continue to participate in a reading public rather than in a public constructed around performance.

Rashed associated modernism with a critique of ideology, and he wrote sharply against both religious and Marxist critics of his work. Beginning with his second volume, his most important claim for literature was that it should be free from any external ideological program, whether of a religious group or a political party.[12] Instead, he argued that the poet should give answer to "life" in all its manifestations, based on his own "internal and external experiences." What is significant here is that Rashed is not only challenging what he would call "ideological" poetry, written under an "external precept," but is also emphasizing a model of artistic subjectivity that takes into account the murkiness of internal life, as opposed to just a rationally ordered subjectivity, as is frequently the case in realism and secular nationalism. In place of an experience of the soul, as in religious writing, he stresses the topic of literature to be the "self" of humankind, "error-prone" and "lost" as it may be.[13]

Finally, Rashed also challenged the assumption that his diasporic writing should reflect exclusively on the experiences of his national and literary community by arguing against the confinement of thought or of art to a particular locality. He first articulated a position against the constraints of thought to a particular territory in his first volume, as he argued that modern poetry must embrace nontraditional, global modes of understanding.[14] In his third volume, he wrote against the assumption that the poet must "write about some country or some thing," outlining a process of abstraction. His focus was more properly "circumstances" themselves, which are not necessarily unique to a particular geographical or historical context. He argues in this sense that the poet of one country is not different from that of another, as all bear a responsibility before a "vaster humanity." At the same time, Rashed defended his work against the charge of "distance" from his community by stressing that the "vision" of a poet always has certain local roots in some "present and immediate reality." Yet that vision is not confined to those circumstances, or to a particular nation, as the poet's vision extends not only to what is absent in the world but to what "should be present" in it.[15]

With its emphasis on critical individuality, experience, and a dispersed reading public, Rashed's conception of modernism largely aligns with what contemporary theorists have identified as "geomodernism."[16] His modernism is rooted in place yet also disruptive of local poetics and open to the world beyond the nation, especially to what Laura Doyle has described as a "geopolitical history" of "multiple empires and multiple resistance movements." In other words, it attends to the ongoing imperial settings of modernist style, as noted by Edward Said among others.[17] Rather than just addressing Pakistan or South Asia, Rashed's modernism aligns with an understanding of geomodernist writers whose "horizon is global and [whose] voicing is refracted through the local-global dialectic of inside and outside, belonging and exile, in ways that disrupt conventional poetics."[18]

At the same time, in its creative use of Urdu's linguistic range, Rashed's poetry asserts a regional modernism, with clear links to South Asia and the Middle East. It is in this way that Rashed's poetry differs from this self-presentation: his work does not discard Urdu literary tradition so much as disrupt it. Particularly in his last two volumes, this disruption is facilitated by the poetry's engagement with global forms of thought. The major transformation one sees in later works is a shift from capturing experience to capturing thought, in a way that challenges tradition and articulates new dreams of liberation for the present and future.

N. M. RASHED: BIOGRAPHY

N. M. Rashed was born in the Punjab on August 1, 1910, in the town of Akalgarh, in the district of Gujranwala, now in Pakistan. His mother tongue was Punjabi, and he received his education in Urdu, English, and Persian. His father, Rājah Faẓl-e Ilâhī Chishtī, was an inspector of schools and a follower of Sufism. His mother is remembered as a pious woman, and also an interpreter of dreams. In biographies of the poet, this is often presented as a melding of modernity and tradition. Rashed's grandfather, Dr. Ġhulām Rasūl Ġhulāmī, a poet in both Urdu and Persian, played an important role in his early education.[19] Rashed excelled at his studies, and he began composing Urdu poetry at an early age.

Rashed attended Government College in the city of Lahore, where he received a BA with honors in Persian in 1930 and an MA in economics in 1932. He quickly established himself within the literary circles of Government College, editing the college magazine *Rāvī* and pioneering free verse.[20] He studied English literature with Ahmed Shah "Patras" Bokhari (1898–1958), a popular writer and Cambridge graduate, who would later become Rashed's superior both at All India Radio and at the United Nations.

Following his graduation, Rashed attempted to make a living out of literature and tutoring, but eventually had to take a job at the commissioner's office in Multan. In December 1935, he married his maternal cousin, Ṣafiyah.[21] While working in Multan, Rashed became an active member of the primarily Muslim Ḳhāksār movement, which emphasized military-style discipline and social service and aspired to free India from the British.[22] Rashed's involvement in this organization was enthusiastic, but brief.[23] As I will discuss later, though his family members and friends remembered the poet's opposition to the movement's regimentation, later writers have seen his involvement as proof of his ever-present Muslim consciousness.

Like many South Asian literati of his generation, Rashed began a career in radio and then joined the army. From 1939 to 1941, he worked at All India Radio, first at Lahore and then in Delhi. There he published his first collection of poetry, entitled *Māvarā* (The Beyond) in 1941. From 1943 until 1947, he took up a temporary army commission with the rank of captain in the Inter-Services Public Relations Directorate of the British Indian Army.[24] He began in Delhi, and then spent time in Iraq, Iran, Egypt, Jerusalem, and Ceylon. Rashed's experiences in Iran became the subject of his second collection of poetry, *Īrān meñ ajnabī* (A Stranger in Iran), which he published in 1957.[25] After leaving the army in 1947, he returned to All India Radio, working as a director in Lucknow. With the Partition of British India, All India Radio also split in two.[26] Rashed elected to serve in Pakistan, where his family lived. He moved up the ranks in Radio Pakistan in various locations—Peshawar, Lahore, Karachi.[27]

In 1952, Rashed joined the United Nations as an information officer, a post that would take him to a number of countries in his later life. He lived in New York until 1956, then Jakarta until 1958, and Karachi from 1958 to 1961. Just before returning to New York in 1961, his wife passed away. Two years later, he married Sheila Angelini, an Italian-British teacher. He returned to Tehran in 1967 and remained until 1973, where he gave numerous lectures in Persian, which he spoke fluently, as well as a number of interviews about his own writing.[28] He also wrote extensively in Urdu about modern Persian poetry.[29] In Iran, Rashed completed his third collection, *Lā = Insān* (X = Human) in 1969.[30]

Though he had earlier hoped to return to Pakistan, Rashed retired to Cheltenham, England.[31] One of the main considerations Rashed mentioned was the comfort of his wife.[32] There he spent time writing and researching.[33] Shortly before his death, he completed his fourth volume of poetry, *Gumāñ kā mumkin* (The Possibility of Supposition).[34] Rashed passed away from a heart attack on October 9, 1975.[35] Contrary to the burial practices preferred in Islam, his body was cremated.

There are a number of competing narratives about Rashed's cremation, which still remains controversial. According to Saqi Farooqi, a younger poet and friend of Rashed's living in London, as well as Rashed's son Shahryar, the poet had voiced a desire to be cremated.[36] Rashed's daughter Yasmin Hassan, however, has blamed Rashed's second wife for his cremation and charged that Rashed never communicated a desire to be cremated to anyone.[37] As I will discuss below in regard to Rashed's critical reception, absolving Rashed of the posthumous sin of cremation has opened up readings of the poet as a committed Muslim and a Sufi that had previously been foreclosed by what one contemporary Urdu weekly described as a rebellion "against Islam and God," and an indication of the poet's arrival at a "place of apostasy and heresy."[38]

RECEPTION OF RASHED'S WORK BY URDU CRITICS

Much of the critical writing in Urdu on N. M. Rashed speculates on the effect of his time spent abroad on his poetry. This sort of reading coincides with Rashed's own initial concern with capturing experience, but opposes the terms in which he later wrote. In his first two volumes, the settings of Rashed's poetry followed the contours of his life, though his poems employed a variety of narrative techniques designed to signal the distance between the poetic voice and his own. Later, his poetry left aside concrete geographical reference points, although the poems rested on the imaginative geography of Urdu literary tradition. The poet consistently subverted the organic relationship between poetic setting and national geography that some critics desired, eventually fashioning poetry that addressed universal themes of human life. But as the universality of his poetry's address increased, so did the intricacy of its ties to the history of Urdu literature. In his prose writing, Rashed articulated his desire to separate culture from geography. Yet Rashed chose to write his "universal" poetry from the position of Urdu, a language that had been rendered "particular" and attached to the national project of Pakistan over the course of his life.

Rashed's opposition to common uses of place as a marker of identity was present in his poetry even before Pakistan was created. It began with the poems in his earliest volume, which were set in the urban spaces particular to late colonial British India. Critics like the poet Mīrājī found these settings distasteful, as they appeared more "Western" than Indian.[39] Rashed's second volume, *Īrān meñ Ajnabī*, which was published ten years after Partition, invoked the more general geographical category of "Asia," which included both Iran and India. The poetry also used modern Persian references to signal the common contemporary experience of the region. Not only was the charge of "Westernness" continued here but, as I will explain in chapter two, the poetry became caught up in the larger critique of the Persian legacy in Urdu. Rashed's later, more "difficult" works treated landscape in more loosely metaphorical terms, building upon the genealogy of Urdu poetry most often associated with the establishment of Pakistan. In this poetry, he addressed the general problems of "man."

Many critics attributed Rashed's critique of place and identity to his biography, questioning his commitment to the situation of his own national and religious community as opposed to universal human problems. Rashed's literal distance from his homeland became a proxy for a larger set of discussions about the relevance of his poetry to society. Charges levied against modernism itself—its supposed excessive internality and distance from the common people—continued to be associated strongly with Rashed's poetry. More sympathetic critics followed Rashed's own suggestions to interpret his poetry as increasingly cosmopolitan, concerned with the human world as a whole.

These readings are primarily interesting insofar as they signal the difficulty that modernism faced in the Urdu literary sphere. Rashed's poetry attempted to posit literature as a form of critique rather than a space of common purpose or communion. That was literature's purpose, as far as he was concerned.

Shortly after N. M. Rashed's death in 1975, the poet Faiẓ Aḥmad Faiẓ artfully described Rashed's position in the field of Urdu poetry. Noting the length of time Rashed had spent outside of Pakistan since joining the United Nations in 1952, Faiz spoke of the "distance" between the poet and his public as a loss, not only to his public but also to Rashed himself. "When a man is overseas," Faiz wrote, "then his own self *(żāt)* cannot stand in for society, and, in a way, his own self becomes a separate country." Instead of focusing on his own society, such a poet becomes at once too preoccupied with "looking inside his self" *(darūñ-bīnī)* and too prone to transcendent pronouncements. Rashed's cosmopolitanism had left him disconnected from the specific concerns of his people, Faiz argued. He became focused on his own estranged self and on the "international problems" of man devoid of any regional or national specificity.[40]

Faiz's argument pivots on the distinction between "inner-looking" *(darūñ-bīnī)* and "outer-looking" *(jahāñ-bīnī)* poetry—a distinction that had emerged among Urdu progressive *(taraqqī pasand)* critics by the early

1940s. These critics were associated with the extraordinarily influential All-India Progressive Writers Association, an anticolonial literary organization that formed in London in 1935 and quickly spread through India. Modeled on the Writers' International and Popular Front, it worked through manifestos, local branches, and national conferences, and quickly established a national presence.[41] By the early 1940s, some "progressives" were perceived to be ousting from their fold some of Urdu's most beloved writers, who were deemed too sexual or obscene, as well as those who were not politically aligned with the Soviet Union and Communist Party.[42] Many progressive critics, embracing aspects of socialist realism, condemned the "classical" tradition of Urdu poetry as well as modernist writings for focusing on the inner world at the expense of the outer one, in the manner done by Faiz in his review of Rashed's later work. They demanded that literature instead be mimetic and realistically depict the problems of India's peasants and workers. At that time, the critic Āftāb Aḥmad defended Rashed's poetry using language grounded in these terms, calling Rashed a poet of the "external through the internal."[43] But even Āftāb Aḥmad complains that in Rashed's later volumes, "it seems as if he has stepped off of the earth and entered a strange and personal/internal *(żātī)* world." Like Faiz, Āftāb Aḥmad blames Rashed's time away from Pakistan. "Far from the nation, in foreign lands," Āftāb Aḥmad explains, "the very circumstances of his personal life pushed him far away from the world of external realities."[44]

Critics wishing to recuperate Rashed's later poetry from this criticism often invoke his appeal to universality. They cite the example of the Urdu and Persian poet Muhammad Iqbal, who similarly moved beyond national concerns to address the global Islamic community. This interpretation emerged after the publication of N. M. Rashed's 1969 collection, aptly titled *Lā = Insān* (X = Human), which Rashed described in its preface as addressing "the suffering soul of mankind as a whole."[45] The volume was published soon after the 1965 India-Pakistan war, which had exacerbated national tensions in the Urdu community.[46] For those Urdu literati concerned with developing ways of thinking beyond the nation, Rashed's poetry was particularly attractive. In an Indian journal and edited volume published shortly afterward, Indian critic and philosopher ʿĀlam Ḳhūndmīrī described Rashed as "from his first period to the last, concerned with the collective human station."[47] Pakistani poet and critic Vazīr Āġhā agrees that Rashed's "revolutionary voice" is in fact "more concerned with the future of the race of man than the future of his own country."[48]

Critics who follow this mode of reading also frequently comment on Rashed's freedom from ideology. Muġhannī Tabassum, an Indian critic and poet, describes one of Rashed's later poems as bearing a "sensitivity and consciousness of his age [that] is not bound by any principles or point of view." The poem in question shows that Rashed "holds such a cosmic consciousness" that his poetry, too, "is not bound to time or place," but instead is deeply fixed on the "human predicament."[49] Reading today, we can recognize these discussions as both cosmopolitan—the practice of writing a universal account of human life from within a position of difference—and secular—writing under a universal understanding of humanity as sovereign.

More recently, critics from Pakistan have reversed both of these readings to incorporate Rashed as a national poet, seeing him primarily as a Pakistani and a Muslim. In a series of revisionist readings published during Rashed's birth centenary celebrations in 2010, critics tied Rashed's poetry much more closely to Pakistani politics and history. To these writers, Rashed's focus on the "human predicament" was a cover for a Muslim worldview made necessary by his work at the United Nations. Much of the recently published work focuses, therefore, on Rashed's "religious consciousness," and many critics read his late poetry in particular as involving Rashed's experiences of the soul.[50] Research into his earlier involvement with the Khaksar movement, as well as the denial of his desire to be cremated, enabled his canonization as a properly Pakistani Muslim poet. Many of these volumes simply ignore much of the writer's criticism of Sufism and of nationalism.

The most significant of these volumes is perhaps that of Fateh Muhammad Malik. Malik follows the cosmopolitan narrative to argue that Rashed was not bound to any particular "political or literary movement," such as the Progressive Writers Association or the symbolist followers of Mīrājī. Malik finds in Rashed's poetry a political consciousness arising from the "bounty of his spiritual experience," that is, from the poet's inner recesses rather than from outside. He sees Rashed as a poet focused strongly on message, whose purpose was to free "the world of the East from political and civilizational slavery to the West." Malik provocatively writes that Rashed was more "connected in an unbreakable and instinctive way with the destiny of the Indian Muslims" than any of his contemporaries, even Faiz.[51] As in his treatments of other writers, Malik interprets whatever universality may be present in Rashed's text as a result of the poet's deep and spiritual experiences of his contemporary world, and particularly his feeling of "Pākistaniyāt," or care for Pakistan.[52]

These revisionist readings of Rashed's poetry collapse into a Pakistani Muslim identitarianism the far more subtle and critical kinds of readings that his poetry actually attempts to make possible. The main project of Rashed's poetry is exactly the escape from such representative and ideological reading practice through consistently iconoclastic and formally complex writing. While Rashed addressed the Urdu literary community, the manner in which he made that address emphasized shared knowledge and experience over the more foundational identities fundamental to nationalist discourse. The conventions of Urdu poetry, as a whole, require an ability to read about Muslim experience. But to collapse Rashed's poetry into "Muslim" experience requires a misreading of much of his poetry, which invokes but critiques religious tradition, particular the Sufi experience so crucial to many ways of thinking about being Pakistani. In place of identity, this present study finds that the overarching concern of Rashed's poetry is freedom, both from political formations and from ideology. Rashed nominated literature as the appropriate discursive space for free critique. So while this study largely agrees with the cosmopolitan reading of Rashed's poetry—chapter 3, for example, sees Rashed as imagining new ways of visualizing the human collective—it also reads Rashed's verse as involving literary and religious traditions primarily in order to critique them.

CHAPTER OUTLINE

The first chapter of this book places N. M. Rashed's controversial volume *Māvarā* (The Beyond, 1941), the first volume of free verse in Urdu, within its properly multilingual literary milieu. The poems are written in opposition both to classical forms of poetry, like the ghazal, and to previous attempts at literary reform. Reform movements in South Asian languages depend on the association of language with a regional or religious community. Attempts to naturalize the Urdu, Hindi, and Bengali languages and attach poetry to the moral life of the community were countered by romantic movements in those literatures. In his poetry, Rashed tried to move beyond both of these approaches by responding to his contemporary circumstances. To respond to the domination of colonialism required a break with poetic form, particularly so that poetry could properly represent sexual desire. *Māvarā* opposes embodiment to transcendence, arguing that the forms of romantic vision or a metaphysical beyond advocated for by previous poetry were insufficient to the contemporary moment. The poetic subjectivity that emerges in Rashed's poetry opposes the rational subjectivity of literary reform as well as the lyrical subjectivity of romanticism, which is associated with figures like Rabindranath Tagore in Bengali and Akhtar Shairānī in Urdu.

By focusing on the significance of literary reform and romanticism, chapter 1 challenges a frequent mode of reading modernism, and *Māvarā* in particular, as a reaction to "progressivism," or *taraqqī pasand adab*. Modernism and progressivism began to solidify as opposed positions only after the publication of the volume. Rashed's poems clearly explore the intersection of power, psychology, and sexuality, employing what I call a form of psychological realism in critique of British imperialism. To some progressive and nationalist critics, who insisted on a less psychological realism, the poems' descriptions of escapism through the romantic couple appeared as apolitical, asocial, and dangerously perverse. Like Rashed's poetry, which employs loosely Freudian concepts, these critics also turn to psychoanalytical models, even as they decry the poetry as too Western and insufficiently indigenous.

Chapter 2 examines Rashed's formally innovative poem "Īrān meñ ajnabī" (A Stranger in Iran), which was the centerpiece of a volume of the same name. Published in 1957, ten years after the formation of Pakistan, this long poem articulates the resistance to both ideology and the politics of representation that came to exemplify his work overall. In the movement to establish Pakistan as a separate nation for the Muslim community, Urdu literature became a symbol of an Indo-Muslim culture built, in part, on a historical relationship with Persian language and literature. Rashed's poem is set in Iran and engages with Urdu literary debates about the role of Persian language and culture. Its series of poetic fragments describe the experiences of an Indian Muslim soldier in the British Indian Army occupying Iran during World War II. Rashed's narrator searches in Iran for his cultural past, but instead finds an extension of his colonial present in a Tehran divided between European and Soviet powers and filled with war refugees. Rashed exemplifies the contemporaneity of Iran by including modern Persian vocabulary in his Urdu poem.

This gesture is meaningful in the context of a movement, articulated by many progressive critics, to deemphasize Persian and promote a Hindustani language that bridges the gap between (Muslim/Pakistani) Urdu and (Hindu/Indian) Hindi. Modernism *(jadīdiyat)*, the literary movement with which

Rashed was most closely associated, tended to emphasize the Persian roots of Urdu, in a gesture that we can recognize as strongly identitarian—one that was dismissed by progressives as socially regressive. By setting the poem in Iran and by using modern Persian, Rashed confronted a readership for whom those gestures could only be signs of Indo-Persian nostalgia. Instead, the poet articulated a common contemporary experience of an oppressed "Asia."

For Rashed, Asia was not a marker of cultural heritage, but was closer to what Gayatri Spivak has recently called a "position without identity"—a geographical category grounded not in a timeless culture but in an experience of power. The ephemeral and contingent experiences of Iran presented in the poem provide the poet evidence for his critique of the two modes of belonging then prevalent in the Urdu literary community, progressivism and Indo-Muslim identitarianism. In occasionally parodic poetic fragments, Rashed reveals both to be ideologies mired in imperial projects. Soviet internationalism is revealed as Russocentric imperialism, while Western imperialism provides stronger connections between India and Iran than does the Indo-Persian tradition. In addition, the poem employs rich citations of modern Persian poetry in order to critique an Iranian nationalism based on continuity with a lost imperial past. Rashed proposes a category of Asia too vast and heterogeneous to collapse into ideology, and imagines, in vague detail, the emergence of a "new human" not bound by any current identitarian or political structure.

Chapters 3 and 4 explore Rashed's late poetry, which was collected in two volumes. That poetry deepens and extends the poet's critique of representation and ideology, casting doubt on the relationship between word and meaning, both in the context of postcolonial states like Pakistan and in relation to metaphysical meaning in general. A particular target of these poems is the reliance of Urdu literature on Sufi ideas of the self, which the poet dismisses as insufficiently attendant to the body and psychology. Rashed's third volume, *Lā = Insān* (X = Human, 1969), questions the meaning of the word "human" and opens up the possibility of new, unconventional forms of subjectivity. The poet celebrates the malleability of language as a sign of the possibility of the transformation of social life in order to allow individuals greater freedom. In chapter 3, I explore how Rashed's poetry uses a modernist form of allegory to envision a fully embodied collectivity that does not follow the false certainties of symbolic politics. As allegory, this poetry incorporates elements of literary tradition, ensuring the effectiveness of its address to the transnational Urdu literary community. By reinterpreting and compounding elements drawn from the ghazal, Iqbal, Sufism, and Rumi, it critiques tradition in order to emphasize the instability of meaning and to celebrate bodily life.

In his late poetry Rashed engages most closely with the writing of Muhammad Iqbal, who, despite his opposition to the form of the nation-state, had become accepted posthumously as the poet-philosopher of Pakistan. In the Pakistani nationalism derived from Iqbal's work, Islam, as an "ethical ideal plus a certain kind of polity,"[53] provides the cohesion of a nation for Indian Muslims despite—or perhaps because of—its fundamental difference from Western nationalism. Rashed's critique of the symbol as vulnerable to ideological reification, discussed in chapter 3, is directed toward Iqbal's poetry. Iqbal's writing on time is a focus of chapter 4. Though Iqbal was critical of the conception of time in Sufism, the mystical practices of Islam that are frequently valorized as a marker of Pakistani cultural particularity, Rashed's late poetry asserts that Iqbal did not go far enough to disrupt the temporality that has been conventional to cultural nationalism.

In both chapters 3 and 4 however, I observe, how Rashed finds in Iqbal's writing the raw materials for the new form of collectivity that he proposes. Working again in an allegorical mode, Rashed's poems on time continue to critique the idea that national identity—that marker of modernity—is an organic attribute of human beings. It does so using an allegorical technique that incorporates aspects of literary and religious tradition and inverts their significance. In other verse, Rashed also deprecates Sufi withdrawal from the world, much as does Iqbal, yet he does so in order to celebrate the uncertainty of language and the instability of social forms.

In these chapters I detail a move in Rashed's poetry to carve out a position for literature from which it can challenge ideology. In the late colonial period, reform movements and identitarian political projects used the medium of Urdu poetry, which also became a site for the articulation of Islamic modernism. Rashed's poetry maintains a close proximity to religious discourse, but through literature it presents a different sort of critique. It sees in literature possibilities for deeper understanding of the relationship between the body, the self, and the social world. For Rashed, modernism is a means to sustain doubt and to challenge the certainty and the veneer of naturalness taken on by conventional ideas. His poetry emphasizes change over continuity, and limits itself to the exploration of worldly life.

In the conclusion I consider one of Rashed's most popular poems, "Ḥasan kūzagar" (Hasan the Potter). Heralded as one of the greatest statements about love and creativity in Urdu, this poem in four parts, crossing both of Rashed's two final volumes, provides an opportunity to reconsider the themes discussed in the previous chapter—embodiment, position without identity, allegory and collectivity, and temporality—through a reading of each of the four parts of the poem.

ONE

Embodiment

IN 1941, N. M. Rashed published *Māvarā* (The Beyond), a work celebrated as the first volume of free verse, or *āzād naẓm*, in Urdu.[1] The poetry, which vividly describes the subjective experiences of a narrator whose life resembled that of both the author and his readers, solidified Rashed's reputation. The formal experimentation that was the hallmark of this volume remained important throughout the poet's body of work. His association with free verse also led him to be classified as a modernist poet by Urdu critics, and the reception of his poetry remains tied to the category of modernism itself.

For Rashed, to be a modern *(jadīd)* poet was to respond to contemporary experience and to explore changing ideas of the self. The poet understood his social reality, and particularly the political domination of colonialism, through its psychological effects. Rashed adopted a loosely Freudian view of the self that led him to focus directly on sexuality. The need to engage with sexuality, he argued, necessitated a decisive break with traditional poetic forms, which could not accommodate lust. It required the poetry to focus on embodiment rather than transcendence, on material life rather than a spiritual "Beyond." The title of his volume is clearly ironic.

In this chapter I examine what led Rashed to articulate this relationship between experience, psychology, poetic content, and form. I argue that the significance of Rashed's break with form is dependent on both the history of the association of language with political community and the emergence across North Indian languages of romantic forms of poetry that privileged a new kind of lyrical subjectivity. By the late 1930s, when Rashed began to compose the poems included in *Māvarā*, Urdu and Hindi had become mapped upon Muslim and Hindu religious communities. Advocates for Hindi, in particular, had extended their claim to representation to aspire to the status of a national language. Literary reform movements of the nineteenth and early twentieth centuries had associated literature with the moral fitness of these linguistic communities. And while each of these language movements advocated linguistic purification, there were obvious commonalities across languages. As I will describe in this chapter, the literary histories of Hindi and Urdu were both heavily influenced by that of Bengali.

Because of the linguistic diversity of South Asia and the tendency of both language movements and academics/critics to view literatures in isolation from one another, it has been difficult to account for the emergence of these movements across languages. The tendency to focus on individual literatures has been particularly pronounced in scholarship on modernism. In the case of Urdu, this has led authors to ignore the significance of romanticism in the development of modernism, and to focus more squarely on the continuing importance of literary and social reform. This ignores the influence of Bengali, in which romanticism allowed for the articulation of a new form of poetic subjectivity, and Hindi, in which lyrical subjectivity was tied to formal innovation.

This is unfortunate, for as I argue in this chapter, romanticism was the immediate touchstone for the formal experimentation that led to *āzād naẓm*. Romantic poetry in Urdu, with its articulation of a new form of subjectivity, was as important a target of critique for Rashed's poetry as the moral reform movements and community-based address popularized by earlier literary reformers. This chapter therefore begins with a discussion of the politics of literature and language as well as an overview of the key role of romanticism in the emergence of modernism in Urdu, Hindi, and Bengali literatures.

By emphasizing romanticism and the emergence of a new poetic subjectivity, I argue that Rashed's modernist Urdu poetry was less of a reaction to "progressivism," or *taraqqī pasand adab*, than it later appeared to be. Between the time the poems were written and when they were published, modernism and progressivism gradually came to be opposed categories of literary analysis. Because the reception of Rashed's poetry—and with it, modernism in general—has been so closely tied to this distinction, this chapter concludes with an account of slightly later "progressive" condemnations of Rashed's poetry. The focus of those critics is the poetry's imagination of psychology, which was dismissed as inimical to the realism prized by progressive literature. However wooden and wrongheaded these critical texts, this reception of his poetry is significant because it led Rashed to articulate a critique of progressivism, or more accurately "socialist" *(ishtirākī)* writing, in his later poems and criticism.

POETIC MODERNISM IN URDU AMONG SOUTH ASIAN LITERATURES

Colonial modernity fundamentally altered South Asian literary traditions as vernacular languages were codified and literary histories became attached to linguistic communities. While some languages and literary forms were abandoned, others were invented. Some writers explicitly rejected past forms, while others forged new relationships with reconceived literary traditions. Although scholars typically trace these processes as they affect single languages, it is clear that shared movements can be seen at least across North Indian languages, if not across the entire subcontinent. The contours of these changes are fairly uniform: in the late nineteenth century, movements for morally uplifting and realistic literature emerged in Urdu, Hindi, and Bengali, which led in the first decades of the twentieth century to the emergence of countermovements described as romanticism. In the 1930s, a deliberately crosslinguistic movement for anticolonial and sometimes socialist-realism inspired progressivism gained strength and emerged at the same time as modernism or experimentalism in Hindi and Urdu. The move for experimentalism in poetry in Bengali, however, began earlier in the 1920s in a reaction to the poetry of Rabindranath Tagore (1861–1941). Literary histories of Urdu have overemphasized the distinction between modernism and progressivism and obscured the importance of romanticism as the ground for the emergence of modernism. A comparison between romanticism and modernism across these three languages is therefore particularly revealing of the certain lockstep in which these literatures developed that would otherwise be obscured in a single-language approach.

Among these literatures, the literary history of formal experimentation in Urdu has depended on a distinction between "progressivism" and "modernism" that obscures what these movements have in common. That is less the case in Hindi and Bengali, where the emphasis placed on the lyric poetry associated with Rabindranath Tagore has allowed for the articulation of what constitutes modern poetry. What emerged in the early twentieth century across these languages was a new idea of poetic subjectivity, one that would necessitate the development of new poetic forms. While this entire discourse is modern, in the sense of being a product of colonial modernity, the link between an emergent literary subjectivity and formal experimentation came to be defined as modernism in all three of these South Asian languages.

The history of literary innovation in the vernacular languages of South Asia must be understood as emerging from a colonial discourse of literary reform. An important aspect of British colonial hegemony was the idea that earlier South Asian literatures, understood as shaped by feudal forms of patronage, were fundamentally escapist and morally reprehensible. This escapist character was tied to descriptions of writing filled with embellishment and lacking realistic description. Colonial state patronage sought to distinguish itself from this past by encouraging movements in literature that emphasized the moral benefits of realism and the movement of language toward common speech. The Victorian novel became an important model for Indian vernacular writers, and with literature considered a means for social improvement, the writer was burdened with the project of social uplift.

As Vasudha Dalmia, Aamir Mufti, and Farina Mir have all discussed, movements for literary reform were grounded in new ideas about vernacular languages. As these scholars have argued, modern languages were established to serve social communities bounded by religion and place, and became crucial to the conduct of politics in the late colonial period. The nineteenth-century debate over Hindi and Urdu involved their codification as separate languages and their attachment to Hindu and Muslim religious communities, respectively. It was a result of the languages' emergence as a single lingua franca of the subcontinent, for "only on this geographic and linguistic terrain could the question of *national* language have arisen."[2] Farina Mir's work on Punjabi shows how unique the national ambitions of Hindi and Urdu's reformers were. Although the colonial state designated Urdu as a vernacular literature in the Punjab, Mir tracks the emergence of a Punjabi literary formation spanning domains of class, caste, religion, and, after 1947, two postcolonial nations.[3]

Mir has marked the beginning of these historical processes with the replacement of Persian with Urdu (referred to in this period by the British as Hindustani) as the language of the lower courts.[4] Dalmia, by contrast, looks to the period of the 1860s, when Hindi nationalists moved to establish a separate Hindi language, built upon the common vernacular of Hindustani but written in the left-to-right *devanāgarī* script. Hindi, distinguished from Urdu, was promoted as a national language, depending on the association of language, religion, and territory, or, in a common slogan, "Hindi, Hindu, Hindustan."[5] As Dalmia argues, the proponents of linguistic modernization fully disavowed the composite character of literary production in order to attach the modern literature of Hindi to the "pre-Muslim" literary archive of Braj Bhāshā, a "medieval" language associated with Vaishnavism, and of Avadhī, an "Eastern" form of Hindi best known for the *Rāmcharitmānas* of Tulsīdās.[6]

The movement for poetry in modern Hindi is tied to the work of the Benares-based Hindi nationalist, Bhāratendu Harishchandrā (1850–1885).[7] Hindi poetry only really emerged in the early twentieth century, however, after Braj Bhāshā was displaced by colonial objection to its religiosity, sensuality, and courtliness.[8] Allison Busch's account of *rīti* literature includes an analysis of this decline. She notes how Braj conformed to an image of precolonial decadence more closely associated with Urdu and its legacy of Persian motifs.[9] Busch indicates how strong parallels can be drawn between Mahāvirā Prasād Dwivedī's promotion of Hindi literature and the work of the Urdu writers Muḥammad Ḥusain Āzād (1830–1910) and Ḳhvājah Alṭāf Ḥusain Ḥālī (1837–1914). Frances Pritchett has established how these figures recast the Urdu canon in relation to a critique of Persianate forms and language and gave strong recommendations for the reform of Urdu writing.[10]

As Pritchett details, Āzād called for a new poetry in Urdu based on English models, criticizing both the *maẓmūn* (themes or symbols) of Urdu poetry as too limiting and the language of poetry as ridiculously magniloquent. Āzād's "natural poetry" movement depended on the new conception of the relationship between language and community associated with figures like Harishchandrā. For Āzād, Urdu literature was tied to the particular conditions of a *qaum* (community/nation) and its rise and fall. In his account, the state of Urdu literature was as debased as that of the Indo-Muslim community, for it continued to serve the tastes of the now-disenfranchised nobility.[11] Āzād followed the contours of the colonial critique of Mughal rule in order to recommend changes to language and literature that also required changes in the structure of Indo-Muslim society.[12] For Āzād, Urdu literature was a primary site for moral self-improvement, and the goal of self-improvement was greater success in public life.

Ḥālī focused more squarely on remaking the canon of Urdu poetry, targeting in particular the form of the ghazal. Ḥālī shared Āzād's objections to the falseness of figurative language, but he also objected to the depiction of love in the ghazal, finding it immoral, damaging to the community, and in need of reform.[13] Ḥālī objected to the ghazal's overt eroticism as a paradoxical sign of a lack of virility. He argued that sexual desire—the "hidden secret"—must be restricted from literary expression in the service of the collective good of the community. But even as he condemned the content of the ghazal, Ḥālī recommended the continued use of its form because of its popularity and ease of transmission.[14] Formal experimentation, he asserted, would estrange readers and interfere with natural poetry's moral project. Ḥālī's influence may be one reason for the relatively late emergence of formal experimentation in Urdu poetry. Though Ḥālī and Āzād both condemned "Persian" influences on Urdu, there were still fewer moves in Urdu toward linguistic purification than in Hindi.

Formal experimentation in Hindi poetry came earlier, in the early 1920s movement called the *Chhāyavād yug*, or era of romanticism (literally "shadowy age"). Formally experimental poets like Nirālā, Mahādevī Varmā, and Pant all countered the poetry supported by social reformist Dwivedī. Karine Schomer argues that, unlike the overt social messages advocated by Dwivedī, "Chhayavad quietly reflected on the cultural heritage of the nation and strove to make it meaningful."[15] Lucy Rosenstein describes the poetry as preoccupied with "a cosmic realm, an idealized world of intense beauty, mystical love and profound harmony." She also has argued that this poetry translates the "desire for political independence" into "a quest for individual freedom," in which "tradition was reclaimed not as a public patriotic statement, but in a personally meaningful way."[16] These accounts prize the emergence of lyric poetry that projects a literary subjectivity as a marker of the poetry's modern character.

It is possible to trace the emergence of this lyrical subjectivity in the poetry of Rabindranath Tagore. Dipesh Chakrabarty has argued that while Rabindranath Tagore's prose fiction became a site for a critical eye, for reform and improvement, Tagore's Bengali poetry depicted a world outside historical time. It provided a space of unreality, which allowed the poet to explore the beautiful and the sublime. This space of love allowed for what Tagore called "piercing the veil" of the objectively real. Chakrabarty explains that, for Tagore, "the poetic then was that which, in the middle of the everyday, helped to transport one to the level of the transcendental" while "the prosaic, in contrast, pertained to the realm of needs and utilities." The poetic self for Chakrabarty represents an indigenous subjectivity that "helped transcend the mere thingness of things by letting us see beyond the real or *bastab*," and that contrasted with the subjectivity of prose, which is public and focused on the objectively real, as in Tagore's novels.[17] Tagore's advocacy of this poetic subjectivity was fiercely debated by Dwivedī-era Hindi critics, who saw Tagore's influence in the poetry of the Chhāyavād, which they condemned.

Romanticism emerged in Urdu in the work of Akhtar Shairānī in the early 1930s, even while he was seemingly writing in isolation from these movements in Hindi and Bengali. Shairānī's poetry was Rashed's immediate object of critique in *Māvarā*, though he also tied his poetry to the larger genealogy of literary reform in Urdu described above. Rashed's poetry shared the preoccupations with literary subjectivity of his immediate contemporaries, including Faiẓ Aḥmad Faiẓ, whose poetry is one focus of Aamir Mufti's work.[18] But while Faiz continued to accept Ḥālī's advocacy of the popular form of the ghazal, Rashed insisted that an aesthetic intervention in Urdu poetry must involve both form and content. In his critical writings and introductions, Rashed stresses that the new sort of lyrical subject he is describing, who has a very obvious heterosexually oriented libido, can only be made manifest in a new form of poetry. It is to this material then that I now turn.

THE LOOSENING OF VERSE

In the introduction to *Māvarā*, Rashed describes *āzād naẓm* as an attempt to find from within the qualities of the Urdu language a new form of poetic expression capable of engaging with the new demands of the modern condition. The traditional forms of Urdu poetry, such as the ghazal, appear to him as too limiting. Moreover, the lyrical poetry written in the style of Tagore, such as the *gīt* (song), also appeared insufficient in the modern era. The centrality of Rashed's volume in the Urdu literary canon can perhaps be accounted for by the fact that his formal experimentation is so obviously recognizable as Urdu rather than as Bengali, English, or Hindi. Yet Rashed describes his central concern as finding a poetic form allowing for the conveyance of feeling, which includes sexuality, not just the chaste emotions of the social reformers or the romantic experiences of "piercing the veil of the real" as in Tagore.

Rashed grounds his argument in a discussion of musicality *(mausīqī)*. Normally, he states, the individuality of the rhyme and meter of a language's poetry comes from the melody *(tarannum)* and proportionality of sound *(tanāsub-e aṣvāt)* of a country's traditional music. Yet the classical poetry of Urdu, he explains, is based not on "national music" but rather on a "mechanical" system of prosody that came to India from Arabia through Iran, as the meters of Urdu poetry are those of Persian. Yet, he argues, the Indian people have internalized the ghazal to such an extent that it is an "individual tradition." As such, it has also greatly affected India's musical traditions.[19]

For Rashed, grounding in music is not enough, however. As evidence for this claim, he describes the recent attempts to write Urdu *gīt* in non-Persian "Hindi" meters by poets such as Mīrājī and others. As Geeta Patel has argued, Mīrājī worked across the Hindi and Urdu divide, whereas Rashed places his poetry much more obviously in the camp of Urdu and Persian.[20] Yet Mīrājī also incorporates, at times, the poetic aesthetic of Tagore. Rashed acknowledges the *gīt* form as a measure of a growing national consciousness. Though the *gīt* is "in harmony with the nation's musical consciousness *(ḥiss-e mausīqī)*," Rashed is certain that poetry in that form is not suitable for representing "lofty thoughts or for unveiling life's secrets." *Gīt* is also unsuitable for "approaching the intellectual traditions brought forth in our country through the effects of the rest of the world's culture."[21] Rashed frames his rejection of the suitability of the *gīt* within a statement about the global nature of modernity. He further explains, "Whether you like the modern thoughts of foreign countries or not, today our thoughts and ambitions are certainly within their grasp, and we definitely cannot escape from them, because civilization *(tahżīb)* and culture *(ṡiqāfat)* have left all geographical boundaries and now have a global grasp. Despite this, these new thoughts have granted us a new wakefulness, a new capacity, and a new moving life *(mutaḥarrik zindagī)*, which cannot but affect our literature."[22] Because of the global reach of modern life (despite its origin), Rashed sees no possibility of a return to folk tradition or to the traditional Urdu literary genres, such as the ghazal. Due to their constraints on form and content, they do not in his estimation have the capacity to adequately reflect and respond to modernity. In their place, he argues for *āzād naẓm* as a form that is both organic and musical, yet capable of abstraction.

For Rashed, musicality does not require strict adherence to form. Like Ḥālī before him, he focuses on the role played by rhyme in poetry, yet he insists, "[in *āzād naẓm*] rhyme is merely a servant to the poem, not its master." Rashed does not reject rhyme completely, but he looks past rhyme to highlight the importance of musicality itself. While Ḥālī acknowledged that rhyme could restrain poetic expression, he never advocated abandoning it.[23]

Rashed, on the other hand, contends that form can be abandoned for the sake of "feeling" *(ĕḥsās)* if and only if it maintains the musicality found at the heart of poetry. He identifies the musical strength of his free-verse poetry as the impression of rhyme without its formal presence and restraints.[24]

Employing a familiar meter and the impression of rhyme, Rashed set his sights on a poetic form not overly bound by convention but still acceptable to its local audience. Urdu poetry tends to presuppose performance in a *mushā'irah* (poetry gathering) or other collective setting. Rashed struggled to find a favorable reception for his work and to fend off the charges of unaesthetic Westernization that were lobbed at earlier modernizers of poetic form and content. In his free-verse poems, Rashed provides rhyme and its expectation—which may or may not be fulfilled. At the same time, the poems are not bound further by poetic conventions, such as the *mazmūn* ("themes" or "symbols") of ghazal poetry, or formal limitations, such as a fixed number of metrical feet. Unlike other forms of modernism prevalent in South Asia, such as painting, in which the expectation was of some familiarity with an already established international modernism, Rashed's poetic modernism deliberately presupposes an audience educated in the classical forms of Urdu poetry. Rashed's break with poetic form assumes knowledge of its conventions.

One of Rashed's key rhetorical moves is to insist that his true innovation was less in form than in content. Rashed highlights his use of erotic content as his key break from the approach of earlier literary reformers, such as Ḥālī. While Rashed characterized the natural poetry movement as full of "good intentions," he declared it incapable of advancing Urdu poetry, precisely because of its understanding of literature as "a means of expressing moral and social thoughts." Instead, Rashed argued that poetry can advance only when "that adaptability and that capacity can be found, in terms of forms of expression, such that erotic/passionate thoughts *('ishqiyānah khayālāt)*, freed from worn-out symbols, can be made manifest in it. . . . [T]his is the only way our poetry can be saved from being frozen artistically—not by finding morality or so-called 'realism' *(ḥaqīqat nigārī)*."[25]

Rashed agreed with Ḥālī that the conventions of classical Urdu poetry were too limiting. Yet he took issue with Ḥālī's assertion that poetry could be rejuvenated by properly representing reality. As noted above, while Ḥālī ostensibly wanted poetry to describe things that are "always in the world," he also qualified this statement with "or should be in it."[26] For Ḥālī, this qualification required the suppression of eroticism, which he viewed as the prevalent feature of earlier Urdu poetry, particularly the ghazal, and as a source of harm to the community. For Rashed, "realism" was not the answer, but rather "feeling," which included sexuality.

ANOTHER KIND OF LOVE

The poems of Rashed's *Māvarā*, which are arranged more or less chronologically in the volume, show a steady movement away from the moralistic rejection of sexuality found in the work of the literary reformers. Rashed's earliest poems make a substantive distinction between love *(ʿishq)* and lust *(havas)*. As such, these poems are consonant with the romantic poetry of the early 1930s, particularly that associated with the poet Aḳhtar Shairānī (1905–1948), an early mentor of Rashed's. He was very popular among college students in Lahore, both for his romantic personality and for his rejection of literature as moral reform. The son of a respected professor and scholar, Aḳhtar Shairānī famously fled from his matriculation exam to dedicate his life to poetry.

Aḳhtar Shairānī's "romantic" poetry plots an escape from the pains of the material world into a utopian world of love, wine, and song. His poems address a named female beloved, called Salmâ or Reḥānah. This feature distinguishes his poetry from earlier ghazal poetry, in which the beloved is unnamed and frequently ambiguous—male, female, or divine. Giving a name to the beloved marked his poetry as modern. Yet unlike other poetry from that period, such as the natural poetry movement with its didacticism or Muḥammad Iqbāl's poetry of Islamic revivalism, Aḳhtar Shairānī's poetry appeared explicitly nonpolitical.[27] In place of politics, his poetry instead frequently takes the form of a romantic flight. An example comes in his well-known poem "Ai ʿishq kahīñ le chal" (O Love, Take Me Somewhere):

> O Love, take me somewhere, away from this habitation of sin
> from the abomination of this world, from the cursedness of life
> from these people who lust, from this lust
> far away—take me somewhere else!
> O Love, take me somewhere!
>
> (lines 1–5)
>
> May nature be at my defense, and fate too be in sympathy!
> May Salmâ be at my side, and Salmâ's love as well

May everything be free and may your kindness be there too!
O child of beauty, take me!
O Love, take me somewhere!

(lines 46–50)

May we come to such a paradise, may we arrive in such a valley
where the pain of the world would never cause the heart to writhe
and whose Springs would be filled with the pleasure of living
If you're going to take me, take me there!
O Love, take me somewhere!

(lines 86–90)[28]

This poem calls for a retreat into a paradise of love, far away from the turmoil of the world. The first line of the poem makes a distinction between love *(ʿishq)* and sin/wickedness *(pāp)*. This distinction between love and sin reveals the inherent sexual moralism in Shairānī's poetry. Although the poem mentions Salmâ, Shairānī's named beloved, it does not delve into eroticism of the body. Instead, this poem and Shairānī's poetry in general distinguish love from carnal desire.[29] The poet, in other words, appears in love with love, and his poetry does not represent or give a place to sexual desire.

While Rashed would soon object to such a dismissal of sex, the earliest poems of *Māvarā* mirror Akhtar Shairānī's poetry both in their "romantic" landscapes and in their moral distinction between love and lust. Rashed's sonnet "Bādal" (Clouds, §1) and his poem "Ek din—lārins bāġh meñ" (One Day in Lawrence Garden, §2) are romantic depictions of nature and the poet's relationship to it. Echoing Akhtar Shairānī's landscape poems, such as "Gujrāt kī rāt" (A Night in Gujarat), they are filled with moonlight and stars.[30] Similarly, Rashed's sonnet "Sitāre" (Stars, §3) depicts the world as a dusty place of suffering far from man's "lost paradise" *(gum-shudah jannat)*. This "lost paradise" is a recurring site of romantic retreat in these early poems, and it is the very subject of the poem "Vādī-e pinhāñ" (Hidden Valley, §4), an edenic valley filled with angels, melodies, dreams, music, and mirth—the same general destination as that of Akhtar Shairānī's "O Love, Take Me Somewhere."

Nowhere is the distinction between love and lust clearer in Rashed's earliest poetry than in his short poem "Gunāh aur muḥabbat" (Sin and Love, §5). Set in the age of youth, the first part of the poem, "Sin," depicts that period as one of lust *(havas)* and carnal desires, devoid of both the god of love *(ʿishq devatā)* and the houri of chastity *(ḥūr-e ʿiṣmat)*. The "Devil," referred to as Ahriman, the Zoroastrian spirit of evil, dominates that period. The references found in this poem are noticeably secular. The "god of love," the "houri of chastity," and Ahriman all, in a sense, sidestep the question of religious piety—a feature Rashed's early poetry shares with Akhtar Shairānī's. The poem contrasts the sinful time of youth to the period when the narrator has fallen in love and been lifted up from depravity to a new morality, as a "healthy/morally-right longing" *(ārzū-e salīm)* takes the place of his earlier "bestial desires" *(bahīmānah khvāhish)*. As in Akhtar Shairānī's poetry, Rashed's earliest poems revolve around a conventional opposition between love and sex. In this way, his work aligns itself with the moral reform of natural poetry. However, instead of aiming to uplift its community, this "pure love" became an end in itself.

The next set of poems in *Māvarā* reject this moralistic, if secular, opposition between love and sex and seek a new relationship between the body and desire, and with it a new morality. According to these poems, sexual desires should not be repressed, and youth should not be betrayed. The poem "Mukāfāt" (Retribution, §6) announces this new position. Its narrator claims that he has lived a chaste and holy life, committed to "the Lord God" *(hazrat-e yazdān)*, using the term *Yazdān*, the Zoroastrian spirit of good. He has struggled against the "Devil" *(ahrimān)*, the spirit of evil. In so doing, he has repressed his desires, and he has never shown his soul to anyone; he has never expressed passion; he has only nurtured "sins" in his thoughts and never let them enjoy expression in his life. As a result of this repression, the narrator's youth is filled with poison. The desires he struggles against return in his dreams as the poem concludes:

> Look, they have come as terrifying images,
> those desires that I murdered
> Look, those same followers of the Devil have come,
> those I made miserable through my chastisement
> I never saw this excruciating torment in my soul,
> never before, Oh my unfortunate fate!
> But no matter how much trouble they give me, it is not enough
> I have abased my soul so thoroughly
> I could not let it sing with youth
> or let the spell of desire be cast upon it
> Oh, if only I had secretly committed one sin,
> If only I had filled my youth with sweetness
> Why have I still not committed even one sin?
>
> (lines 21–33)

The narrator has defiled his soul by not allowing his desires to partake of his youth. He wonders why he has never sinned. Yet this statement is ironic, because by never committing a sin, the narrator has in fact committed one: the betrayal of his youth. This poem too is secular, examining the internal, psychological consequences of sexual repression. Its framework, moreover, is generally Freudian, since the content of repressed desires comes forth in dream-images.

To represent love as material—focused on and originating from the body—appealed to Rashed as a critique not only of prevalent prudery but also of literary tradition. He based this critique in contemporary urban experience. Though Rashed came to reject Akhtar Shairānī's dichotomy between love and lust, he continued to see elements of his own critique in Akhtar Shairānī's poetry, which he understood as a substantial break from literary tradition. In a contemporary essay, Rashed explained:

> Although [Akhtar Shairānī's] love, following the pretension of every Urdu poet, is free from "lust" *(havas)*, still in it there is no lack of sexual feeling. Akhtar's love is earthly. It is completely material . . . and truly it is not that love which by being called metaphor *(majāz)* is understood to be a staircase to so-called truth *(ḥaqīqat)*; it is not that love which is explained away to a ridiculous degree through useless exegesis, and which people try to paint in the unexhilarating colors of Sufism and mysticism in a futile effort to expose its imaginary, hidden message! Akhtar's love is the earthly love of a sensitive and young urbanite *(shahrī)*; divinity and spirituality are meaningless words for him. . . . Akhtar's thoughts are overflowing with this other type of love.[31]

The experience of the "sensitive and young urbanite" of "material" love provides the basis for a secular critique of Urdu literary tradition's reliance on the sacred. Literary tradition here is synonymous with the exegesis of Sufism, understood as the mystical practices of Islam. The poetry of the ghazal, with its focus on unrequited love, is read under the lens of Sufism as metaphorical. Accordingly, the beloved and the erotic desire of the lover serve as metaphor *(majāz)* for a reality *(ḥaqīqat)* beyond the phenomenal world.

In *Māvarā*, Rashed rejects this Sufistic formulation. In a poem titled "Ḥuzn-e insān: aflāṭūnī ʿishq par ek ṭanz" (The Affliction of Man: A Satire of Platonic Love, §7), which is framed as a poem of seduction, Rashed writes:

> You are deprived of the concord of body and soul!
> Otherwise these winter nights would not be worthless,

and the days of spring would not be without benefit!
Ah man, who now is a worshiper of illusions
Beauty tricks the poor fellow,
forces him to have a taste for the sacred!
Someday the strings of the instrument will break
Smile, for your youth right now is glowing
This is the answer to the joke of the Lord God!

(lines 19–27)

The poem voices a critique of Plato's abstraction and idealization of beauty, which causes man to become devoted to something that is illusory instead of physically present. His apprehension is limited to that which is sacred *(taqdīs)*, and hence he censures erotic experience—here evoked through the image of winter nights *(shab-hā-e zimistāñ)*. The poem, which addresses a woman, ends with a call for her to seize the period of youth (and the narrator) before their youth inevitably passes.

Perhaps the most successful of these representations of a modern, secular sexuality is the poem "Ittifāqāt" (Accidents, §8), which was written around August 1934.[32] It takes place on a beautiful winter's night in a garden, the common meeting place of lovers. The narrator's sweetheart rests, full of pleasant dreams, while he, afflicted, struggles against sleep. In the narrator's view, the lovers are young, and the night is beautiful—they should take advantage of the situation. The poem is about seizing the moment of youth, but also about discarding religious morality, which is expressed in a recurring line, "Why do you care whether God exists or not?" (lines 20, 24). In the final stanza, the narrator ponders a romantic flight away to the heavens and starting a new life in the stars. But he rejects this notion in favor of the earth: "The heavens are far away, but this earth is near." Bodiless love is rejected as an illusory impossibility: "If souls cannot meet, then let these lips meet." The poem ends with a final rejection of religious morality: "let two frozen bodies be found on the dewy grass, / and if there is a God let him be ashamed!" (lines 28–35). The key word in these lines, of course, is bodies, which Rashed's poetry was trying to reinsert into romance.

Rashed's early poetry moves away from literary tradition, understood as incorporeal love, to the realism of sex. In place of a retreat to the beyond of Sufism or the romantic experience of love, the poems represent an actual romantic couple in a secular, modern, and urban challenge to both religious and moral authority. Unlike the earlier literary reformers and romantics,

Rashed asserted that sexuality was part of the modern condition and it should not be kept hidden from literature.

FLEEING FROM LIFE

In the final poems of *Māvarā*, we find a slightly older protagonist trying, like the poet, to make a living in late colonial India. In contrast to the earlier poems, here the challenges of life under colonial rule penetrate the private sphere of the couple. By showing different images and kinds of couples, the poems represent the internal, psychological effects of this condition. At this point, the category of experience that structures *Māvarā* acquires more psychological depth. Like "Accidents" (§8), many of the later poems of *Māvarā* represent the voice of a male protagonist addressing his lover. Unlike the earlier poem, set in the any-place of a "garden" in the any-time of "youth," these poems are clearly situated under colonialism.

One such poem is "Wretched Poet" (Shāʿir-e darmāndah, §9), in which a narrator addresses, presumably, his wife. Its first stanza reads:

> Life for you is a bed of fur.
> And for me, begging from the Europeans
> Because of the retreat of my forefathers,
> I am a miserable and helpless littérateur
> worn out by the worries of my livelihood!
> In need of a piece of barley bread
> are we—me, my friends, my thousands of fellow countrymen,
> that is, the flowers of the Europeans' gardens!
> You did not hope for a wretched poet
> On the day your star was bound to me,
> you thought that one day my clever mind
> and my knowledge and skill
> would bring pearls to adorn you from the land and sea
> When ill-fortunes block my path,
> why shouldn't your prayers,
> your nightly prostrations and supplications, be useless?
> (My disbelief, too, is its reason!)
>
> (lines 1–17)

The narrator describes himself as a littérateur *(adīb)* and a poet *(shāʿir)*. The learning presumed by this social position—training in Persian, perhaps

Arabic, and certainly Urdu—would not help the narrator's job prospects, as would an English-style education. The narrator's lover admires his education, even though it is of the wrong kind. She prays for his success, but he dismisses her devotion as useless in their condition.

In contrast to Rashed's earlier poems, the narrator exhibits a distinct and identifiable social consciousness. He likens his state to that of his friends and thousands of countrymen *(arbāb-e vaṭan).* Describing his current wretched condition as the direct result of the "the retreat [lit. 'striving for comfort'] of [his] forefathers" (line 3), the narrator echoes a common assumption of both British colonial and Indo-Muslim historiography: that the decadence and escapism of the Mughals caused the decline of Muslim rule and culture. As mentioned above, this assumption of decadence prompted the literary reform of the natural poetry movement associated with Ḥālī and Āzād. The narrator sees himself as quite literally an inheritor of that history. However, by mocking his wife's prayers, asserting his own impiety, and, later in the poem, questioning the very existence of God in the East, the narrator's heretical words make clear that he does not believe that the deliverance of the "flowers of the Europeans' gardens" (line 8) lies in religion.

Unsuccessful in the public sphere, the narrator proposes a retreat to the private sphere of the couple, to a place where he can be a man:

> O my candle of the chamber of faithfulness,
> forget it all for my sake
> Life is the tranquil forgetfulness of dreams!
> You know well there is no god of the East,
> and if there is, then he is behind a curtain of forgetfulness.
> You are my "joy"; you are my "wakefulness"
> Take me in your embrace
> so two "I's" may become one and set the world ablaze,
> so the era you seek in your prayers
> may manifest itself on its own.
>
> (lines 18–27)

Through a focus on the couple, this poem exposes the impact of colonial rule on the private sphere and on the interior life of the self. The narrator tells his beloved to forget her dreams of future prosperity and to seek immediate fulfillment in their romantic relationship instead. In place of "joy" and "wakefulness/vigilance" in public life, they should seek completeness in each other. For the protagonist in the poem, the romantic relationship offers a retreat from the harshness of the world.

In his own critical writings from this period, Rashed explained this retreat using psychoanalysis. For these poems are psychological portraits rather than autobiography. An example is found in his explanation of another poem about a romantic couple titled "Raqṣ" (Dance): "'Dance' is just an excuse for a title. Every art is born from a mentality of man called the fleeing-from-life mentality *(zindagī se gurīz kī żahniyyat)* that comes into being with every culture, with every civilization, and with every slavery to doors and walls. This poem is based on the tenet that when man stands ready to flee from life, he then takes shelter in the skirt of art or in a woman's embrace, which is the fountain of all the arts."[33]

In this statement, Rashed claims that civilization itself, which his poems frequently describe as "doors and walls" *(dar-o-bām)*, gives rise to the "fleeing-from-life mentality." This impulse to retreat from reality leads men to art; indeed, it can be seen as art's purpose. Rashed argues that these "escapist" poems are really descriptions of the psychology of the modern condition. The escapism was not his own, but rather a report of experience.

While not cited in Rashed's statements, the "fleeing-from-life mentality" is a direct translation of Freud's "pleasure principle." Freud first used the term in his seminal essay "Formulations on the Two Principles of Mental Functioning" (1911).[34] The pleasure principle refers to the tendency of the libido to seek situations of satisfaction, in which the self experiences as little stress as possible. Forced by the ego to face the demands of "reality," the self must sublimate its desire for pleasure or succumb to neurosis. Freud draws on his tenet that "every neurosis has as its result, and probably therefore as its purpose, a forcing of the patient out of real life, an alienating of him from reality." For Freud, the artist is like a neurotic: he tries to satisfy his unfulfilled erotic desires through the production of art.[35] Rashed's statement follows Freud's depiction of art as a product of the pleasure principle, a turning away from the pressures and disappointments of external reality, conceived as a struggle for survival.

In linking artistic production to libidinal energy, Rashed makes no distinction between desire for a woman's body and desire in both the production and the reception of art. In his exegesis, a "woman's embrace" is the "fountain of all the arts." Both draw on the same economy of energy. This argument is in tune with Freud's critique of Kantian aesthetics in *Civilization and Its Discontents*: despite the aestheticians' "flood of resounding and empty words" about the "conditions under which things are felt as beautiful," "all that seems certain is its derivation from the field of sexual feeling."[36]

It is clear then that Rashed used elements of Freudian psychoanalysis to explain his own poetry. In doing so, he marked his subjects as modern. Nevertheless, the voice of his narrator is clearly a colonized subject, who, like the "wretched poet," is unprepared for the demands placed on him by British bureaucracy. So it is the demands—perhaps unusually unfair—of colonial modernity in particular that force the narrator's retreat. In this social context, the poems articulate the struggle between reality and the desire to retreat from its challenges as an opposition between life *(zindagī)* and pleasure *('aish)*.

COLONIAL NEUROSIS

The life that Rashed's *Māvarā* describes is particular to colonized societies. Through its methods of characterization, it presents a psychological portrait of the times that opposes British empire. The internal life of the characters in the poems is not particularly obscure, and it does not dwell in psychological or metaphysical symbols. The poems are therefore all fairly straightforward and easy to interpret, unlike much of Rashed's later work. It seems quite obvious from our contemporary moment that the poems were using a method of psychological realism to criticize imperialism. For Rashed, this psychological language was modern and not particularly colonial.

His most notorious poem from the volume, "Revenge" (Intiqām, §10), describes the conquest of a white woman by a brown man, clearly depicting what Frantz Fanon would later describe as the "sexual myth" of the colonial subject's "desire for white flesh."[37] Fanon critiques this desire as a "sexual myth" in an effort to overcome the stereotypes of a racial psychopathology. Reading fictional relationships between black men and white women, Fanon describes the black protagonist, who bears certain similarities to Rashed's narrator, as displaying the "structure of an abandonment-neurotic of the negative-aggressive type." The terms here are Adlerian.[38] At the same time, Fanon discourages linking that behavior directly with "the greater or lesser concentration of melanin in his epidermis."[39] He counters scientific racism based in evolutionary arguments with a notion of experience formed in racist social structures.

For Fanon, to focus on social structure was to critique Freud and Adler's grounding of psychology in the individual's experience of development. In *Black Skins, White Masks*, Fanon argues that to understand the psychology of the colonized the unit of the individual is not enough. "If there is a taint," he writes, "it lies not in the 'soul' of the individual but rather in that of the environment."[40] The psychology of the colonized, he argues, is not a natural result of racial constitution, but rather is rooted in the particularity of the colonial situation. Therefore, the unit of his analysis moves from the individual to the social and from ontogeny to sociogeny. In contrast to an Adlerian response, which would treat a colonial neurotic solely in terms of his individual development, Fanon writes, "I will tell him, 'The environment, society are responsible for your delusion.' Once that has been said, the rest will follow of itself, and what that is we know. The end of the world."[41]

What Fanon does through psychoanalysis, Rashed does through poetic representation. For both, the psychology of the individual must be approached from his social conditions, but the analysis of the individual also leads outward to address social and political concerns. Rashed's characters are clearly neurotics, but their neurosis is rooted in their historical conditions, which constitute their psychology. It is precisely the intersection of sexuality, psychology, and power that Rashed's poetry works to expose. His acknowledgment of this relationship prompts his emphasis on the importance of representing sexuality in literature. Rashed's early poems, such as "Accidents," expose the presence and force of sexuality in modern life. In the later poems, such as "Wretched Poet," sexuality is viewed in its social context, as the narrator assumes a definite identity as a colonial subject.

For Rashed, the social world cannot be separated from issues of the subject. Like Fanon's work, Rashed's poetry presumes that the fundamental problems of society can be addressed only by attention to psychology. As a result, the poems should be seen as addressing the social concerns of its readership. Unlike the earlier literary reformers, the point of his poetry is neither imitation nor moral improvement. Instead, through his early poetry he aimed to represent a contemporary experience of late colonial society. The poems are, as Rashed wrote, "expressions of the powerlessness, frustration, mental struggle, disappointments, and lusts of the youth of this age."[42]

THE DANGERS OF MODERNISM

While the poems of *Māvarā* were written as a particular form of intervention, upon publication they became controversial in a new way, for the volume was published at a moment when progressivism and modernism were fast becoming two separately defined positions in Urdu letters. The focus on sexuality and internality in Rashed's poetry became cause for concern for those progressive critics whose professed allegiance to realism rejected "psychological" or "modernist" writing as obscene. Rashed was placed in the company of some of the best-loved Urdu writers, such as Saʿādat Ḥasan Manṭo, ʿIṣmat Chuġhtāʾī, and Mīrājī, whose work was rejected by some "progressive" critics as obscene. While portions of these debates are no longer terribly relevant, the reliance of critical discourse on questions of the individual's subjectivity remains significant. In particular, the opposition critics employ between the inside and the outside is not only familiar in various aspects of South Asian historical writing, particularly in regard to nationalism, but it became an important figure in Rashed's poetry itself.[43]

The Progressive Writers Association, which formed in London in 1934, came to contain writers from all the linguistic regions of India, who united to oppose traditionalism and regressive tendencies and to strive to liberate the nation from imperial rule. The organization drafted manifestos and organized conferences, and it drew support from a vast political spectrum. Communists among its leadership eventually came to insist on bringing its aesthetic closer to something like socialist realism, which had become the preferred aesthetic under Stalin.[44] As I mentioned earlier, N. M. Rashed became much more critical of "socialist" *(ishtirākī)* writing in his next collection, particularly in regard to Stalinism, but there is nothing of the sort anywhere in his first volume. There is a critique of "realism" in the introduction, but no condemnation of progressivism per se. The preface to the volume is in fact written by Krishan Chandar, a communist and progressive writer, and the book is dedicated to Faiẓ Aḥmad Faiẓ, who is usually remembered as *the* progressive Urdu poet, though his writing is generally quite far from realism.

Two publications from 1945, four years after *Māvarā*'s publication, point to this new terrain. ʿAzīz Aḥmad's history of progressive literature in Urdu describes Rashed's poetry as follows: "Ignoring a few exceptions, the collective inclination of Rashed's poetry and temperament is to flee and escape from life, and it is inclined towards regression. . . . The reason is that there are just two forces that rule over his mind and heart: sex *(jins)* and, because of sexual desire, a death-will *(k͟hvāhish-e marg)*. Sex for him is life's greatest force."[45] Here ʿAzīz Aḥmad employs the binary categories often found in progressive rhetoric. He accuses Rashed of escapism, as opposed to the expected focus on the world. He also finds Rashed's poetry to be regressive rather than progressive. Rashed's poems about sex are a sign first of Rashed's preoccupation with himself, rather than society, and, second, of a certain psychological deviance and emphasis on "sexuality" *(jins parastī)* that Aḥmad argues Rashed shared with other writers, such as Iṣmat Chughtā'ī.

Also in 1945, Ḥayātu'l-lâh Anṣārī published a book-length psychoanalytical study of N. M. Rashed that argued that Rashed was a sexual deviant and that his poetry was morally corrupt.[46] The study uses an Adlerian framework.[47] Anṣārī writes that he felt the need to write the book after reading Rashed's "Intiqām" (Revenge, §10), mentioned above. He describes Rashed as suffering from sadism deriving from an inferiority/superiority complex that inhibits his "social feeling."[48] In diagnosing this sickness, Anṣārī quickly moves from the narrator to Rashed himself, and traces this "illness" through many of Rashed's poems to prove that he suffers from an inferiority complex. Rashed is "so unknowingly a victim of sadism and masochism that he proudly expresses his faults."[49]

Following a description of Rashed's neurosis, Anṣārī points out the dangers of modernism. Because of the entrance of psychoanalysis, as well as Marxism, into literature, people are "afraid to trust their literary taste." As a result, the emergence of modern literature was not sufficiently open to critique. Rashed's poetry was therefore fundamentally dangerous for his readers: "If a non-critic reads his writing, then he will swim away in the flow of [Rashed's] defective emotions, and if the reader's emotions are not strong, then he will fall into hedonism and other such types of base illnesses. Only an individual with deep vision, who can keep firm his personal resolve, can grasp Rashed's vices, and there are very few people like that."[50] The danger of modernism is that unlike "proper" literature, which aims to improve the reader, modernism encourages moral weakness. Only one who can see psychology for what it is will be able to peer into the depraved depths of Rashed's own character in his poetry.

Underlying Anṣārī's diagnosis of Rashed as a neurotic and sexual deviant is the accusation that Rashed is "somewhat English."[51] The Westernness of Rashed's sexuality in particular is the source of its immorality. As elsewhere, literary modernism in South Asia would be criticized for its "European" bourgeois decadence and its emphasis on sexuality and the unconscious.[52] For Anṣārī, the poems of *Māvarā* represent a sexuality enmeshed in psychology that is aligned with the West and opposed to Indian and Islamic tradition.[53] He draws on the examples of the Ellora caves, where the god Shiva and goddess Parvati assume sexual positions, and a sixth-century Arabic *qasīdah* ("ode") by Imrū al-Qais, which depicts a man and a woman happily engaged in lovemaking with their child in between them. In Anṣārī's analysis, these works of art present an indigenous model of sexuality unfettered by psychological complexes, quite unlike Rashed's poetry.

In looking to these ancient models of sexuality, Anṣārī skips over the entire history of South Asian Muslims. Anṣārī, then a member of the Indian National Congress, bypasses the erotic history of the Mughals, for instance, to find in the Hindu mythological past an indigenous prehistory of sexual neuroses, devoid of the conflicts that psychology attempts to describe. Like Ḥālī, Anṣārī viewed literature as a means of promoting a moral subject. His departure, however, was his implicit focus on Indian tradition as an alternative to the problems of modern life, and his criticism of Rashed is that as a modernist he was simply not Indian enough.

CONCLUSION

Both N. M. Rashed's *Māvarā* and the criticism it provoked should be seen as part of a larger debate about the proper lyrical subject of poetry and the status of subjectivity in general. Rashed's poetry was a pointed critique of literary tradition. Rashed conceived of literary tradition primarily through the ghazal. His poems argued that the ghazal could not sufficiently acknowledge bodily desire, preferring to dwell on the immaterial sacred or a potentially allegorical and not necessarily heterosexual beloved. Rashed criticized reformers and realists, who were also critical of literary tradition, for not giving sufficient attention to psychology, especially issues of sexuality and desire. Rashed considered the psychological model of the self to be both modern and universal. The volume's later poems depict the interior life of various romantic couples, representing colonial neurotics in what amounts to a critique of colonialism. After *Māvarā*'s publication, progressive and Indian nationalist critics decried the poems for failing to represent a properly socially oriented and rational subject. Much of this criticism conflated Rashed the author with the lyrical subject of his poetry, criticizing both the author and his writing as too Western and therefore too sexually deviant. But the accusation of the poet as insufficiently concerned with society proved to be a durable criticism, because it fell into a more general distrust of modernism itself.

Rashed asserted that the lyrical subject of modernism should be an individual, not a type. This led him to oppose the anonymous lyrical subject of romanticism just as much as he rejected the traditional lover of the Urdu ghazal. He justified his break with literary tradition, both in terms of form and content, on the grounds of individualism. And yet, even as Rashed criticizes the literary tradition of Urdu poetry he also carefully constructs a genealogy for his writing to oppose. He begins in that volume to assemble the literary tradition that he rejects, both there and, even more thoroughly, in his last two volumes.

Māvarā remains significant in the Urdu literary canon because while breaking with the classical form of the ghazal Rashed maintained many familiar formal qualities, such as most elements of its prosody and its expectations of rhyme. His poetry therefore assumes an audience familiar with the conventions of Urdu poetry, including elements derived from Persian poetry. His argument in *Māvarā* was that these elements were now indigenous to India and not just a part of Muslim experience. Rashed shared this opinion with his contemporaries, though he differed from them in approach. The poet Mīrājī made similar overtures to an audience beyond the limits of Urdu, but he did so by adopting the lyrical forms associated with Tagore or "Hindi." The poet Faiẓ Aḥmad Faiẓ, who was perhaps even more concerned with maintaining poetic community than Rashed, was more attendant to the familiar language and structures of the ghazal and of the *mushāʿirah*. For Rashed, musicality was the touchstone of Urdu poetics, and that was enough of a connection to past forms.

All three of these Urdu poets also shared a preoccupation with questions of subjectivity. The way that Rashed thought of subjectivity in *Māvarā* was through psychoanalysis. In his second volume he turns away from psychoanalysis and toward an idea of experience, where poetry is meant not to analyze the psychic situation of people like him but instead to concern itself with more fleeting experiences, many of them involving geopolitical situations. It is to these concerns that I turn in the next chapter. So while the defining concern of his poetry remains subjectivity, his formulation of what that means changes over time, in a more profound way perhaps than in his contemporaries.

TWO

Position without Identity

THE CENTERPIECE OF N. M. RASHED'S *Īrān meñ ajnabī aur dūsrī naẕmeñ* (A Stranger in Iran and Other Poems) is a formally innovative free-verse poem in thirteen parts that describes the experiences of an Indian soldier in Iran during World War II. British and Soviet armies had invaded Iran in 1941, pushing aside Reza Shah Pahlavi and dividing the country between them. N. M. Rashed arrived in Iran two years later, serving in the Inter-Services Public Relations Directorate as part of the occupying British Indian Army.[1] Although his poem records the impressions of an Indian soldier-poet, its setting in Iran represents more than the happenstance of Rashed's military postings. As the motherland of the Persian language and culture that pervades Urdu, Iran became in the twentieth century a sign of tradition, the foreign point of origin for Indian Muslim identity. The poem's narrator, an Indian Muslim soldier, arrives in Iran in search of the past, yet finds, instead of a common heritage, an extension of his own colonial present. What is truly shared by Iran and India, the poem contends, is the experience of imperialism. The poem thus assumes a critical position grounded less in the authenticity of language, religion, or culture than in the similarities between India's and Iran's contemporary predicaments.

Rashed's volume of poetry was published ten years after the Partition of British India, an event that divided the Urdu literary community between India and Pakistan and intervened in the ongoing reconsideration of Indo-Muslim identity and the status of Urdu as both the assumed "national" literature of Pakistan and a "minority" literature of India. The poem's setting thus allowed Rashed to carve out a third space between a dominant strand of Urdu modernism that was associated with Indo-Muslim identitarianism and the socialist-realist progressive literature well established in the 1940s and early 1950s. Indeed, the poem dismisses these positions as it engages in a larger critique of both literary movements' investment in collective identity.

To describe what India and Iran held in common, Rashed turned to the idea of Asia. This was an unusual strategy—only one other Urdu poet had explored Asia as a potential source of identity, and the differences between these two attempts at Asian Urdu poetry are instructive. In 1952 ʿAlī Sardār Jaʿfrī (1913–2000) published *Eshiyā jāg uṭhā* (Asia Awakes) in response to the Korean War. Jaʿfrī's long poem describes Asia as the "womb of civilization, the motherland of culture," where the "sun opened its eyes." He cites historical figures—the Buddha, Firdausi, Hafiz, Sur, Tagore, and Lao Tzu—as well as artifacts—Mohenjodaro, the Vedas, and the Great Wall of China—in opposition to the so-called civilization *(tahẕīb, tamaddun)* of Asia's colonizers. Denouncing colonialism and American imperialism, Jaʿfrī calls for Asian unity. He also demands support for the Soviet Union—"the star in whose fearless light the people of Asia see [their] destination"—and threatens that "if any tongue says one word against it / then we will pull out that black tongue from the throat."[2]

Rashed, by contrast, criticizes the Soviet Union in his poem, describing it as an imperial force not unlike Europe or America. Furthermore, although Rashed agrees with Jaʿfrī about the effects of colonial rule, he differs markedly in his conception of Asia. Rashed does not treat Asia as a common civilization or offer a roll call of historical figures or cultural achievements. Instead, his Asia is closer to what Gayatri Spivak has described in a more contemporary context as a "position without identity," a geographical category that both Iran and India can claim and yet not fully possess. For Spivak, Asia provides a "position from which to view" that resists "identitarian politics," offering the possibility of a "critical regionalism" at the moment of the alleged postnationalism of globalization.[3] At the much earlier—and profoundly nationalist—moment of decolonization, Rashed makes a similar claim for Asia, and does so in a manner that also evades identitarianism. That is, by invoking Asia, Rashed is able to talk about India and Iran in terms that presage what will later be called subaltern by Spivak and others: a position without identity in which "social lines of mobility, being elsewhere, do not permit the formation of a recognizable basis of action."[4]

This move stemmed from Rashed's desire to produce a kind of literature that could not be considered "representative" in a way most often associated with a "national allegory," Frederic Jameson's term for both the interest in the "national situation" among many third-world intellectuals and the tendency of first-world readers to focus on the "radical difference of non-canonical texts."[5] Furthermore, although Rashed began his career during the movement for *taraqqī pasand* or "progressive" literature, by the time he wrote *Irān meñ ajnabī*, he had begun to reject the requirement that a writer represent a collectivity—whether it be nation or class.[6] Yet even though Rashed's position is clearly outlined in the collection, contemporary readers have consistently misrecognized its point. For example, Aijaz Ahmad has cited Rashed's verse as progressivism's Other—socially isolated, politically quietist, and formally experimental[7]—while other critics would collapse Rashed's anti-identitarian position into the cultural conservatism that had come to be associated with Urdu modernism.

Because the "progressive" elements in Urdu literary culture oppose "Persianized" language in favor of more colloquial and understandable common speech, Rashed's use of Persian in *Irān meñ ajnabī*, along with the general association of Iran with the Indo-Muslim past, encouraged the misapprehension of his collection as a regressive *(raj'at pasand)* statement of Indo-Persian nostalgia.[8] The volume was also considered conservative because, by the 1950s, Urdu *jadīdiyat*—a term that means both modernism and modernity—had become associated with a particular form of Indo-Muslim identitarianism, especially in Pakistan, where some of the most articulate supporters of *jadīdiyat*, such as Muḥammad Ḥasan 'Askarī, increasingly looked to "tradition" *(rivāyat)* to provide the basis of a precolonial Indo-Persianate Islamic civilization. Although it is certainly not inaccurate to describe critics like 'Askarī as modernist—the desire to recapture a lost tradition is, after all, a frequent aspect of literary modernisms—I will here adopt, in order to disambiguate the traditionalist position of critics like 'Askarī from the iconoclasm of Rashed, Aamir Mufti's term "auratic criticism" as a more useful description of 'Askarī's point of view. Mufti defines auratic criticism as a mode of endowing particular postcolonial cultural practices with an aura of authenticity,[9] transforming them into "the unsubsumable Other to the dominant culture of the modern West, the authentic embodiment of difference that the great equalizing engine of modern culture would annihilate, and the means of restoring to itself the shattered totality of life in modernity."[10]

In this chapter, I will show how the ephemeral and contingent experiences of Iran in Rashed's title poem situate the poet in opposition to each of the two modes of belonging then prevalent in the Urdu literary community: progressivism and auratic criticism. At the heart of this reading is a reconsideration of the poem's "Persianized" language. To an Indian soldier, particularly one who, like Rashed, had studied Persian as his own heritage, the experience of modern Iranian Persian was defamiliarizing. In response, Rashed reproduces the literally uncanny effect of Iranian Persian in his Urdu verse. By insistently maintaining the foreignness of this familiar language, the poem avoids resolving what had become known as the "problem" of Persian in Urdu literature in either of the manners then currently in vogue. As a result, his poetry was criticized as avant-garde formalism, on the one hand, or asocial and derivative bourgeois individualism, on the other.[11] Yet Rashed's approach to the category of experience hardly denies its social life. Rather, through the representation of particular experiences his poem obtains a critical purchase that does not correspond to easily recognizable political modes. At the same time, Rashed's poem reflects a moment when the alignment of modernism with tradition and progressivism with Marxism was still vital, and it constitutes commentary on both of these trajectories. Against progressive writers who favored Marxism, the poem represents Soviet internationalism as imperialism, citing specific experiences of the Soviet Union in Iran. But it also opposes the grounding of identity in tradition, both by exposing a connection between India and Iran rooted in the experience of imperialism and by explicitly criticizing forms of Iranian nationalism based on continuity with a lost imperial past.

THE PERSIAN PROBLEM

For twentieth-century Indian Muslims, and Urdu poets in particular, Iran was the homeland of Persian language and culture. In fact, as the language of the Mughal court, Persian had once been an elite lingua franca in India. Urdu contains many Persian words and shares its right-to-left script. "Classical" Urdu poetry grew out of the matrix of Persian poetry, taking on its poetic forms and conventions, and most classical Urdu poets also wrote in Persian.[12] Until the early twentieth century, learning Persian was viewed as necessary for a full understanding of Urdu and as central to the comportment of a respectable North Indian Muslim man.[13] N. M. Rashed was educated in this fashion; although he was also educated in English, he learned Persian as a child and earned his first college degree in Persian from the elite Government College in Lahore.[14]

As explained in chapter 1, Rashed quickly gained a reputation as a poet while a college student, and by the late 1930s he had forged a new poetic form, *āzād naẓm* (free verse), in order to overcome what he (and others) believed to be the overly restrictive rhyme scheme and meters of classical Urdu poetic forms, especially the ghazal, as well as the figurative conventions shared by classical Urdu and Persian poetry, which frequently address an ambiguous and cruel beloved using such themes *(maẓmūn)* as moths chasing after flames, eyelashes impaling the hearts of lovers, birds singing of their love to unresponsive roses, and so on.[15] Despite this obvious formal and thematic innovation, however, the use of the Persian register in Rashed's *Īrān meñ ajnabī* appeared both excessive and odd to his contemporaries. This criticism can even be found in the foreword to the volume itself, which was written by Ahmed Shah "Patras" Bokhari, a prominent man of letters and important diplomat.[16] In it he highlights in particular two lines from the title poem: "*shakr aur qahve ke malfūf-e arzāñ / jo bāzār meñ intihaʾī girāñ the* (cheap envelopes of sugar and coffee / that were extremely expensive in the market)."[17] Although these lines are intelligible in Urdu, they diverge from colloquial language in a number of ways. The word *malfūf* (envelope) would normally be *lifāfah*, a different form of the same Arabic root. The unfamiliar phrase *malfūf-e arzāñ* is generated through the Persian *iẓāfat* (-e), an enclitic that joins nouns with a following adjective, which in colloquial Urdu is used primarily in fixed phrases. The Persianized word *arzāñ* (cheap) sounds a little precious in Urdu, and its Persianized opposite, *girāñ* (expensive), more frequently means "heavy" or "difficult." There are many such passages in the poem, which in one critic's words enlist "weighty Persian words" that are "new and strange" but at times "difficult" *(girāñ)* for the reader.[18]

Yet however much these "new and strange" aspects of the poem's language may draw on the Urdu readership's familiarity with classical Indo-Persian, they actually reflect the poet's encounter with modern Persian. For example, the words used for cheap and expensive *(arzāñ* and *girāñ)* in the passage quoted above are perfectly colloquial in modern Iran. Writing for an audience for whom Persian is read as a sign of the Indo-Persian tradition—a connection alluded to through stock phrases replete with historical connotation—Rashed uses contemporary Persian to balance legibility with shock. The effect is not unlike Freud's description of the uncanny *(unheimlich)*, a "harking-back to particular phases in the evolution of the self-regarding feeling, a regression to a time when the ego had not yet marked itself off sharply from the external world and from other people."[19] To readers like Bokhari, Rashed's verse likewise appears to regress to a precolonial stage when Urdu and Persian were less bound to particular territories.

As a result, Bokhari takes issue with Rashed's use of Persian, declaring that Rashed is not the "stranger in Iran" that he should be: "the mental and emotional world in which [his] poetry grows is not far from Iran; in fact, it is perhaps farther away from India."[20] In Bokhari's estimation, all modern Urdu poets are false modernists, because they still rely on a traditional method of lexical innovation that consists of bringing Persian words into Urdu. He accuses them of using Persian vocabulary as a sign of high culture even though, as he sardonically writes, "those who are born *shudra* (low caste) cannot be made the equal of Brahmans." Indeed, modern Urdu literature cannot be *ṭheṭh* (real, authentic) if it is divorced from the common speech *(bol chāl)* of the nation's people. "How long," he laments, "will Persian and Arabic travel on the shoulders of our poetry? When will that day come when our poets will favor our own language?"[21]

Because the rejection of Persian had long been a touchstone of progressive politics, Bokhari's desire for *ṭheṭh* literature echoes the notion that a vernacular, Hindustani language is the common core of the increasingly divergent, and communally overcoded, languages of Hindi and Urdu.[22] While director of All India Radio in the early 1940s, Bokhari had followed the lead of the Indian National Congress and supported broadcasting in a common Hindustani language, stripped of words too close either to Sanskrit, on the one hand, or to Persian and Arabic, on the other.[23] The Progressive Writers Association took a similar stance, at least at first.[24] Their goal was to produce literature in a natural, vernacular language understandable by the common people and so, in Premchand's words, "to change the standards of beauty" by shifting the writer's gaze from "palaces and bungalows" to "huts and shanties."[25] If common people were to be the focus of progressive art, then Persian, a vestige of feudal social relations associated with well-educated people and the court, had to be avoided.[26]

Following the creation of Pakistan in 1947, a number of prominent cultural critics, and in particular the circle of Muḥammad Ḥasan ʿAskarī, inverted this value judgment, claiming Urdu, rather than Hindustani, as the cultural inheritance of South Asian Muslims. To preserve the Persian vocabulary and grammatical forms of Urdu intact was to retain the cultural and moral integrity of that community. Thus, as Aamir Mufti has noted, the Indo-Persian regional tradition came to be reenvisioned as Islamic rather than Indian, with the mystical worldview of Sufism as the metaphysical ground of an Indo-Muslim culture displaced by colonial modernity.[27] Whereas earlier reformers saw Persian as a source of artificiality, these auratic critics increasingly came to regard the more Indic components of the language as foreign.[28]

Despite his enthusiastic advocacy for modernism *(jadīdiyat)*, Rashed did not share these auratic critics' view of the precolonial Indo-Muslim past as the source of authenticity for modern Urdu culture. But although Rashed's use of modern Persian words thereby resists the conservative investment in Persian tradition, to Bokhari, who advocated the progressivist notion of Hindustani, Rashed's use of the Persian register could only be both politically and aesthetically conservative, at once elitist and opposed to the native language of the people. Bokhari thus overlooks the ways in which Rashed's poem actually exposes the ability of Urdu to accommodate modern Persian as a language that is at once foreign and paradoxically familiar to Urdu speakers. By exploiting the unique relationship between Urdu and Persian, his poetry makes visible the practice of translation that was central to the experience of being a foreigner in Iran.

FRAGMENTS OF EXPERIENCE

The poem "Īrān meñ ajnabī" attempts to challenge both progressive and auratic orthodoxies by capturing the fragments of experience. In advocating a literature for the people, progressive writers and critics aimed to avoid focusing on bourgeois experience by describing instead the objective conditions of workers and peasants. For many of them, modernism's focus on the internal life of the self was excessively psychological and signified a lack of interest in society. Oddly, auratic critics such as ʿAskarī and (later) Salīm Aḥmad, also believed that modernism's preoccupation with individual experience encouraged the fragmentation of a self cut off from a perennial "metaphysical tradition," which they associated with Sufism.[29] Both positions emphasize "reality" *(ḥaqīqat)*—otherworldly in the case of auratic critics, material and social in the case of progressives.

For Rashed, however, individual experience formed the proper subject and substance of literature, although not to the exclusion of social life. His poem represents this-worldly, even mundane, experiences that both escape the auratic critics' focus on transcendence and, given their individual and psychological nature, diverge from progressive realism's concentration on social conditions. In his words, "Īrān meñ ajnabī" "bears the impressions of an Indian soldier who is mentally the resident of one continent and physically a member of a foreign army."[30] By means of a poetic form that Rashed calls the *qiṭ'ah* (fragment or section) and describes as "scattered images" the poem explores a feeling of disjuncture similar to the division between the mind and the body.[31] He further notes that the thirteen *qiṭ'ah* that make up "Īrān meñ ajnabī" lack narrative continuity: some form part of an abridged poetic story, some depict particular characters or events, and others resemble sketches or autobiography.[32]

Rashed wrote his *qiṭ'ah* after abandoning work on a novel about the life of Indian soldiers in Iran that was to capture the "social and individual effects" of the "unprecedented political and economic crisis" of Iran's occupation by foreign armies.[33] In a 1946 letter, he reports that he had written seven or eight chapters; in a late interview, he remembers writing twelve or thirteen, half of which were published "in some journal out of Delhi." In that same interview, he also recalls that he "began to feel that the experiential matter collected in [his] mind" would be better expressed in verse, because the novel form's demand for a connective narrative "stood in the way of putting together different types of impressions."[34] When the fragments of "Īrān meñ ajnabī" were originally published in an Urdu journal, they were called "cantos," not *qiṭ'ah*, with the earlier term functioning as an allusion to the cantos of Lord Byron (in "Childe Harold's Pilgrimage") and Ezra Pound. Rashed reports that he originally thought "cantos would be the best poetic form for depicting wartime Iran, since the form is especially adaptable for different types of poems." Because he came to view his long poem as too fragmented to fulfill the requirements of the canto form, however, in "repentance" for that incompleteness—or so Rashed claims—he adopted the term *qiṭ'ah*.[35]

The *qiṭ'ah* mostly record the responses of an Indian soldier in Iran to the city of Tehran and its wartime inhabitants. In one poem, the soldier reflects on the reign of Reza Shah while looking up at his statue. In another, the soldier bids farewell to a Polish refugee while considering the future of Europe. Several *qiṭ'ah* focus on the psychological and sexual issues confronting Indian soldiers in Iran; others explore the paradoxes of Stalinism, the common problems of Asia, the consequences for the poor of anti-begging legislation enacted by newly independent countries, and the stupidity of certain Iranian government ministers. Nearly all of the *qiṭ'ah*, even the more psychological ones, refer to specific events or locations. According to Rashed, the poem was "formed by embroidering individual emotions on the veil of the politics of the time." He also calls it (more prosaically) an attempt to "analyze the struggle of emotions that were created by particular political circumstances."[36] Anticipating progressivism's demand for social engagement, Rashed contends that emotional response is part of social life. Rashed's poem also denies auratic critics their "tale of the tribe," to borrow Pound's phrase; he does not indulge in nostalgia for the Indo-Persian past. Rather, Rashed attempts to make his outsider's experience of the recent past an intervention into contemporary debates about literature and social life.

In a seminal essay, historian Joan Scott has argued that if experience is assumed to be "transparent," it "reproduces rather than contests given ideological systems." Moreover, she continues, because typical definitions of experience—as an external event or condition that leaves an impression or as internal knowledge acquired over time—presume an autonomous and reliable individual as their starting point, they "naturalize categories such as man, woman, black, white, heterosexual by treating them as given characteristics of individuals." As a result, the historian should attend to how experience itself is a "linguistic event," "always already an interpretation and something that needs to be interpreted." In short, "What counts as experience is neither self-evident nor straightforward; it is always contested, and always therefore political."[37]

Rashed represents the personal experience of an Indian soldier in the manner called for by Scott—that is, as constituted by a rich and contested field of interpretation. As he explains in his introduction, "the modern poet, like his respectable forerunners, does not merely express thoughts and feelings. Many types of shadows appear mixed along with them. Because they are important creatures in his mental world, he also tries to illuminate these shadows as well."[38] Rashed criticizes both progressivism and auratic criticism for erasing the uncertainty of individual experience by demanding that literature conform to prescribed ideologies. In a September 1956 speech to a literary group in Lahore, for example, he declares that the greatest threats to literature are "political and religious groups" who use it instrumentally ("like a weapon") as a "means of interpreting nonliterary aims." These groups "take advantage of the common human weaknesses of the reader and wish to make him a slave of their particular religious or political ideology." To Rashed, literature should offer an interpretation of experience without recourse to totalizing objectives. He continues,

> In reality, the purpose of literature is not ideological instruction. The point of literature is not to change the reader's thoughts or to convince him. The

> point of literature is to give birth to those tiny changes in the reader's mind that can become the basis for free thought and reflection so that he can better understand the meaning of life, so that not through knowledge or reason but through emotions he can reflect and illuminate the most subtle meanings of life. The purpose of literature is to give to your eyes a third magnifying glass so that you can see more clearly the small vicissitudes of life.[39]

Rashed's experiences are ends in themselves; they are not meant to reflect either a typical or an essential experience of a particular community.

PANTHEISM

At its heart, Rashed's poem critiques all ideology as totalizing and deceiving. Addressing both auratic criticism and progressivism, he argues that neither can fully represent individual experience. His most important critical strategy is to combine these two normally opposing positions. He does so by likening communism, the political ideology advocated by many progressive writers, to pantheism *(hamah-ūst)*, which was associated with auratic critics. *Hamah-ūst*, a Persian phrase that means "all is He," specifically denotes monistic pantheism—an idea of a unity of being *(vaḥdatu'l-vujūd)* stressing the immanence of the divine—propagated by certain Sufis, especially Ibn 'Arabī. Indeed, auratic critics (especially 'Askarī) conceived of *vahdatu'l-vujūd* as the central component of the Indo-Persian "metaphysical tradition," a component that offered a different conception of the human subject from that found in European modernity.[40]

Although Rashed does not make explicit the links between communism and pantheism, his use of the metaphor *hamah-ūst* describes communism as a political ideology bound to a single, universal theory and teleology that is, like pantheism, everywhere visible to its adherents. Moreover, just as the deferral from "I" to "he" in the phrase "all is He" *(hamah-ūst)* mirrors the subsumption of the individual self in the totality of the party collective, so the metaphor also draws on many Islamists' tendency to associate pantheism with moral corruption.[41] Like religion, communism appears as an all-encompassing ideology not open to doubt. As such, in Rashed's view it gives short shrift to the rich possibilities of individual experience—and of literature as an interpretation of that experience.

Rashed first uses this metaphor in his satiric poem "Hamah-ūst" (Pantheism, §15). The first scene in the poem takes place at a Russian bookstore on Saʿdī Avenue in Tehran. The narrator, an Indian soldier, has come there with his new friend Ḳhālid to buy a history of Russian artists for an Iranian woman named Marsīdah. Although the narrator has "no affection for the Russians' 'political pantheism,'" Khalid (a soldier who had been living with his unit in a "faraway desert") does, and he tries to chat up a "robust but enchanting" bookstore clerk from the Caucasus by professing his love of the Russian language and "socialist civilization" *(ishtirākī tamaddun)*. When Khalid asks her if she will teach him Russian, because he "wants to see the wellsprings of Russian writers," she brushes him off, and as they leave the bookstore he covers his embarrassment by mouthing communist slogans to the narrator: "If you need to learn a language, learn it from a woman / There is no second to Russian literature anywhere in the world / That beauty from the Caucasus is a working woman! / If all the workers of the world unite, / a new age of happiness will begin!" (lines 61–65). The scene ends with the narrator observing that many of his communist friends try to console one another in this manner, especially after failed romantic ventures. A second scene takes place at Marsidah's wedding, where the bride suddenly approaches the narrator and asks if he has seen Khalid. She recalls last having seen him sitting alone and despondent on a sofa. When they are unable to find him at the reception, they search outside and eventually find him silent and unresponsive. The poem ends with the narrator wondering if Khalid has "found the wellsprings of Russian writers" (lines 72–93).

Although this poem is obviously (and broadly) satirical, it also makes a number of subtler points. While Khalid clearly identifies himself as a communist, his enthusiasm for all things Russian is also a badly concealed attempt to pick up the bookstore employee. Furthermore, when Khalid mouths the Soviet slogans, the details in the poem suggest that his statements are in fact imperialistic. In Urdu, the word *tamaddun* is frequently used to talk about and critique Western civilization.[42] By using this term, Rashed likens the Soviet Union to the British Empire, a connection reinforced by the clerk's homeland, for the Caucasus is a region that has long been subject to Russian conquest. Khalid's declaration of the greatness of Russian language and literature also reflects an ideological shift away from proletarian internationalism—an identity based in class consciousness—to what David Brandenberger has described as "Stalinist russocentrism," a form of Russian nationalism that appropriated symbolic elements of the czarist regime.[43]

In another *qiṭʿah* focused on the Soviet Union, Rashed further explores the disjuncture between communist ideology and Soviet practice. "Tel ke saudāgar" (Oil Merchants, §12) warns Iranians to beware of Soviet "robbers" disguised as "old oil merchants" who have pitched their tent near the city walls. If invited to feast in the city, they will drink, sing, dance, and warm everyone's hearts with their laughter. But when the dawn breaks, the residents will "dig the graves of [their] dead with [their] eyelashes" and "shed tears" at the "ashes of the banquet's spread" after their guests have attacked them in the night. The poem urges Iranians to "strengthen the low walls" and "post sentries at every tower and gate" of their "tall, shining cities" of "Tehran and Mashhad," both of which were in areas of Soviet influence during World War II.[44]

The casting of the Soviets as oil merchants clearly reflects the two major crises in relations between the Soviet Union and Iran at the time, both of which involved oil concessions. The oil crisis of 1944 occurred after the defeat of the German army at Stalingrad, when the Iranian prime minister, Mohammad Said, rejected the Soviets' demand for a huge oil concession in northern Iran. In a press conference at the Soviet embassy in Tehran that the *New York Times* described as "notable for the frankness of views expressed by the representative of one power in the capital of another," Soviet Assistant Commissar for Foreign Affairs Sergei I. Kavtaradze stated that the "disloyal and unfriendly position taken by Premier Said toward the Soviet Union excluded the possibility of further collaboration with him."[45] Members of the communist Tudeh Party staged large rallies in Tehran against Said, and he resigned two weeks later. A second crisis followed in 1946, during which the Soviet Union held up troop withdrawals until securing from Iran's prime minister the promise (later voided) of a joint Iran-Soviet oil company.[46] These events also highlighted the lack of autonomy characteristic of national communist parties such as Iran's Tudeh Party. For following the oil crisis of 1944, the Tudeh were forced to adopt a pro-Soviet attitude that was not necessarily in the best interests of Iran or the international proletariat.

Rashed tells his story using literary and historical allusions that clearly link Soviet actions—metaphorically described as "pantheistic"—with imperialism. He begins the poem with a reference to one of the best-known couplets of Hafiz Shirazi, a fourteenth-century Persian poet:

> If that Turk of Shiraz would take my heart
> I would grant Samarqand and Bukhara for his black *(hindū)* mole

Although Bukhara and Samarqand (now in Uzbekistan) were both centers of Persian culture and Islamic learning, Hafiz offers to trade them both for the black (literally *hindū*, Hindu or Indian) mole on the cheek of his beloved

Turk. In the *qiṭʿah*, Rashed alludes to this verse to call attention to the Bolshevik conquest of the two cities in 1920, both of which were then absorbed into the USSR:

> Bukhara and Samarqand for a Hindu mole!
> Very well, but what remains of Bukhara and Samarqand?
> Bukhara and Samarqand are intoxicated in their slumber,
> covered in blue veils *(ḥijāb)* of silence,
> their doors closed to travelers
> like the eyelids of sleeping moon-faced women,
> two moon-faced women
> crippled by the whips of Russian "pantheism"!
>
> (lines 1–8)

The inaccessibility of these two "moon-faced" cities—"their doors closed to travelers"—starkly contrasts with their historical significance as sites on the Silk Road and as cultural and intellectual centers.

Rashed makes this warning against Soviet expansionism even more explicit by comparing the Iranian experience of Soviet imperialism with India's suffering under British rule:

> We too have shed tears!
> —though now the Hindu mole has no value
> that deep, oozing boil on the cheek of the world
> that arose from the West's blood-thirsty desire—
> We too have shed tears
> Our eyes have seen
> cities dissolving like flowing shadows,
> falling roofs and doors
> and minarets and domes
>
> (lines 34–42)

The "Hindu mole" from Hafiz's couplet returns as a graphic metaphor for colonized India—but now as a symptom of Britain's imperial desires rather than a mark of beauty. Dismissing the structural differences between European colonialism and Soviet communism, the poem finds a common content in India and Iran's experience of foreign domination: "cities dissolving like flowing shadows" and "falling roofs and doors / and minarets and domes."

For Rashed, the idea of "all of the workers of the world unit[ing]" is an ideological myth contradicted by the actual experiences of Soviet rule represented in his poem. Writing from the perspective of occupied Iran, he depicts the Soviet Union under Stalin as an authoritarian imperial power dedicated to imposing its Russocentric culture on an ever-expanding empire.

ASIA

To the ideologies of auratic criticism and Soviet-aligned progressivism Rashed opposes images of an Asia constituted through a common experience of foreign domination. For Rashed, it is this contemporary history that India and Iran hold in common, not a traditional past or a socialist future. Articulating the experience of domination is a central theme of "Īrān meñ ajnabī" and the specific subject of its first *qiṭʿah*, "Manna and Quails" (Mann-o-salvâ, §13). In form, this *qiṭʿah* echoes the *savāl-o-javāb* (question and answer), a rhetorical device common to classical Urdu and Persian poetry, and it recounts a series of misrecognitions. First, the Iranian populace hails the soldier-narrator as a *hindī* (Indian), not, say, as Asian or Indo-Persian. Second, seeing his uniform, they assume he is powerful. The voice of "Iran"—who is called *ʿAjam*, which perhaps means something closer to "Persia"—asks why Indian soldiers are occupying the country. The soldier replies that he does not choose to do so and that British colonialism is really to blame. India and Iran share the same position in regard to imperialism, he argues, a position he describes using the popular Orientalist trope of the harem. The "European" is a "highway robber" *(rah-zan)*, who imagines Asians as "a languid race of ancient eunuchs" and Asia itself as a "barren and rich widow, being pressured for her unprotected wealth" and longingly awaiting his embrace. The Indian soldier is likewise a "eunuch": "we [Indians] have become the house-lizards in the heights of his civilization," in which Europe's exclusive claim to modernity leaves the peoples it colonizes behind.

As with many of the *qiṭʿah*, the general reflections in "Manna and Quails" are specific to a very particular time and place. Details in the poem refer to the bread shortages in wartime Tehran that led to rioting in late 1942: a poor wheat harvest, coupled with poor food distribution (vehicles and trains were requisitioned by the Allied troops) and Soviet claims on Azerbaijani wheat supplies, resulted in massive bread shortages in a city whose wartime population had rapidly increased with an influx of refugees.[47] The poem's title, "Manna and Quails," which refers to the sustenance provided to the Israelites after their exodus from Egypt, appears in an image of a beggar's hand opening before Indian soldiers in the hope that "a chunk of bread would change into manna and quails."

Because the Indian soldier fails to provide either liberation or relief, he imagines that "Iran"—or ʿAjam, his interlocutor—believes he is "bound in a chain of indecent love for the Europeans." Yet the soldier responds:

> This is not indecent love
> but just a chain,
> one great iron noose
> which spreads
> from one end of the East to the other,
> from my homeland to yours
> There is just one spider's web in which
> we Asians are bound and writhing!
> From the blood-shedding morning of the Mongols
> to the fatal evening of the Europeans!
> We are writhing
> in one single pain without cure,
> and even this prized partnership
> of shared, soul-destroying afflictions
> has not yet let us
> come close to one another!
>
> (lines 68–83)

The common experience of imperialism produces a strange "partnership" between Iran and India, binding them together while also keeping them apart. One line in this stanza—which mentions the "blood-shedding morning of the Mongols"—even suggests a longer history of domination by alluding to the Mongol conquest of Iran in the thirteenth century, and the subsequent sacking of Delhi by Timur in 1398. Although this sort of reference might often support a claim to cultural unity, in Rashed's poem it only emphasizes the ways in which India and Iran are linked by conquest. "Asia" refers to an experience of power, not of heritage—of position, not identity.

In a similar fashion, the poem's language invokes the Indo-Persian heritage—but only to critique it. In Arabic, *ʿajam* literally means "to mumble" and denotes a non-Arab, especially a Persian. In its common usage, it also connotes Persian civilization, as distinct from Islam. It should come as no surprise, then, that in its opening question, ʿAjam enumerates the glories of Persian civilization and imitates a prayer:

> God on high,
> this land of Darius the Great,

these courts of Naushirvan the Just,
these galleries of Sufism, wisdom, and literature,
why today, in the presence of dark-skinned enemies,
are they again becoming a festering sore?"

(lines 1–6)

The Indian soldier responds by relativizing, if not denying, his complicity in Iran's occupation:

We are not guilty of this crime, beloved Persia *(jān-e ʿajam)*, we are not.
That first Englishman
who brought his wares
to the shore of India
it is his fault
that we are trampling
the rose-covered soil
of your homeland with our dark feet!

(lines 7–14)

This passage is one example of the ways in which Rashed attempts to capture modern Persian in his poetry by making specific—if often somewhat obscure—references to the poetry of Iran's Constitutional Revolution (1905–1911). Indeed, ʿAjam's initial question closely resembles lines from the famous "Musammat-e vaṯanī" (National Poem) composed in 1910 by the Constitutional poet Farrūḳhī Yazdī:

Is this the same Iran that was the halting place of Kai Kavus?
The resting place of Darius and the abode of Cyrus?
The land of Zal, Rustam, Gudarz, Giv, and Tus?
Never was it so trampled as by the oppression of the English and Russians![48]

Because Farrūḳhī's poem accuses the state of collaborating with imperialist domination, it allegedly so enraged the governor of Yazd that he ordered Farrūḳhī lips to be sewn together.[49] Rashed's subtle reference to Farrūḳhī text reminds the reader that the wartime occupation of Iran had several historical precedents at the same time that his ventriloquism of the voice of modern Persian poetry allows him to stage a dialog between his Indian soldier and modern Iran.

The poem represents two collective identities—Iranian and Indian—in flux. Moreover, the experiences of Rashed's narrator clearly have some relationship to his own. Shortly before the Partition of British India, Rashed chose to live in Pakistan, which he left a few years before the publication of *Īrān meñ ajnabī* to begin working as an international civil servant for the United Nations. When Rashed calls the soldier "Indian," he refers to an undivided geopolitical entity that no longer exists and to which he no longer has any claim. That is perhaps why the soldier in "Manna and Quails" uses the Persian and broadly geographic term *hindī* in place of many of the more common Urdu terms for the modern Indian nation-state. As with the name ʿAjam, the geographical entities Rashed names do not necessarily correspond to national identities.

Given the historical moment of its writing and publication, the care with which Rashed addresses these issues of naming and geography immediately raises the specter of Partition. Although Rashed never openly discusses the Partition of the Indian subcontinent in his poetry, his treatment of geography raises the question of the extent to which his poetry is a reaction to that historical trauma. Aamir Mufti's recent work on Rashed's more popular contemporary, the Urdu poet Faiẓ Aḥmad Faiẓ (1911–1982), provides a useful point of comparison on this question. Mufti parts ways with progressive criticism, which frequently reads the ghazal-like beloved of Faiz's lyrical poetry as a metaphor for socialist revolution by arguing instead that Faiz "imbues the lyric experience of separation from the beloved [in the classical ghazal] with a concrete historical meaning—the parting of ways or leave-taking that is partition." Faiz's poetry thus makes available "an experience of self that is Indian in the encompassing sense, across the boundaries of the 'communal' and nation-state divides." In doing so, however, Faiz neither upholds the "fragment" (Muslim experience) as a totality, as in auratic criticism, nor does he seek unity-in-diversity, as in Indian nationalism. Instead, Faiz reveals that "the truth of the self is its contradictory, tense, and antagonistic reality." Mufti concludes that Faiz "pushes the terms of identity and selfhood to their limits, to the point where they turn upon themselves and reveal the partial nature of postcolonial 'national' experience."[50]

Like Faiz, Rashed rejects nationalism as a source of individual identity. The experiences described in his poem take no recourse to a sense of national belonging based either on indigeneity or tradition. What differentiates Rashed from Faiz, however, is that Rashed is reluctant to subsume his poetic project into even such a self-effacing mode of political representation as Partition. Indeed, Rashed's critique of Faiz's poetry is particularly revealing in relation to his own project: "Faiz approaches his reader at two levels at the same time: the level of the ordinary lyrical poet, with a direct emotional appeal; and the level of a socially conscious poet, in terms of a political metaphor. His reader has thus to make a slight mental adjustment to arrive at the underlying meaning of his poetry, particularly when Faiz's poetry is not a poetry of intensely subtle personal experience, which the ordinary reader would find difficult to share with him."[51] Rashed rejects Faiz's approach—which requires that readers relate the lyrical experience produced by a poem to its political metaphor—because for him poetry is first and foremost the communication of individual experience. As such, it replaces the pleasure of identification with the difficult ethical step of acknowledging difference. It requires the reader to realize, first, that the author of the text is a unique individual different from him- or herself and, second, that the author can be understood despite that difference. And because the poetry of individual experience requires readers to doubt their own assumptions, this encounter becomes a vehicle for free thought, reflection, and, crucially, critique.

From Rashed's point of view, Faiz's poetry is simply too easy, written "with a clear awareness of a multitude behind him." Moreover, Faiz's poetry is also too sensuous and so never sufficiently iconoclastic or subversive. Instead of being confronted with difference, Faiz's reader is lulled into a sense that the poetry in front of him is the same old lyric poetry, which verges on kitsch, or what Rashed calls a "white narcissus or calendar art."[52] Although this emphasis on personal experience may very well be Rashed's response to the devastation wrought by Partition on claims to identity, emphasizing personal experience is not the same thing as turning away from the social realm, as progressivist critics would frequently contend. For Rashed's emphasis on subtle, individual experience relies on an ethical belief that experiences can be conveyed and that difference can be acknowledged and maintained. This ethic informs his identification of "Asia" as an experience of domination that both Iranians and Indians share but which nevertheless does not create a unified Asian identity.

CTESIPHON AND TEHRAN

Rashed extends his critique of identity to nationalism in its Iranian form in a *qiṭʿah* that focuses on an experience of Tehran. Like his critique of communism and his concept of Asia, Rashed grounds his criticism of nationalism in an opposition to yearnings for domination that are cloaked in auratic approaches to the past. Ironically, he finds this desire to revitalize an imperial national past in the poetry associated with Iran's Constitutional Revolution, which itself aimed to limit the power of the Shah. Rashed contrasts these dreams of "imperial dignity [and] the nimbus of grandeur" *(jalāl-e shahī, farrah-e kibriyā'ī)* with true freedom from domination—a liberation that can occur only apart from nationalism.[53]

The final *qiṭ'ah* of the poem, "Tamāshā-gah-e lālahzār" (The Tulip Field Theater, §14), is a response to an opera staged at a Tehran theater. The title of the *qiṭ'ah* refers to an actual theater in Tehran's Lalehzar theater district.[54] However, the title can be read as "the Tulip Field Theater" or "the theater of the tulip field." Collapsed into its component parts, the word for theater, *tamāshā-gah*, can also be read as "place of *(-gah)* spectacle *(tamāshā)*." This rather complicated poem employs the "tulip field theater" as a metaphor, drawing on the rich associations of the tulip *(lālah)* in Urdu and Persian literature. In the first stanza, the theater becomes a synecdoche for Asia. It reads:

> The Tulip Field Theater
> my eyes were fixed on the "théâtre"
> my ears were set on the treble and bass of "musique"
> but my heart kept on
> counting the pains of Arabia and Persia
> the theater of the tulip field!
>
> (lines 1–6)

Sitting in the actual theater, his senses fixed on drama and music, the narrator's heart dwells on the suffering of Arabia and Persia *('arab-o-'ajam)*. The words in quotation marks in this passage are the modern Persian words *tiyātar* (theater) and *mūzīk* (music)—French words incorporated into colloquial Persian that have no currency in Urdu. Highlighting their European etymology makes these cultural forms appear as a derivative and inauthentic appropriation of cultural modernity. In the last line, after the narrator recounts the pains of Arabia and Persia, the meaning of *tamāshā-gah-e lālahzar* (Tulip Field Theater) shifts from the particular theater to "the theater of the tulip field," or Asia itself.

The narrator identifies the performance he is observing as a staging of the verse opera "Rastaḳhīz-e salāṯīn-e īrān" (Resurrection of the Sovereigns of Iran) by Mirzādah 'Ishqī (1893–1924), an Iranian nationalist associated with the Constitutional Revolution. Mirzādah 'Ishqī composed the opera in 1915 as a response to a visit to the ruins of Madāyīn (Ctesiphon), the former capital of the Sassanid Persian Empire that is located near Baghdad. In the opera he decries Iran's loss of imperial might, contrasting Iran's contemporary weakness with its military power and territorial holdings under the Persian emperors. At the start of the opera, a character named "ʿIshqī the Traveler" arrives at the ruins of the ancient imperial city and laments its dilapidated state. He falls asleep and dreams of a wailing woman, who emerges from a tomb wearing a burial shroud. She identifies herself as the daughter of the Sassanian emperor Khusrau II (r. 590–628) and his Armenian queen Shirin, who were among the last Persian rulers before the Arab conquest. Their daughter laments the state of Iran, repeating the line, "This ruined graveyard is not my Iran / This desolate abode is not Iran. Where is Iran?" She describes the ancient Persian rulers as brokenhearted, and they then appear one by one—Cyrus, Darius, Naushirvan, Khusrau, and Shirin—and grieve for an Iran that has lost its former strength. Together, they invoke the soul of Zoroaster, who appears like an angel dressed in white. He points at the audience and declares that the royals are right to grieve, for their sons have forsworn their forefathers.[55]

Rashed's *qiṭʿah* paraphrases ʿIshqī's opera while also drawing on other poetic conventions associated with the tulip field:

> The Tulip Field Theater,
> where is Iran now?
> this masterpiece of ʿIshqī—"Iran's Resurrection!"
> Now Iran is an old woman in mourning
> whose beauty faded years ago
> Persia weeps on the ruins of Ctesiphon,
> that Naushirvan and Zarathustra and Darius,
> that Farhad and Shirin, that Kai Khusrau and Kai Qubad
> "We are a legend; they were a legend's characters!
> We are a caravan; they were a caravan's chiefs!"
> whose tombs are beneath the dust
> the theater of the tulip field!
>
> (lines 7–18)

The question "where is Iran now?" echoes the lament of the daughter of Khusrau and Shirin in ʿIshqī's opera. In addition to the Persian royals Naushirvan and Darius, the poem's narrator also mentions Farhad, the legendary architect and sculptor who fell in love with Shirin, as well as the Kayanian kings Kai Khusrau and Kai Qubad from the Persian epic *Shāhnāmah*. The penultimate line, "whose tombs are beneath the dust," paired with the final line, "the theater of the tulip field," activates the literary associations of the tulip as a marker of martyrdom in Persian and Urdu poetry, for the red tulip has been associated with both love and death since at least the time of the *Shāhnāmah*, where it is identified as the "Blood of Siyavosh," the martyred father of Kai Khusrau. In classical Urdu and Persian poetry, the tulip marks the tombs of those who have died in the battle of love. It also became the prominent symbol of revolutionary martyrdom during Iran's Constitutional and Islamic Revolutions.[56] In this stanza, the tulip field, following convention, becomes a marker of the graves of the martyrs of Iran's past.

Ultimately, however, ʿIshqī's poetry serves as fodder for a general criticism of Iranian nationalism. For ʿIshqī's strategy of glorifying pre-Islamic Iran reflects a maneuver during the Constitutional movement to invert the understanding that Islam brought civilization to Iran, by resignifying the pre-Islamic Iranian past as the prehistory of the nation and its civilization. This Persian chauvinism was also a secularist strategy to subsume Shia religious identity under a generally nationalist frame.[57] Reza Shah continued this strategy, a point that Rashed notes in another *qiṭʿah*, "The Alchemist" (Kīmiyāgar), in which an Indian soldier addresses a statue of the founder of the Pahlavi dynasty as "O successor of Darius and Cyrus *(ai dāriyūsh aur sīrūs kā jā-nashīñ)*."[58] For Rashed, Iranian nationalism is simply another form of ideology, either a cover for corruption (as in the case of Reza Shah) or a crippling self-delusion. Rashed's narrator derides ʿIshqī's focus on the "lost pride of ancient rank and glory," asking, "how long will the melancholy of singing laments last? / for the journey from grief to eternal grief is arduous" (lines 20–21). ʿIshqī's yearning for the past thus not only becomes tiresome but also threatens to turn into melancholia, a crippling "eternal grief" *(ġham-e jāvidān)* for that which is lost.

In place of dreams of former glory, the narrator proposes a new dream of a world without domination. In doing so, he activates another meaning of the tulip field:

> The Tulip Field Theater
> the young bride of tomorrow, concealed in veils
> upset with hungry-eyed and hasty men
> but now our dreams are not the nightmare of the past,
> our new dreams are the dreams of a new Adam,
> dreams of a world of striving!
> A world of striving, not Ctesiphon
> not the palaces of Faghfur and Khusrau

These are not the abode of that new Adam
  new habitations and new kings
    the theater of the tulip field!

(lines 31–41)

The "young bride of tomorrow, concealed in veils" is a familiar metaphor for the self. It draws on the mystical convention of the soul as the bride of God. Here, however, the desired end is not a mystical union but a new mode of selfhood, one that demands the cultivation of generosity and patience. In place of fantasies of restoring the lordship of the past, the narrator imagines new realms of political and existential sovereignty. He envisions a "new Adam"—a new subject, one without dreams of domination, the "nightmares of the past." Instead of the fixities of palaces and imperial pomp, the narrator imagines a new Adam who strives, or literally "runs about" *(tag-o-pau)*, and is defined less by what he is than by what he is not. The narrator rejects the nostalgia of nationalism as well as contemporary associations of modernity with Europe. In their place, he imagines a new form of sovereignty that would also entail liberation from all existing forms of identity. There is no definite metaphysics attached to this self-assertion. To provide one would, no doubt, be to fall into ideology.

In its attempt to reclaim a lost past, the Iranian nationalism described in this *qiṭʿah* mirrors the auratic criticism of the Urdu literary community, since it aims to tether postcolonial modernity to tradition. By criticizing Iranian nationalism as both nostalgic and aligned with domination, Rashed counters a similar nationalism within his own literary community, which also inhabits the metaphorical tulip field of the poem. Against auratic preoccupations with historical and civilizational unity, Rashed searches for a category of individual experience that would not fall into any such identitarian trap. This desire leads him to the "new Adam," a category of the individual that, like "Asia," signifies not a fixed identity but the possibility of a more inclusive form of belonging that is no longer grounded in dreams of resurrecting the dominance of the past.

CONCLUSION

In the literary history of Urdu, modernism *(jadīdiyat)* is typically negatively presented in two ways: first, as a translation of Western modes of subjecthood and literature, and, second, as a movement primarily concerned with form. Both qualities differentiate it from auratic criticism and progressivism. Auratic criticism represents a desire for a more authentic relationship between the self and the metaphysical world, and progressivism, in its socialist realist mode, a less individualized relationship with the social collective. Both view modernism as either a superficial and decrepitly bourgeois formalism or a problematic imitation of the West. In this and the previous chapter, I have shown that Rashed's poem is more than mere formal experimentation or imitation of Western modes. But I also hope I have demonstrated that the poem's auratic and progressive critics—who argue that it fails to be properly representative, either of tradition or of the people/nation—are exactly right. It is precisely because of this resistance to representation that Rashed's poetry remains both perplexing and controversial.

Despite his resistance to a politics of representation, however, Rashed's poem does attempt to reconsider what India and Iran might share. This move was itself tendentious, because Iran, conceived as the motherland of Persian, had become a sign of an Indo-Persian past that was upheld by auratic critics and rebuked by locally focused progressives. Not surprisingly, then, Rashed's poem was misrecognized by some as an identitarian statement of Indo-Persian nostalgia, because of its focus on Iran and the Persian inflection of its language. Yet the narrator hardly finds his cultural heritage in Iran. Instead, he finds himself caught in an antagonistic relationship brought on by the circumstances of the colonial present. The experience of domination is what constitutes the relationship between the Indian soldier and Iran and defines the geographical category of "Asia," from which Rashed imagines the emergence of a "new Adam." This man, like this Asia, captures an experience that is at once shared, essentially individual and—happily, for the poet—entirely incapable of giving substance to collectivity.

THREE

Allegory and Collectivity

SOON AFTER INDIA AND PAKISTAN GAINED INDEPENDENCE, N. M. Rashed articulated a theme of separation between word *(ḥarf)* and meaning *(maʿnī)* that he reworked in a number of ways in his later poems. On the one hand, this separation referred to the disconnection between state ideology and practice, particularly, if not exclusively, in the context of Pakistan. On the other, it signified a gap between human language and metaphysical meaning in general. Though Rashed's poetry mourns this disconnection, it also doubts that such a connection was ever truly present. His late poetry consistently challenges the certainty of conventional meanings and assertions, while also holding open the possibility of new ways of understanding the human subject and social life.

Rashed's final two volumes address this new set of concerns. The title of his final collection, *Gumāñ kā mumkin* (The Possibility of Supposition, 1976), explicitly called into question the status of meaning in general.[1] Rashed introduced his concerns in another way with the title of his penultimate volume, which took the form of an equation, handwritten on its title page, *Lā = Insān* (X = Human, 1969).[2] The title seemed to suggest that the poet had left the bounds of national culture and even Asia behind, addressing universal questions of the human condition.[3] While his 1940s and 1950s poems explored the psychological and political effects of colonialism and imperialism, his later work suggests that the postcolonial condition was little improved. Rashed witnessed the violent Partition of the Indian subcontinent at the moment of its independence from colonial rule. Then, as an employee of the United Nations, he had a front-row seat to decolonization on a global scale. His reflections on decolonization from this period, in prose and in verse, question the vitality of the self and its freedom in postcolonial nations. His poetry considers the possibility of other forms of collectivity and different models of the self. He continued to oppose ideology, which he viewed as intellectual and creative laziness. In keeping with that critique, he also criticized the reliance of modern Urdu poetry on the symbol. Rashed's late poetry, by contrast, is largely written in an allegorical form. It attempts to imagine an alternative form of society—a collectivity of individuals. In this chapter I will address both the significance of the disconnection between word and meaning in Rashed's poetry and his efforts to envision an alternative form of collectivity.

In its imagination of collectivity, Rashed's poetry directly confronted the poetry and legacy of Muḥammad Iqbāl (1877–1938), whom the Pakistani state canonized as its poet-philosopher. Before studying in Europe just prior to the First World War, Iqbal had penned some of the most beloved poems of Indian nationalism. On his return, the gaze of his poetry extended beyond India to focus on the global Islamic community *(ummah)*. Though he came to strongly oppose territorial nationalism as counter to the universalism of Islam, the Pakistan movement embraced him as its official philosopher on account of his call to create a separate Muslim state within (or without) British India.[4] In this chapter I will explicate how Rashed expanded on Iqbal's sense of collectivity while also criticizing his use of symbols, which would unite word and meaning, by instead emphasizing their disunity. In chapter 4, I will discuss in more detail how Rashed disputed Iqbal's sense of teleology, especially as applied to Pakistan.

Rashed's use of modernist allegory is the formal expression of his rejection of symbolism: allegory's ability to sustain two parallel systems of signification allows him to emphasize the disjuncture between word and meaning. Instead of seeking out symbols that would bridge the visible and invisible worlds, as Iqbal tried to do, Rashed incorporated into his poetry aspects of Indo-Muslim literary tradition and repurposed them, juxtaposing and reinterpreting them in ways that broke with their original meanings. Rashed's modernist allegories, such as "Heart, My Old Desert-Wandering Heart," try to imagine new forms of collectivity and freedom while remaining immersed in the textual tradition that called forth Urdu's transnational literary community. In the process, these poems uphold the possibilities of literature as an independent discursive space for creativity and critique involving, but not subservient to, religion or politics.

THE BROKEN HARMONY OF WORD AND MEANING

The first of Rashed's poems to address the disjuncture between word and meaning, "Namrūd kī k̲h̲udā'ī" (The Lordship of Nimrod, §15), is clearly about Pakistan. The narrator of the poem addresses a "philosopher" *(falsafī)*, who dreams of a new land. Rashed's readership immediately recognized this philosopher as Muḥammad Iqbāl.[5] We know from a recently published interview that Rashed composed the 1949 poem in Lahore, a city where Iqbal spent much of his life and was buried in 1938.[6] A site of Partition violence, Lahore was overrun with refugees when Rashed composed the poem.[7]

"The Lordship of Nimrod" commences by recounting the philosopher's dream of a new land and by addressing the disjuncture between that dream and current reality:

> This land of the holy,
> where in his early morning sleep the philosopher saw
> a ray of longing for a fresh wind, a lush field, and a soul-quenching stream!
> Arriving here a traveler has begun to wonder:
> "Was that dream a nightmare?
> —Was that dream a nightmare?"
>
> (lines 1–6)

The "early morning" *(saḥr-gahī)* of the philosopher's dream is the time of prayer, and Iqbal himself famously rose early and slept little. The philosopher's dream of a place where people can dwell in comfort is generally commensurate with territorial nationalism. His message, as interpreted by the narrator, is a demand for a separate and "soul-quenching" Indo-Muslim homeland.

Instead of these early morning dreams, in which the divine plan and the human world would unite, the people are left with the "lordship of Nimrod." In the Islamic and earlier Judaic tradition, Nimrod is an idolatrous king and oppressor of Abraham. The term therefore indicates a period of darkness:

> O philosopher,
> where is that heavenly vision?
> And in its place this lordship of Nimrod!
> With broken strings you've woven the nets of your illusory philosophy

Today we have lost hope
in that certainty, in that action, in that love!

(lines 7–12)

The second and third lines of this stanza set up an opposition between the vision and the reality. The disillusioned people have lost faith in the dream of a land of prosperity that might quench the soul. All the concepts that governed that dream—*yaqīn* (certainty/belief/faith), *'aml* (action/work), *muḥabbat* (love)—these "strings" of Iqbal's philosophy, so filled with meaning in his poetry, have all broken. This line is a response to a verse from one of Muḥammad Iqbāl's most famous Urdu poems, "Ṭulū'-e Islam" (The Rise of Islam): "unwavering certainty, eternal action, world-conquering love— / these are the swords of men in the jihad of life."[8] That poem describes the rejuvenation of the Muslim community, and in it Iqbal identifies the qualities of the *mard-e momin*, the "man of faith."

Rashed's narrator recounts the greatest ruination of Islamic history, the destruction of Arabia and Persia by the Mongols, only to conclude that the current situation is far worse. In that earlier period of defeat, material objects and cultural treasures were destroyed. And although Arabia and Persia grieved for the shattering of a beautiful enchantment conjoining "iron, wood, stone, and silver," now, the narrator declares, "we are the helpless prey of worse days." For around him now are the "hearts' ruins." The "ruined cities" of these hearts now lament the "broken harmony of word and meaning" (lines 13–19).

A final stanza of the poem, excised in a later version of the text, describes the consequences of this breaking of the bond of word and meaning in further detail.[9] It reads,

I tremble with fear for the days to come
My eyes see
that the pleasant dream
    of the connection of word and meaning has shattered
for the roads are filled with halfwits
with sleepwalking beggars
with "Sufis"
Life is void of striving
Our civilization is ancient, sick, on its last breath!

(lines 32–40)

Here, the dream of finding a fullness of being through the realization of an Indo-Muslim civilization—the communal actualization of what Iqbal would call *ḳhvudī* (selfhood)—appears to be foreclosed. So too is the dream of the union of word and meaning, of the external and the internal, that Iqbal believed would be possible though the centralization of Indian Muslims in a particular territory. Though that dream brought pleasure *(lażżat)*, through an expectation of harmony between spiritual meaning and social life, it appears now as mere words and a nightmarish fantasy. Now there is neither certainty *(yaqīn)* nor *ārzū*, the will to seek and strive—a preoccupation of Iqbal's poetic vision. Those who offer airs of intelligence are fools; the hope of social equality and provision for the poor in an Islamic country is lost; and those self-proclaimed "Sufis" are frauds. Instead of finding its actualization in Pakistan, Indo-Muslim civilization is near death.

Rashed's later gloss of the poem states the obvious: the poem is "a gesture towards the effects of the breaking of the connection of word and meaning which we began to feel after the formation of Pakistan."[10] Unlike in the majority of his later poems, Rashed clearly refers to Pakistan, yet Pakistan here is also an allegory for the status of language more broadly. For the poem evokes the separation of language and metaphysical meaning in general. Through its insistence on the separation of word and meaning, the poem addresses the disconnection between ideology and practice, and it also challenges a teleological vision of Pakistan as a natural and inevitable formation arising from a separate Indian Muslim nation. Yet this critique of nationalism can also be made more generally. Rashed's poetry offers alternative ways of conceptualizing collectivity, while at the same time addressing the transnational Urdu literary community.

X = HUMAN

Through an emphasis on the lack of concord between word and meaning, Rashed's late poetry challenges other realms of thought as well. Though this poetry, like *Irān meñ ajnabī*, is often read as nostalgic, it should be noted that there is no lost period of totality in it. Rashed's writing remains distinct from that of the auratic critics who subscribed, in various degrees, to a perennialist philosophy that emphasized a premodern "metaphysical tradition." Instead, Rashed describes the separation between word and meaning as a constitutive characteristic of language. Especially distrustful of claims of unity, his late poetry questions conventional beliefs and emphasizes, in particular, the uncertainty of the meaning of the word "human" *(insān)*.[11]

In the poem "Vuh ḥarf-e tanhā" (That Lonely Word, §16) Rashed holds up the writings of the blind Arab poet Abu'l-'Alā' al-Ma'arrī (973–1058 CE) as a model for this sort of skepticism. Ma'arrī refuted claims of religious authority and challenged religious doctrine.[12] The poem begins with its narrator asking why we raise "our" arms in desperate prayer, describing what is, for South Asian Muslims, among others, an emphatic gesture calling for divine intervention. Are the arms of the prayerful raised in the hopes of avoiding imminent harm, the narrator asks, or are they a delusional proclamation of certainty in God in the absence of genuine knowledge, "a deception to hide from us our deprivations?" In order to keep the addressee from deferring to the Almighty, thereby avoiding the question, the narrator, in a parenthetical remark, calls out, "Don't look at the sky!" He then declares,

> Great and high God (Paradise is a certainty) will sometime
> deliver us from god
> for we on this earth are like that lonely word
> (but it won't be such a world) silent as well as articulate,
> which lives in longing for union with meaning,
> which has craved the concord of word and meaning!
>
> (lines 5–10)

The separation of word and meaning prompts the narrator to question the validity of inherited religious beliefs. As M. A. R. Habib notes, in the statement that "Great and high God" will "grant us salvation from god" (lines 5–6), there is "an implicit recognition that the 'reality' of God has been passed down through language."[13]

The statements in this poem border on apostasy, but the narrator's interjected comments, marked in parenthesis, soften its radicalism. For instance, belief in the "resurrection" *(qayāmat)*—and, by extension, paradise—constitutes one of the pillars of faith *(arkānu'l-īmān)* in Islam.[14] The interjection by the narrator "Paradise is a certainty" *(bihisht bar-ḥaq)* states that belief—although the following statement, "but it won't be such a world," questions whether the world beyond will correspond to the desires of the outwardly pious.

Having likened human existence to a word, silent and articulate, whose meaning is unknown, the narrator prays for the "dreams of Ma'arrī," who had the courage to face this uncertainty, and the "agitation of Maʿarrī's soul" so that "through courageous sins we find the salve for sacred pain" (lines 11–14). Instead of bland and blind holiness *(taqaddus)* in life, the act of sin *(gunāh)*, the "twisted works" that strengthen the heart, would open the possibility of greater self-understanding (lines 32–33). For the "lightless and dark eyes" of the blind Maʿarrī "pierced the dark nights / of man's inner being *(darūñ)*" where they could see "the heart-breaking separation *(firāq)* of word and meaning" (lines 15–19). Unlike the Sufi, presumably, the narrator states that Maʿarrī found no unity *(viṣāl)* in the inner world.

Instead, Maʿarrī questioned accepted beliefs, especially the existence of an afterlife. For him, the narrator states, the belief in paradise was a form of escape *(farār)* for the "innocent and simple" from the oppression in this world, from "tyrants' whips on naked bodies." The narrator later criticizes visions of a paradise of pure delight, proposing that oneness without any contradictions would actually be a sort of hell. In place of certainty in paradise, the poem calls for a focus on the question of human life. "Paradise," the narrator remarks, "is a great zero"—the word used here, *ṣifr*, also means "cipher." Whereas "we are those lost numbers," of the arithmetic sort, "without which no equation can be made" (lines 27–28).

This likening of human life to an equation forms the title of Rashed's third volume, *Lā=Insān* (X=Human). In its introduction, Rashed explains the title as meaning, "[I]n life's equation, human is a lost figure whose value is not known, and, whether one is a poet or an artist, all are trying to obtain this value. The original value of X perhaps will not be known; but in this exercise, there is enjoyment for all, and our reward is ourselves."[15] As in "That Lonely Word," the meaning of "human" here is left open—an algebraic X—without any sense of certainty. It is a word without a known or perhaps knowable inner meaning. Instead of putting forth a universal philosophy of the subject, as did Iqbal, Rashed's poetry focuses on the uncertainty of the human subject and the disconnection with metaphysical understanding.

"ARE YOU AFRAID OF LIFE?"

In Rashed's poetry, the lack of connection between word and meaning is an occasion not for mourning but rather for the exploration of new possibilities. He expresses this view most clearly in what has become one of his most popular poems, "Zindagī se ḍarte ho?" (Are You Afraid of Life?, §17).[16] Like

"That Lonely Word," it questions established values and raises a cry of revolt against tyranny. Addressing the uncertainty of the meaning of "man," the poem's narrator challenges existing social forms:

—Are you afraid of life?
You too are life, we too are life!
Are you afraid of man?
You too are man, we too are man!
Man is language, man is expression,
You are not afraid of this!
Man is bound to the iron bond of word and meaning
Life is bound to the garment of man
You are not afraid of this!

(lines 1–9)

The description of the relationship of "word and meaning" as "iron" is ironic, for the poem on the whole is about the production of new meanings for old words. Just as "That Lonely Word" called for deliverance from God, as understood through language, so too this poem calls for a redefinition of the meaning of "human" and a break with existing forms of oppression, whether social or ideological.

Though presented in this poem in an unusually direct and optimistic form, this view of language is part and parcel of Rashed's approach. For Rashed, language does not coincide with truth, or inner meaning *(maʿnī)*. He questions any claims of unity between spirit and matter, in the present or in the past. These claims should be met with skepticism, as delusionary constructs or as ideology in support of oppressive power relations. Yet despite his commitment to skepticism, the condition of uncertainty is for Rashed an opportunity to challenge the status quo and to explore new possibilities for the present and future. This requires, however, searching for the possibilities latent in this world, not for a reflection of a world beyond.

FROM SYMBOL TO ALLEGORY

In his well-known poem "Dil, mirā ṣaḥrā-navard-e pīr dil" ("Heart, My Old Desert-Wandering Heart," §18), Rashed plots his reflections on the possibilities of human life within one of the most prominent and often-debated landscapes of Urdu poetry, the desert. In the early twentieth century, writers who called themselves "natural poets" and sought a literature more connected to the everyday life of India dismissed the desert as a conventional landscape of Arabic and Persian poetry. To them and their British supporters, the desert appeared exogenous to India and far removed from the subcontinent's verdant, and therefore edifying, nature. For Muhammad Iqbal and others, writing shortly afterward, the desert similarly, but more positively, served as an index of the Arab origins of Islam. To critics influenced by this literature, Rashed's desert landscapes, like those of Iran in his earlier poetry, provided further proof of his distance from South Asia or revealed his attachment to the sacred geography of Islam or of Arabia.[17] Others read this poem, composed in 1961, as a direct commentary on political developments in the Middle East.[18]

This criticism considered the desert as a literal geographical space. But that is not how the figure of the desert functions in Rashed's poem. The desert is a much richer metaphor, with referents that go far beyond geography. In this regard, Rashed's poem is similar to the poetry of the ghazal, in which the desert is often used metaphorically to situate the lover's state of passion or to portray the world as a place of ruin. A similar richness is found in Iqbal's poetry, where the caravan in the desert overcomes the attachment to place characteristic of territorial nationalism.

Rashed's poetry involves those meanings, but it goes further. It uses the material nature of sand to celebrate bodily rather than spiritual life, to emphasize the impermanence of oppression and imperialism, and to counter the metaphysical understanding of community upheld by Iqbal. These meanings emerge strongly only when one considers the symbols of Rashed's poem—sand, fire, the dawn, arriving caravans—in relation to one another. In other words, it is necessary to see Rashed's poem as an allegory rather than simply as a symbolic poem. In allegory, signs simultaneously carry multiple meanings because they are assembled into a narrative that says one thing but also means something else.

By reading Rashed's poem as an allegory, it is possible to square his use of this densely intertextual symbolic vocabulary with the rest of his oeuvre. As described above, a distrust of the symbol, as a unity of word and inner meaning, pervades his later poetry. That suspicion joins his critique of ideology, a guiding principle of his writing closely connected to his focus on the instability of meaning. In personal correspondence from around this time, Rashed described his own struggle in his poetry to record his "dreams" in a way that is "abstract" rather than "detailed," and he associated the latter, negatively, with "ideological poets."[19] In his later work, including this desert poem, it is possible to see how, through allegory, the poet sought to solve the problem of intelligibility, while maintaining his commitment to recognize the instability of meaning.

ALLEGORY IN URDU

Rashed's poem is a modernist form of allegory, which differs considerably from the moral didacticism for which allegory is normally decried in Urdu criticism. As in other languages, allegory *(tamsīl)* in Urdu opposes symbol *(ʿalāmat)*, the latter implying an immediate unity in language with an inner truth. The truth of the symbol can be psychological, as it was for the "symbolist" poets of Urdu, inspired by the poet Mīrājī.[20] Or, in opposition to what was often dismissed as a "Western" position, symbols *(mazmūn)* can contain metaphysical truths, which auratic critics like Muḥammad Ḥasan ʿAskarī considered to be an authentically "Eastern" approach.[21] In either case, advocates of the symbol in Urdu prize a seamless relationship between sign and meaning. Modernist allegory, by contrast, makes a virtue out of disjuncture, relying on an extended narrative that builds meanings. If the symbol in Urdu signifies synecdoche, a sign contiguous with what it represents, allegorical signs often exploit a deliberate separation between what is said and what is meant.

Allegory *(tamsīl)* is a modern concept in Urdu, coined by the natural-poetry advocate Muḥammad Ḥusain Āzād in the later part of the nineteenth century. Azad came up with the term as a way to describe a series of English allegorical essays, primarily by Johnson and Addison, which he translated into Urdu with a few additions and transformations. Azad hoped through this experiment to modernize Urdu literature by following English models, and in the process to enhance the moral fiber of the Indo-Muslim community.[22] The critic Gyān Chand Jain notes that "allegory" existed in Urdu literature long before it was named as such, although it does not correspond exactly to any concept in Urdu's traditional poetics. Contemporary Urdu critics, noting the awkward history of the term, tend to use "allegory" to describe a very limited number of texts and genres, particularly those that take the form of extended narratives. In addition to Azad's writing, these include a few earlier Sufi romances. Though some scholars have found allegory in more contemporary texts, it is very uncommon.[23] Further, after

Azad, allegory as a technique has often appeared outdated; it is, Jain writes, "a memorial of the past," with no "reflection of the future in its mirror."[24] This denigration of allegory in Urdu closely follows its treatment in European romanticism, which generally privileged the symbol, as did many later forms of modernism.[25]

Interestingly enough, Rashed's use of modernist allegory can best be understood through the concept's rehabilitation in the field of postmodern art criticism.[26] Craig Owens's transformative pair of essays, "The Allegorical Impulse: Toward a Theory of Postmodernism," is extraordinarily useful insofar as it reevaluates and redefines allegory, stripping it of the distasteful charge of didacticism and artifice and emphasizing its appropriation and reuse of existing symbolic vocabularies.[27] Owens follows Walter Benjamin in noting that allegory frequently comes into prominence at moments when there is a breakdown of traditional forms of representation. When the certainty of the symbol—the connection with an inner or metaphysical meaning—is called into question, as in postmodernist art, the self-consciousness of allegory becomes useful. Postmodern allegory works primarily through appropriation, Owens observes. Unlike the symbolist, the allegorist "does not invent images but confiscates them," he writes. The writer "does not restore an original meaning that may have been lost or obscured," but rather "adds another meaning to the image."[28] The meaning of the allegorical artwork compounds with the gathering together of images from previous art and tradition. Instead of maintaining the original authority of the appropriated elements, their unusual juxtapositions call attention to the artwork's estrangement from tradition.

Owens usefully describes how allegory preserves symbolic correspondences while also extending their meanings through the production of narrative. Unlike the romantic symbol, prized for its immediacy, allegory "superinduces a vertical or paradigmatic reading of correspondences upon a horizontal or syntagmatic chain of events," writes Owens.[29] Reading vertically, allegory employs metaphors, or signs that stand for something else. But those metaphors extend, horizontally, over time, taking on metonymic meanings.

These horizontal and vertical aspects are central to the effect of Rashed's allegory, as is its appropriation of imagery from literary tradition. The thick descriptions of sand, fire, and the dawn take place in a horizontal, generally narrative sequence. The storytelling aspect to the poem is familiar, not unlike the analogical stories *(ḥikāyat)* told by Sufi poets like Rumi, who in his *Maśnavī* expresses subtle spiritual points through such tales, or those told by Iqbal, who followed Rumi's model to present moral, philosophical, and spiritual lessons. Rashed's text similarly leads the reader to decode the meaning of these elements as metaphors. But instead of maintaining continuity with that analogical tradition, his poem juxtaposes aspects of literary tradition in order to signal its distance from traditional symbols and understandings. For as it incorporates and compounds traditional images, it disrupts the usual ways those symbols and literary elements are understood.

Rashed's descriptions of sand, fire, and the dawn draw heavily on Indo-Muslim literary tradition. Reading vertically, across the disparate or even conflicting meanings of individual metaphors, it is possible to see how appropriated symbols in the poem refer to and contrast with those symbols' meanings as enshrined in literary tradition. Compounding these symbols, the poem supplements and therefore subverts their usual understandings. By appropriating traditional imagery, while also avoiding creating either personal or metaphysical symbols, Rashed's poem presents a unique vision of human life, but one free from the programmatic and didactic certainties that he so keenly wished to avoid. The poem includes references to the history of imperialism in order to present an alternative, utopian vision of freedom from bodily and social constraints.[30]

"HEART, MY OLD DESERT-WANDERING HEART"

To understand that utopian vision, it is important to trace the development of allegory in the poem both vertically, through Rashed's development of metaphors, and horizontally, through his use of narrative. The narrator describes four elements of the desert landscape: the sand, the bonfire, the rising morning, and the caravan. As they appear in the narrative of the poem, the first three elements stand for the essential role played by materiality, desire, and the self or soul in human life, while the fourth—the caravan—offers a new model of community, an alternative to both the nation-state and the global Islamic community.

In the first lines of the poem, the narrator describes his "old desert-wandering heart" as enthralled near the "endless bonfire of desires" (lines 1–3). He then explores the nature of sand and its relationship with his heart (lines 4–32) before turning his attention to the bonfire of desires, including its connections to sand and to community (lines 33–91). He describes his dream of a new caravan of "solidarity" *(yak-dilī)* characterized by the freedom of the individual (92–115). This caravan finds in the desert the awakened dawn, which the narrator describes using Sufi imagery for the soul (116–154). In the final stanza (155–160), the narrator brings all these elements into further relationship with one another. In the analysis that follows, I will explore how the images of the poem—desert sand, the bonfire of desire, the caravans of solidarity, and the dawn—invoke the Urdu ghazal, Iqbal's imaginations of the global Islamic community, and the Sufi poetry of Rumi, while, through the compounding of imagery, presenting an alternative vision of human life.

DESERT SAND

Rashed's poem defines the desert landscape by contrasting it with the city, as is common in Urdu literary tradition. Rashed's poems typically extol the city, but not in this poem, where the narrator beckons a community away from urban sites of "deceit and dissimulation" (line 15). The desert, in this poem, becomes a site of passion and of ruin, as in the ghazal. However, while the desert in the ghazal usually is the place of the solitary lover, in Rashed's it also becomes a place of community.

The poetry of Mīr Tāqī Mīr (1723–1810) provides some insight into how the desert functions in the Urdu ghazal. By convention, the desert is the place of madmen who have been driven from the city by their passion. Mir therefore at times refers to the "desert of passion" *(saḥrā-e ʿāshiqī)*, at several points warning away from it even Ḳhvājah Ḳhiẓr, the legendary and saintly "green" figure who drank the "water of life" and now wanders the earth helping lost travelers.[31] The beloved of the ghazal usually remains in the city, and the lover haunts her/his alleyway. At times, the lover must take recourse to the desert. Mir writes,

> *ham se dīvāne raheṅ shahr meṅ subḥānu'l-lâh*
> *dasht meṅ qais rahe kūh meṅ farhād rahe*
>
> Would madmen like me remain in the city? Good God!
> Qais stayed in the desert; Farhad in the mountains.[32]

Qais is another name for the famous desert-wandering lover Majnun, inflamed with passion for his beloved Laila. Farhad is another legendary lover and stock character of the ghazal, who killed himself after nearly completing the seemingly impossible task of carving a mountain after being falsely informed of his beloved Shirin's death.

In the Urdu ghazal, the city can also refer to the abode of human life within the desert of the destructive forces of nature. Mir writes of the leveling of a city,

> *ab shahr har ṯaraf se maidān ho gayā hai*
> *phailā thā us ṯaraḥ kā kāhe ko yāñ ḳharābā*
>
> Now, in every direction, the city has become a plain
> Why had ruin spread out here in that way?[33]

Verses such as the above can sometimes be read as an expression of Mir's times, as Mir witnessed the destruction of his city, Delhi, twice, by the forces of Nadir Shah in 1939 and the Marathas in 1761. Because the city here is not explicitly named, however, the critic Shamsur Rahman Faruqi explains, the "'city' is not only the city of Delhi or any city but holds the place of the whole world; the entire world appears a ruin."[34] As a place of ruin, the world takes the metaphorical form of the desert. Mir therefore counsels against the permanence of any settlement in this world,

> *us kuhnah ḳharābe meñ ābādī nah kar mun'im*
> *yak shahr nahīñ yāñ jo ṣaḥrā nah hu'ā hogā*
>
> Don't settle in that old ruin, benefactor
> There is not a single city here that will not have become a desert

Other verses by Mir similarly describe the "sand-heap of the desert" as "once a caravan," and the desert's "whirlwind" as "once a desert-wanderer."[35]

Rashed's image of the "desert-wandering heart" immediately invokes these earlier meanings, and the description of sand involves these metaphorical possibilities. In Urdu literary tradition, as elsewhere, the heart *(dil)* is the seat of passion *('ishq)* as opposed to reason *('aql)*, and it offers a different way of perceiving than do the eyes or ears. The narrator describes his heart as the "joyous citizen" of the desert and, in fact, as sand itself. Sand is "glorious and golden," like the morning of festival *('īd)*, and "free and great like moments of passion." It is timeless—the "beauty of centuries" and the "meeting place of those separated at the birth of Adam." The "fragrance of sand" is in the heart's form *(paikar)* and soul *(jāñ)*, and sand alone is what it seeks (lines 3–10).

The narrator differentiates the sand of the desert from that of the city, as material nature free from commodification:

> Sand strikes a tune
> as its grains are those ancient anklets
> that the hand of the vile cannot grasp
> Sand of the desert is far away from the sand-waves of the goldsmith,
> far away from the fountain of deceit and dissimulation, from cities!
>
> (lines 11–15)

The figures of water—waves, fountains—are those of flowing matter. In the conventions of Persian poetry, the sand of the desert, like the water in the ocean, is in a state of constant movement. Distinct from the flow of "sand-waves" crafted by the city's goldsmith—associated in the poem with hypocrisy, deceit, and artifice—the waves of the desert sand appear to be of a different, purer nature. For the desert sand is, the narrator explains later, nature free from thought (line 30).

As material nature, the sand is a power that cannot be contained or ever entirely appropriated by human force. It cannot be grasped by the "hand of the vile" (line 13). The sand presents a counter to all forms of despotism because it destroys any semblances of permanence:

> Sand keeps awake at night; it hears the footsteps of every tyrant
> Sand keeps awake at night; it keeps watch like a herald
> It sees the footsteps of the dictator's shadow
> Sand, the death of every agent, of every plunderer
> Sand, the death of the tumult of despotism's transgression
> When sand arises, the sleep of every conqueror flees
> The dreams of all emperors are wounded by the spears of sand!
>
> (lines 16–22)

In this passage, sand watches for the approach of tyrants, dictators, and plunderers only to overcome and destroy them. Forms of oppression tend to describe themselves as representing a permanent and natural order. Like Shelley's Ozymandias, however, they are not outside the forces of history. For in their material nature, they are subject to decay and to destruction. By describing the "dreams of all emperors" as "wounded by the spears of sand," the narrator explains that what appears to be timeless in the social world is in fact impermanent.

Rashed's poem adopts the ghazal's view of the world as a desert of ruin, but his insistence that the world's most oppressive structures are impermanent opens the possibility of overcoming negative aspects of social life. Sand, as nature—and even as death—can provide a source of hope. It signals the eventual end of all forms of despotism, as the desert sand exposes the transitory nature of human history. The narrator therefore asks the desert to "give him a new interpretation of the dreams of your awakened grains [of sand]." The grains of sand are the "rising dawn," as the "day of joy" has reached the edges of the desert. The narrator calls to his heart to embrace its nature and "come and kiss the sand" (lines 23–30).

THE BONFIRE OF DESIRES

Just as the narrator urges his heart to give in to its desire, he also insists that the sand itself is incomplete without the "endless bonfire of desires." Desire for a divine or metaphorical lover, is, of course, the driving force propelling the Urdu ghazal. In Sufi cosmology, God created the world out of love, and so love permeates the universe. That permeating love becomes the medium through which one can know and experience the divine. As a result, desire is understood to be the soul's need for union with the divine. Like Rashed's description of sand, which plays on the geographical imagination of the ghazal, his references to the bonfire are consonant with that tradition. But in place of the Sufi emphasis on spiritual union, Rashed's poem advocates for desire as a force for the creation of human community.

Rashed's narrator describes the bonfire conventionally through a number of typical Sufi metaphors. These include the description of the bonfire as a "ladder" *(mĕʿrāj)* a common Sufi motif for the celestial journey of the mystic. The sparks of the bonfire are in different stages: some are "lost in the embrace of the wind," others are "climbing, rung by rung, up the tower of flames," and others are "still in the depths of the fire / agitated but hesitant like a young child" (lines 40–43). The fire, a "treasure-trove of color" (line 44), feeds the flame of the Sufi "lovers" *(ʿushshāq)* (line 46). Without it, the narrator says later, the desert would "remain in its lightless, self-absorbed solitude / acclaiming its own uniqueness" (lines 83–86). These descriptions all conform to the Sufi understanding of the origin of the universe in God's love. The last phrase refers to God's desire to perceive his own attributes in the world. By applying that conventional description to the desert itself,

Rashed's narrator implies that the desert can take on the attributes of the divine.

In Rashed's poem, breaking with Sufi tradition, the bonfire of desire also serves as a sign of human creativity. Fire is therefore described as "freedom," "joy," "creation," "growth," "adornment," and "elegance" (lines 52–55). It is "that purity by which all sins are washed away" (line 56), and not something that could be extinguished or denied by "holy" action—a line of thought that is also found in "That Lonely Word" (§16). For the fire of desire is a "gift" on the same order as the "first breath of man" (line 57). Like so many of Rashed's other poems, "Heart, My Old Desert-Wandering Heart" emphasizes the importance of desire as a component of human life.[36]

As a sign of the force of creativity and growth, the fire is at the core of social life. The "torch for those who have lost their way," the fire serves as a "guide for travelers, for desert wanderers," and as "an aid for caravans as well" (lines 35, 72–73). Around the fire, a group of "storytellers wrapped in wool and turbans"—like a "crowd of lashes around an eye"—cause the "grains of sand to glisten with their astonishing, heart-gripping experiences" such that "each grain [of sand] resounds like the instrument of the soul" (lines 75–80). The fire also protects against predatory or destructive forces—whether of imperialism, as the political references later in the poem might suggest, or of any other form—as without the fire, "wolves" *(bheṛiye)* would enter the desert (lines 59–60).

Desire as a creative force in social life also protects against the perpetuation of colonialism. Without desire, the narrator continues, Asia and Africa would be just an empty space for the possession and dominance of Europe and America:

> If there were not this endless bonfire of desire,
> Asia and Africa would be the name for an empty space
> (the name for a useless space)
> Europe and America the name for dominance
> (the name for reiteration of dominance!)
>
> (lines 87–91)

The term for "dominance" in this passage, *dārā'ī*, contains associations with the Persian king Darius *(Dārā)*, and so brings to mind an earlier form of empire. The word for "reiteration," *takrār*, from the Arabic root *k-r-r* (to return), means repetition as well as struggle. As such, the evocation of "Europe and America" as a "reiteration of dominance" indicates the impulse to perpetuate Western imperialism in the postcolonial period—what Edward Said called "the discourse of resurgent empire."[37]

The fire of desire, as the force of human growth and creativity, counters that oppressive discourse. For the bonfire of desires, with its "song of new joy" (line 37), inspires people to work against forms of oppression. So while the poem's description of desire clearly contains its more spiritual meanings, the narrator also, and unusually, focuses on the effects of desire in the world. In this poem, desire counters oppression and helps people realize the mutability of social life and the possibility of greater freedom.

THE CARAVAN

The poem presents the possibility of new social forms as the narrator's "dream" *(k̲hvāb)* of caravans of "solidarity" (*yak-dilī*, literally "one-heartedness") of the "East and West." The image of the caravan would be familiar to Rashed's readers from the poetry of Muhammad Iqbal. The solidarity described in Rashed's poem is strikingly similar to Iqbal's vision of the global Islamic community, although Rashed's poem does not explicitly refer to Islam as the source of solidarity. But the poem's insistence upon the novelty of the narrator's dreams is grounded in its understanding of the creative possibilities of the individual as physical and social, rather than primarily spiritual. In that sense, this poem is in line with Rashed's more general critique of Iqbal's writing, discussed below and in the following chapter.

Rashed describes the caravans of solidarity as sites of pleasure and empowerment, and suggests that their presence spurs creative activity. The caravans bring two famous objects of Persian legend, "the throne of Jamshed and the crown of Kai," as well as jugs of "the wine of the majesty *(saṭvat)* of the individual." Both signs of power, usually vested in royalty, are made available to the people in the narrator's dream. The caravans also bring the cheer of "hard work done day and night" (lines 111–15). And yet, in the preceding verses, Rashed's narrator also cautions against taking too much pleasure, contrasting his dream with the "indolence" that often follows revolutionary moments (line 102).

In this way, the narrator differentiates his ideal of solidarity from existing political and ideological projects. He explains that the solidarity will "be beyond the understanding of man" (line 95). It neither conforms to existing models, nor can it be comprehended by reason. He then explains what it will be:

> Such a solidarity that we'd all say:
>   "Do not make such haste
>   Do not become a throng of roses!"
> We'd say:
>   "You were not the pain *(ġham)* of all *(kul)*
>   Now don't became the pleasure *(lażżat)* of all as well
>   Do not become the indolence of the day of rest
>   Become solidarity, do not become a stillness
>   in which there is nothing but
>   the fruitless laziness of summer afternoons!"
>
> (lines 96–105)

In this poem, Rashed argues that the people should not bloom too quickly like a "throng of roses." Solidarity should not bring pleasure *(lażżat)*, if it has not been grounded in collective suffering *(ġham)*, the word associated with the suffering of the lover in the ghazal. The passage concludes that solidarity should always be grounded in creative action, not the "stillness" found in the heat of summer. Like Iqbal, Rashed here emphasizes the need for effort and struggle.

The most unusual set of claims in the poem, and the real break with Iqbal's thought, concerns the effect that such a collective project would have on the individual. The poem describes the tangible effect of the caravan's presence on the individual's body as an ecstatic release from societal and psychological pressures. The bodies of the East and West, "barren for centuries," would blossom and open, suddenly, as though from a magician's spell (lines 106–110). In the light of Rashed's interest in Freudianism, this passage could be interpreted as indicating a "harmony" of the reality and pleasure principles—a favorite goal of his critical prose writing.[38] In keeping with the poem's focus on the creative force of desire, the narrator indicates that the cause of this blossoming of the body would be "fruitful love" *(ʿishq-e ḥāṣil-k͟hez)* or the "force of creation" *(zor-e paidāʾī)* (lines 106–110). Rashed focuses his criticism of Iqbal on that author's theory of the individual, and of the ideal relationship of individuals to Islam.

Using the metaphor of the desert caravan, Rashed builds upon Iqbal's descriptions of individuality, freedom, and passion, but takes pains to differentiate his position. Iqbal used the caravan as a sign of the global Muslim community. Writing against the dominance of Sufi thought in the Indian subcontinent, Iqbal celebrates the desert location of the sacred spaces of Islam as an antithesis to the "fragrant rose gardens of Iran or the glittering streets of Europe."[39] An example of Iqbal's preference for Arabia is found in his 1915 Persian maśnavī *Asrār-e k̤hvudī* (Secrets of the Self). He writes:

> You have picked roses in the garden of Persia *('Ajam)*
> You have seen the Spring of India and Iran
> Taste a little of the heat of the desert
> Drink the ancient wine of the date
> . . . . .
> For centuries, you have danced on tulips
> You have bathed your cheeks with dew, like a rose
> Throw yourself onto the burning sand
> Plunge into the fountain of Zamzam [in Mecca][40]

In Iqbal's poetry, the nomadic life of the desert is an alternative to more bounded forms of community, and desert wandering signifies the breaking of attachment to a particular land. In the poem "K̤hiẓr-e rāh" (K̤hiẓr of the Road), Iqbal adopts the voice of K̤hiẓr, the legendary guide to travelers mentioned earlier in connection with Mir's verse, to claim that the "constant endeavor" of K̤hiẓr's "desert wandering" is "proof of life." Iqbal's K̤hiẓr describes the appeal of the desert, "when, in the expanse of the desert, the bell of [the caravan's] departure sounds." Drawing on ghazal convention, he explains that "the passion of love searches for fresh deserts" while people in settlements are "bound to fields and groves."[41] Through K̤hiẓr, Iqbal celebrates rootlessness, travel, and movement as essential to the true message of Islam.

In his Persian maśnavī *Rumūz-e be-k̤hvudī* (Secrets of Selflessness), Iqbal explains further that the Muslim community is not "bound by space," and that the country is not the "foundation of the community." The "purpose of Muhammad's mission," he writes, was to "found Freedom, Equality, and Brotherhood among all mankind." Iqbal's collective finds its perfection when the "community, like the individual, discovers the sensation of self." For Iqbal that sensation can only be "realized through guarding the communal traditions," as it is organized by "Divine Law," as "good communal character" derives from "discipline according to the manners of the Prophet."[42]

Iqbal famously emphasized the importance of the individual self *(k̤hvudī)*, rejecting the Sufi ideal of mystical extinction *(fanā)*, especially in his earlier work *Asrār-e khvudī* (Secrets of the Self). In that philosophical Persian *maṡnavī*, he argued explicitly that the "origin of the system of the universe is [from] the self," and that the "continuity of life" depends on "strengthening the self."[43] Iqbal also wrote that the self needs training *(tarbiyat)*, however; he used an elaborate desert-based metaphor to describe its three stages. First, the self should show the obedience *(iṭāʿat)* of a camel to the regulations of Islam; second, the self must exhibit control *(ẓabt)* over the carnal self *(nafs)*, which like a camel thinks only of itself; then, finally, when the camel of the body is under control, the self achieves divine viceregency *(niyābat-e ilâhī)*. This last stage involves the emergence of a hero, "a rider of destiny," who will calm the noise of the nations of the world, and bring to the human race universal brotherhood, while making the rule of God present in the world.[44]

In Rashed's poem there is no mention of the regulations of Islam. Instead of valuing control over the carnal self, he emphasizes the body's release from moral restrictions. In prose, Rashed described Iqbal as continuing a traditional distinction, also fundamental to Sufi thought, between *havas* (desire) and *ʿishq* (passion). The former, associated with the carnal soul *(nafs)*, leads to baseness, while the latter, associated with the higher soul *(rūḥ)*, leads to greatness and the divine.[45]

Similarly, while both visualize a more liberated community beyond the nation, Rashed's poem does not share Iqbal's faith in the possibility of the social world's transcending itself and becoming spiritual. Instead of Iqbal's "man of faith" *(mard-e momin)*, uniting divine will with human life, Rashed uses the image of the storytellers, awakening hearts with their "astonishing, heart-gripping experiences" (line 78). As a result, Rashed's poetry clearly celebrates the material world of human existence as glorious and beautiful without calling for obedience to divine law.

THE DAWN

The caravan's songs of freedom stir the final element in the poem's allegory, the dawn. The narrator calls out to "Pilgrims, victors, caravans to come," for when they "return from the city" they will find that

> on the border of sand, the eternal soul, which was sleeping,
> has awoken from the "laments of the reed"

That bashful morning planted in the depths of sand
has awoken from the songs of freedom!

(lines 116–121)

The dawn, or "soul of eternity" *(rūḥ-e abad)*, is coaxed awake by the "laments of the reed" *(shikvah-hā-e nai)* and "songs of freedom." The first song, the "laments of the reed," is found in the well-known prelude to Rumi's *Masnavī*, in which a narrator instructs the reader to listen to the reed flute's song mourning its separation from the reed-bed. That passage is normally read as an account of a lover pining for the divine beloved—like the bird of the soul yearning to return to its nest, to use another common motif. Critics have speculated in various ways about the identity of the reed, proposing that it might be seen as Rumi's inner self freed from its outer self, as his soul experiencing divine inspiration, as his spiritual mentors Shams-e Tabrīz and Ḥusāmu'd-dīn, and even as the prophet Muhammad.[46] In any case, Rashed's allusion to Rumi starts a counterpoint with Rumi that influences the interpretation of the allegory on the whole, and of the dawn in particular.

Rashed's narrator addresses the morning as a bride who has consummated her marriage with the divine and can now finally participate in the celebration of the desert. The soul as a bride is a motif of Sufi poetry, used also by Rumi but especially prevalent in the Indian subcontinent.[47] In Rashed's poem, before the dawn's union she was a young and innocent girl who had been living in purdah, so none of her (presumably male) audience would dare speak with her:

The morning was so virgin, had never been touched by men
We couldn't even ask her age!
She did not laugh from pain,
She didn't even laugh at the colorfulness of the grains of sand,
She used to laugh in a shy, careless manner!
Now she celebrates the glory of the desert
as if it were the very arch of the feet of the Glorious and Majestic!

(lines 122–28)

She spent the night pining under that arch, like the lover of the ghazal, hoping for union with her beloved. Now she has emerged from the bridal chamber, "happy [and] bright faced." There the "murderer" *(qātil)*—an epithet of the beloved in the ghazal—has let flow "the shining blood / of thousands of stars." This blood, presumably the redness of daybreak, is also a sign of the consummation of the dawn's marriage, as the murderer let the stars' blood flow "near every flower on the [bridal] bed *(sej)*" (lines 132–36). Now, she too joins in the celebration of the desert, which appears to her like the "arch of the feet of the Glorious and Majestic," which she would surely worship. In other words, she no longer sees the desert as separate from the divine.

The narrator elaborates on his glorification of the material world of the desert by addressing the dawn, asking her to tell him tales of the desert rather than of the past. In his prelude, Rumi's narrator explains that the reed "tells of the Way full of blood" and "recounts stories of the Majnun's passion." Rashed's narrator, by contrast, tells the dawn that he is sick of hearing "tales" of those "martyrs of desire" *(tamannā ke shāhīd)* whom he could never meet. Their longing was not fully ripe, the narrator protests, because they found the dawn's "honey . . . not sweet." Because the lovers of the past sought the spiritual "Way," they undervalued the material world of the desert, just as the dawn had done before her mystical union (lines 137–41).

Rashed's description of the dawn is playful, invoking aspects of Sufi poetry while also insisting upon the importance of material life. The sun was a favorite image of Rumi, whose spiritual mentor was named Shams (Sun). But for Rumi the physical sun is always subservient to its metaphorical referent: the soul, the spiritual mentor, or the divine.[48] In Rashed's poem, by contrast, the sun is part of the physical world: earlier he calls the grains of desert sand, which also make up the narrator's desert-wandering heart, the rising dawn (line 26). The dawn is as much a figure of the self, as of the soul, blurring the distinction between *nafs* (carnal soul) and *rūḥ* (soul) made by Rumi. Rumi's separation between the two is echoed in the duality that Rashed sees in Iqbal's conception of passion, which emphasized the world but turned away from the body. While working within the metaphorical language common to Sufi poetry, Rashed's poem critiques that tradition's denigration of the body. The narrator instead requests the dawn sing praises of the material world of the desert (lines 147–54).

NARRATIVE HORIZON

The conclusion of "Heart, My Old Desert-Wandering Heart" clarifies the relationships between the elements of the allegory:

> Morning, sand, and fire, the majesty *(jalāl)* of us all!
> The caravan of solidarity, their beauty *(jamāl)*

Come!
Let's meet in this circle of praise *(tahlīl)*
Come!
Joy to the endless bonfire of desire!

(lines 155–60)

Sand, fire, and morning, standing for materiality, desire, and the self or soul, respectively, signify the majesty *(jalāl)* of human life. The caravan of solidarity, a collective of free and enlightened individuals, represents their beauty *(jamāl)*. These two attributes—majesty and beauty—are opposed, in the Sufi tradition. Taken together, in the poetry of Rumi for example, they describe the capacity of God to contain opposites.[49] Celebrating the bonfire of desire, the narrator beckons people to meet in a "circle of praise *(tahlīl)*." In its religious sense, the word *tahlīl* refers to the act of "pronouncing, in a high and intelligible voice" the "first and main element of the Islamic profession of faith"—*lā illâha ila'l-lâh* (There is no God but Allah)—which entails a "formal and basic recognition of the divine unity." [50] More informally, however, it means to shout with joy.

These three terms—majesty, beauty, and proclamation—describe the desert landscape. Juxtaposed, they suggest two possible readings for the poem as a whole. Either the poem is making a statement about the unity of being and the immanent presence of God in this world, or it is offering a more secular celebration of this-worldly life. In both cases, the poem emphasizes the importance and significance of the tangible world of the desert, and the effects of desire in it.

In its appreciation of this-worldly life, as well as its insistence on the importance of creative activity, Rashed's poem echoes Iqbal's critique of aspects of Sufism. Both writers appear to oppose the mystical goal of *fanā*, or extinction of the self. Rashed's poem goes further, however, by rejecting Iqbal's choice to privilege spiritual over worldly and carnal forms of desire. For Rashed, desire signals creativity and life, even in its carnal forms. Desire courses through the physical world like an élan vital, to use the favorite term of Henri Bergson, whose work was a central impulse for Iqbal's ideas about temporality and the self. That discourse, and Rashed's intervention in it, is the topic of the next chapter. Rashed's desert poem is mainly critical of Iqbal's insistence upon differentiating love of the soul from love of the body.

By celebrating the material world, Rashed's allegorical writing allows for the imagination of a collectivity not bounded on a spiritual plane. He connects Iqbal's metaphysical certainty to his confidence in the virtues of a separate Indian Muslim homeland. Rashed traces his distrust of such visions to the fundamentals of language—the relationship between word/symbol and meaning—and law—the potential for a moral system grounded in religion to produce real freedom for individuals. While both poets visualize a more liberated community beyond the nation, Rashed's vision involves freedom from moral strictures that would deny bodily desire, because he sees the body as the site of all creative activity. Written in an allegorical mode, Rashed's poem, like his later oeuvre on the whole, works with Iqbal's meanings while assembling an alternative version of that thinker's view of the self and collectivity. Rashed's writing is consistently distrustful of claims of the unity of divine and human will. Instead of transcendence, Rashed's poem celebrates the power of desire, and the mutability and transience of material nature and forms of human life.

THE DISCURSIVE SPACE OF LITERATURE

In "Heart, My Old Desert-Wandering Heart," Rashed places himself within an intellectual lineage or *silsilah*, to use the term preferred in Urdu discourse. His poetry traces a particular genealogy of Indo-Muslim literature by using and altering the imagery of the ghazal, Rumi, and Iqbal. Rashed's model is Iqbal, who saw himself as following in the "caravan of passion" whose "chief is Rumi."[51] While Iqbal was certainly critical of much of the ghazal tradition, particularly the poetry of Hafiz, Iqbal's poetry maintained continuity with its symbols. Rashed's allegorical poem compounds and reinterprets ghazal imagery. It presents a message at odds with that tradition while still remaining recognizably related to it.

Rashed's poetry is most intimately connected to the oeuvre of Iqbal, but that same oeuvre is also the focus of his critique. Rashed is troubled by two interconnected aspects of Iqbal's legacy: the appropriation of his philosophy as the national ideology of Pakistan and his transformation of literature into religious philosophy. As outlined first in his *Īrān meñ ajnabī*, Rashed's late poetry attempts to carve out an alternative set of discursive possibilities for literature that would allow for writing to escape ideological strictures, whether religiously or politically defined. In a sense, what Rashed called for was, indeed, art for art's sake—yet not in the merely aesthetic or escapist way described by some progressive critics. Instead, his poetry argues, literature should provide a place for a particular kind of experience and of critique.

Writing in often veiled or allusive terms, Rashed's poetry constructs a worldly critique by taking or citing elements from Urdu and Persian literary tradition and investing them with new meanings. The reader must be familiar with the Indo-Persian literary tradition to fully understand Rashed's work, but his poetry challenges the original authority of those very assumptions. Although Rashed appeared to many critics to have rejected his responsibilities to the Pakistani nation, and despite Rashed's own universalistic and humanist rhetoric, his poetry is intelligible and meaningful to a deterritorialized and transnational Urdu literary community. Distrustful of claims of organic unity, whether of the nation or the religious community, Rashed presents a discursive ground for community instead. That community is based in a critical apprehension of a shared tradition, rather than in ideology, ethnicity, religion, or territory. Through allegorical appropriation and reinterpretation, Rashed created a meaningful form of poetry in the gap between word and meaning, without seeking to overcome that distance.

FOUR

Temporality

N. M. RASHED'S ALLEGORICAL POEM "Another City" (*Ek aur shahr*, §19) is a densely written meditation on time and progress and their effects on the self. It begins by describing how in the other city, the "desire for self-understanding hides its face in darkness." Knowledge of the self would presumably provide some light, but instead a mountain of "boundless haste" looms on every pathway. The inhabitants of the other city are ironically described as "valiant Western heroes" *(afrangī mardān-e rād)*, using a phrase common to the poetry of Muḥammad Iqbāl.[1] "Thirsty for fresh blood," the heroes' hearts are greedy like the "eye of a hunter" (lines 1–6). The poem goes on to reflect on how the city's inhabitants understand their own progress:

> The river has two shores and both are unattainable
> Evil is a black hand and the bearer of goodness a white face!
> One weighing down the eyes, one with a smile on its lips!
>
> (lines 7–9)

At the poem's end, that river becomes a metaphor for a linear form of time, for which there is neither beginning nor end.

The poem was completed in 1957; an earlier version, titled "New York," was written in March 1955.[2] That location may explain the opposition between the virtuous "white face" and the "black hand," which must cover the tears of those presumed to be wicked. These are simultaneously ironic references to the racialized metaphors of morality common to everyday life of the United States in that era, and inversions of the more commonly used phrases in Urdu: the "white hand" *(yad-e baiẓā)* of Moses and the "black face" *(rū-e siyāh)* of a criminal. The inversion implies that judgments of "virtue" are reversed as well. The poem continues:

> All measures are useless when silver and gold are the scale
> when the fountain of the appreciation of action is meaningless nonsense
> when at every moment terror threatens the soul!
>
> (lines 10–12)

Both experience and an innate sense of justice are irrelevant, the narrator says, when everything boils down to money. "The fountain of the appreciation of action" should not be "meaningless nonsense," of course, and neither should there be the threat of "terror" at every moment. It is not clear from the poem why things are that way. But that state of affairs may suggest that the city is headed toward its destruction:

> These are all horizontal *(ufuqī)* men; these, their high-rising *(samāvī)* cities
> Does a wave of the storm of time lie to ambush them?
> Are all the beloved children of destruction?
>
> (lines 13–15)

These lines imagine time as a river, which if it assumes the form of a tidal wave might destroy the city. The inhabitants' false understanding of progress and virtue, described earlier, leads the narrator to fear for his safety.

In an unusually compact way, this allegorical poem introduces the themes about time that are of central concern to Rashed's late poetry. In "Heart, My Old Desert-Wandering Heart" (§18), as described in the previous chapter, individual metaphors were linked to each other both "horizontally" in a narrative and "vertically" to different points of intertextual reference. By contrast, this entire poem refers simultaneously to two "vertical" genealogies of modernist writing, by using as points of reference the poetry of W. H. Auden and that of Muhammad Iqbal. Sharing Auden's location and sense of temporality, Rashed marks his participation in the global history of modernism, a supposedly universal project. Yet he also dramatizes how that sense of commonality dissolves when the poem confronts the disjuncture between a presumably "universal" conception of time seated in the "West" and the temporal understandings prevalent in Rashed's Urdu literary community.

Rashed's most obvious allusion to Auden is the description of the city's residents as "horizontal," which references Auden's short poem:

Let us honour if we can
The vertical man
Though we value none
But the horizontal one.[3]

There are many possible interpretation of "horizontal" in Auden's poem. It could mean the dead, conformists, or the self-obsessed. Rashed's poem draws in all those meanings to describe the residents of the "other" city. But as I will describe more fully below, by marking the location of his poetic critique of progress in New York, Rashed also refers to Auden's most famous deliberation on temporality and destruction, his "September 1, 1939." In that poem, Auden reflects on the Great War at the start of World War II, while Rashed's 1957 poem reflects, in turn, on World War II from the perspective of the Cold War. There are common elements to both poets' understandings of the self and of society that showcase their common participation in a global modernism.

Alongside its allusions to Auden, Rashed's poem uses vertical and horizontal axes in order to describe time, developing the sense of the horizontal also common to the genealogy of Sufism and its immanent critique by Iqbal. Sufis frequently describe a mystical ascent out of time, as part of an esoteric understanding of time outside the usual, worldly understanding. Iqbal creatively reworked this distinction by taking recourse to the modernist philosophy of Henri Bergson (1859–1941), whose thought he adopted, to a point, but ultimately rejected in favor of a temporality built from within Islamic thought. Iqbal's ideas about temporality, particularly the sense of common movement through time of the Muslim community, were adopted by Pakistani nationalists as the philosophical basis for the nation. By referring to vertical and horizontal axes of time, Rashed's poem intersects with this line of thought. As a result, the poem simultaneously comments on the temporality of the global order signified by the Cold War and that of the national imagination of Pakistan.

In this chapter I will examine N. M. Rashed's reflections on time within this complex and transnational genealogy. The poem "Another City" criticizes the West's (or America's) understanding of its own progress for ignoring human suffering and for placing more value on the unfolding future than on the injustices of the present. Rashed also opposed uncritical adherence to the past or to tradition, as has been discussed. In other late poems, Rashed encompasses both of these criticisms within a larger critique of teleology, focusing particularly on the teleology of nationalism. His poetry substitutes an emphasis on contemporaneity, which can be understood as seizing the moment of the now, bringing doubt to the structures and institutions of the present, and reestablishing a more vital and creative experience, in line with the elusive category of life.

HORIZONTAL MAN

The relationship of the New York poem "Another City" to Auden's work provides concrete evidence for Rashed's complex relationship to global modernism. Auden's "September 1, 1939," set among the "dives / On Fifty-second street," dwells on Europe and America and the flaws and follies leading to war. Like Rashed's narrator, Auden's is "uncertain and afraid" as "The unmentionable odour of death," or the return of war, "Offends the September night."[4]

Both poems reveal the ideologies of progress and of American virtue as merely the display of imperial power. Rashed's "high-rising city" populated by "horizontal men" mirrors Auden's own vision of the city:

> Into this neutral air
> Where blind skyscrapers use
> Their full height to proclaim
> The strength of Collective Man,
> Each language pours its vain
> Competitive excuse:
> But who can live for long
> In a euphoric dream;
> Out of the mirror they stare,
> Imperialism's face
> And the international wrong.[5]

The strength of "Collective Man" to which the American skyscrapers testify reveals to the British poet "imperialism" and "international wrong." In Rashed's poem the "valiant Western heroes," despite their assumption of virtue, are in reality "thirsty for fresh blood." Rashed's poem works, as Auden says, "to undo the folded lie, / The romantic lie in the brain / Of the sensual man-in-the-street / And the lie of Authority / Whose buildings grope the sky."[6] Rashed's reflections on New York during the Cold War are steeped in the experience of World War II. As is clear from his *Iran meñ ajnabī,* that experience of war brought home to him the presence of numerous forms of oppression that the poet saw as imperialist, whether European or Soviet. In "Another City," America is clearly placed within that paradigm.

The conclusion of Auden's poem shows numerous similarities to both Rashed's own poetry and poetic persona:

> Ironic points of light
> Flash out wherever the Just
> Exchange their messages:
> May I, composed like them
> Of Eros and of dust,
> Beleaguered by the same
> Negation and despair,
> Show an affirming flame.[7]

The "ironic points of light," which are able to pierce through the darkness of the "night," should be seen as references to vitalism, which was of great importance to modernism in English. In this reading, Auden's "Eros" and "dust" would correspond to Henri Bergson's division between élan vital and matter. But the more appropriate reference for Auden's figure is Freud, for whom Eros was a force opposed to death. Auden's Freudian understanding of subjectivity, as surrounded by forces of "negation and despair," and his hope for an "affirming flame" are strongly resonant with Rashed's own work. If Rashed's first book of poems introduced the categories of psychoanalysis, his later poetry deepened that engagement, incorporating the poet's reading of radical post-Freudian psychology.

Donna Jones explains the movement from Bergson's category of "life" into Freud's concept of "Eros" as an effect of the Great War. Bergson's "*Creative Evolution* (1907)," she writes, "had captured the optimistic prewar zeitgeist like no other work," as it "culminated in the human mind becoming conscious of itself as the highest expression of . . . an élan vital[,] and life thereby achieving a form with which to beat back matter and even death, against which it had hitherto vainly battled." The "grim pessimism of Freud's [postwar] *Civilization and Its Discontents*"—with its postulation of a "death drive" within humankind—instead "defines precisely the effects of the Great War on European thought." For "Europe," Jones writes, "had come to expect death."[8]

Rashed's pessimism and his opposition of desire to despair are in line with Auden's concerns, and therefore participate, quite knowingly, in a global modernist genealogy of thought. As I will explain later in this chapter, one of the primary concerns of Rashed's poetry is the force of "negation and despair" in everyday life—the subjective experience of death in life. As in Auden's poem, Rashed attempts in his poems to move beyond fear, especially of death, in order to celebrate transitory human life and to rescue experience from negative forces, both societal and psychological.

But as I suggested above, the categories of horizontality and verticality at play in "Another City" also are used to express a different conception of time. In Sufi thought, it is common to differentiate the horizontal experience of days, months, and years from the vertical flight of the mystic outside of measurable time. Finding parallels between this convention and the philosophy of Henri Bergson, Iqbal likened the horizontal span of earthly time to Bergson's "serial time" and the vertical flight out of time to the "intuition" of "pure duration."

Iqbal presents an interpretation of Bergson's understanding of temporality, using the familiar terms of Sufi discourse, in a short poem from his *Payām-e Mashriq* (Message of the East):

> In order to have the secret of life revealed to you,
> Do not separate yourself from the flame like a spark
> For seeing, do not use your familiar eyes
> Do not pass through [your] country like a foreigner
> The image you have formed is entirely false imagination
> Procure an intellect tutored by the heart[9]

Iqbal presents Bergson's method of intuition as a vision from the heart, not the intellect, following the usual Sufi distinction between passion *(ʿishq)* and reason *(ʿaql)*. Ultimately, however, Iqbal criticized Bergson's philosophy as too atheistic, and put forward an alternative vision of time grounded in Muslim philosophy.

In a 1967 address in English to the Asia Society of New York, Rashed took up Iqbal's idea of an alternative temporality, while also implicitly explicating his earlier poem. He characterizes the time of the West as a "civilization which, for all practical purposes, moves forward in parallel straight lines, and is in a position to move with the utmost velocity" unlike the more "curvaceous nature of the Oriental civilization." The forward-moving, continuous (usually *musalsal*) motion of time is visualized in "Another City" as horizontality, where it appears as a river without shores (line 7). Though in the poem the skyscrapers of the city reach into the sky, the people remain confined to this horizontal axis, moving forward with "unbounded haste" and deprived of "self-knowledge." In "Oriental civilization," Rashed explains in his address, curvature reigns. It is expressed in its material culture ("arches and domes of the Oriental buildings," "designs on rugs and carpets," the "arabesques in the paintings," the "circular letters of the alphabet"); in its music ("where every movement is a series of circles, and every note rejoins itself in a large circular motion"); in its "ambiguous" poetry ("where not only the rhyming arrangements are repetitious, but there are often layers of meaning contained within a circle"); and in its "wisdom" ("which is brought out through a series of metaphors, symbols, proverbs and parables, with the understanding that the more roundabout you are, the wiser and more interesting you are").[10] For Rashed, this more curvaceous experience of time opposes the "straight" time associated with the modernity of the West. Like Iqbal, he remained critical of both cultures of time.

Rashed adopted Iqbal's critique of serial (or "straight") time, but he also sought a new relationship to time in his own poetry, one that opposed teleology and that valued contingency and contemporaneity. Rashed identified the Bergsonism of Iqbal, linking him to global literary modernism, in which Bergson's approach to temporality is especially influential. But whereas Iqbal used Bergson to reconstruct religious thought, Rashed's understanding of temporality is grounded in the possibilities of literature. His approach is opposed to teleology as a matter of principle, for in Rashed's mind literature is by definition focused on worldly experience and is therefore shaped by the imperatives of physical and mental life. The kind of nontranscendent thinking found in his poetry, and, as he prescriptively describes, in literature as a whole, serves as a this-worldly alternative to Iqbal's thought. Rashed's work speaks from a position of cultural difference, answering preemptively the accusation of Westernness, but leaves the "now" open to new forms and ruptures of thought in the service of life.

TIME IS GOD

Rashed follows Iqbal in grounding his critique of temporality in the following text, wherein the "Apostle" of God is reported to have stated: "God said: 'The son of Adam should not say, "Curse Time!" For I am Time! I send the day and the night, and if I wished, I would take them away [lit. seize them].' "[11] Muslims recognize this text as *hadīs-e qudsī*, an authentic tradition that reports a statement of the prophet Muhammad in which he transmits a direct communication from God. This *hadīs-e qudsī* is one of the most significant statements about time in Islam. Both poets quote this text in their poetry, but to very different ends.

Muhammad Iqbal engages with the *hadīs-e qudsī* in his poetic and philosophical writings, where the conception of time has a central place. Even beyond his poetic and philosophical contributions, Iqbal holds a revered status in the national history of Pakistan because he proposed, within the forum of the Muslim League, the need for a "consolidated North-West Indian Muslim State" some ten years before the 1940 Pakistan Resolution.[12] According to C. M. Naim, Iqbal's address, when read in its historical context, appears to be advocating for a Muslim provincial self-government within a federal scheme.[13] However, Pakistani nationalist historians read Iqbal's demand for "[s]elf-government within the British Empire, or *without the British Empire*," (italics mine) as a key event in the genealogy of Pakistan as a nation-state.[14] In his broader philosophical writings, however, Iqbal opposed territorial nationalism as counter to Islam. Against the understanding of time that animates conventional nationalism, Iqbal returned to the *hadīs-e qudsī* as an alternative vision of time.

Iqbal first laid out a philosophical conception of time in "Al-vaqt saif" (Time is a Sword), a section of his Persian *maṡnavī Asrār-e ḳhvudī* ("Secrets of the Self") published in 1915.[15] In this passage, deeply influenced by the writings of Henri Bergson, Iqbal draws on both the *hadīs-e qudsī* and on Bergson's distinction between spatialized time and the time of duration:

> You, who are not aware of the essence of time
> who are unaware of everlasting life
> . . .
> You have conceived of time as space
> You have distinguished between today and tomorrow
> O you who have fled from your own garden like fragrance
> You have created your prison by your own hand
> Our time which has never seen beginning or end
> sprouts from the flower bed of our heart
> The living are more alive from knowledge of its essence
> Its life is brighter than the dawn
> Life is from time, and time is from life
> "Do not abuse time" was the command of the Prophet
>
> (lines 16, 21–25)

In this passage, the time of "today and tomorrow"—or a concept of time in which each moment has its own unique space—is differentiated from the "essence of time," which is described as "everlasting life." Iqbal follows Bergson thus far. For Bergson, the immediate data of consciousness are temporal; he names this "duration." Duration is heterogeneous and continuous, a multiplicity of quality rather than quantity. Spatialized time, on the other hand, is a secondary process in which time is treated as a homogeneous quantity. Bergson introduced the philosophical method of intuition as an act of self-sympathy consisting of the experience of duration. For Bergson, to experience one's own duration is to experience all of duration.[16] In this passage, as in the short poem on Bergson quoted earlier, Iqbal refers to the intuition of duration as a perception through the heart, not the intellect.

Yet even as Iqbal was attracted to some of Bergson's ideas, he criticized his methodology and conclusions. Iqbal argued that even though Bergson's intuition was dependent on the self, his misconception was that "pure time [is] prior to [the] self, to which alone pure duration is predicable."[17] According to Iqbal, Bergson does not realize that "Neither pure space nor pure time can hold together the multiplicity of objects and events. It is the appreciative act of an enduring self only which can seize the multiplicity of duration—broken up into an infinity of instants—and transform it to the organic wholeness of a synthesis. To exist in pure duration is to be a self, and to be a self is to be able to say 'I am.'"[18] While Iqbal seems to accept Bergson's premise of duration, he contradicts its implications by arguing that duration must be sustained by something external to it. The qualitative and quantitative multiplicity of the universe requires a self to provide it duration, not just a human self to recognize that it is there. The universe is therefore utterly dependent on what Iqbal calls "the Ultimate Self" or "the Absolute Ego." Iqbal finds "the ultimate Reality as pure duration in which thought, life, and purpose interpenetrate to form an organic unity."[19] For Iqbal, and as in the *ḥadīs̤-e qudsī*, that unity, time, is God.

To Iqbal, the presence of "ultimate Reality" as pure duration, or as the essence of time, proves the integral relationship between thought, or reason, and God. He therefore counters both Sufism's rejection of reason as finite and its conviction that esoteric knowledge is the only path to God, as famously articulated by the eleventh-century Iranian Sufi philosopher al-Ġhazālī. For Iqbal, the "deeper movement" of thought is capable of reaching "an immanent Infinite in whose self-unfolding movement the various finite concepts are merely moments." Thought, he argues, is a dynamic self-expression of the whole which, though it appears to be a "series of definite specifications," cannot be understood "except by a reciprocal reference" to the whole itself.[20]

Iqbal saw the unfolding of history, even as spatialized time, not merely as the unfolding of human events but as the manifestation of God. In other words, history is teleological; it is the continuous and organic actualization of selective possibilities. The future is not predestined. Rather, Iqbal argues, it is formed through intermediate human choices, as a "progressive formulation of fresh ends, purposes, and ideal scales of value."[21] But this new formulation of ends merely expresses the whole that is always already present. Despite its similarity to Hegel's philosophy of history, Iqbal identifies this view of history as the unique position of Islam. He writes of the Muslim historian Ibn Khaldun that "only a Muslim could have viewed history as a continuous, collective movement, a real inevitable development in time."[22]

Iqbal presents this notion of creative teleology as the temporal understanding of the Muslim community. While intended as universal, it was simultaneously bound to Iqbal's audience of Indian Muslims and later mapped onto the nation of Pakistan. The great paradox of this appropriation is that Iqbal was an adamant opponent of territorial nationalism. Although Iqbal declared in his 1930 presidential address that "the Muslims of India are the only Indian people who can fitly be described as a nation in the modern sense of the word" and that "the life of Islam as a cultural force in the country very largely depends on its centralization in a specified territory,"[23] what is often ignored is that these statements were framed within a criticism of nationalism rather than a celebration of it. In the same speech, Iqbal rehearsed the familiar narrative of secularization, arguing that the nation-state developed in Europe only after the displacement of a universal Christian ethics "by national systems of ethics and polity."[24] He marked the Reformation as the point after which the issue of eternal salvation became a private affair divorced from temporal life. In contrast, Iqbal saw in Islam an essential rejection of this split. "In Islam," he writes, "God and the universe, spirit and matter, Church and State, are organic to each other. . . . To Islam, matter is spirit realising itself in space and time." Islam, as an "ethical ideal plus a certain kind of polity," provides the cohesion of a nation for Indian Muslims despite—or perhaps because of—its fundamental difference from Western nationalism.[25]

As Partha Chatterjee has noted in his analysis of anticolonial nationalism, colonial difference—the imperative to be "other" in order to have value—

forced the content of Indian nationalism into an inner or spiritual realm divorced from the public life of the state.[26] For Indians during colonialism, what was available was the development of a particular national genius rather than a more universal experience of historical development. What Iqbal did was to transform the former condition—national genius—into the latter—universal Spirit—by invoking the Islamic community as something larger and more universal than the nation, even as he found its incarnation in the Indian Muslim community.

Other verses from Iqbal's poem illustrate this maneuver. Expanding on the title "Al-vaqt saif" (Time Is a Sword)—a saying associated with the Muslim jurist Imām Shafiʿī—Iqbal writes:

> [O] the memory of days when the sword of time
> was allied with the strength of our hands
> We sowed the seed of religion in the field of hearts
> and removed the veil from the face of truth
> Our fingernails opened the knot of the world
> Our bowing in prayer gave bounty to the world
> We poured rose-colored wine from the pitcher of truth
> We attacked the ancient taverns
>
> (lines 87–94)

In this passage, Iqbal invokes the Islamic past as the moment when the sword of time was in Muslim hands. He states further,

> Our cup, too, has adorned the gathering
> Our chest, too, has possessed a heart
> The new age adorned in all its luster
> has arisen from the dust of our feet
>
> (lines 99–102)

Here, as elsewhere, Iqbal refers to Muslim contributions to modern knowledge, such as the scientific method and mathematics. Recalling the loss of Muslim sovereignty, he continues by addressing Europe:

> Although crown and signet-ring have passed from our hands
> do not look contemptuously on our beggarliness
> In your eyes we are backward
> thinking old thoughts, contemptible
>
> (lines 109–112)

Against this European perception of Muslim backwardness, Iqbal describes the universal value of the national genius of Muslims:

> We are freed from the suffering of today and tomorrow
> We are bound to love One
> We are the secret hidden in the heart of God
> We are the heirs of Moses and Aaron
> The sun and moon are still brightened by our light
> Our cloud is still full of lightning bolts
> Our self is the mirror of the self of God
> The being of the Muslim is among the signs of God
>
> (lines 115–122)

Here Iqbal elevates the Muslim community to a universal level, as the community of God, freed from the suffering of today and tomorrow. Iqbal manages to put forth an understanding of time that is different from what Benedict Anderson has described as "homogeneous, empty time"—the temporal requisite for the imagined community of the nation.[27] Anderson takes the term from the "Theses on the Philosophy of History" by Walter Benjamin, who in turn took it from Bergson.[28] According to Anderson, simultaneity is the premise of print-capitalism's preeminent genres, the novel and the newspaper, which facilitated national imagining in the eighteenth century. The reader of a novel is able to imagine characters who live their lives separately but simultaneously, who are active at the same time in different locations as part of the same society. The nation is imagined in an analogous manner, as a community moving steadily through the homogeneous, empty time of history.[29] In a colonial context, Iqbal presented an inner, spiritual, and essential meaning of time premised on a difference from this homogeneous, empty nation-time of the West. In the history of Pakistani nationalism, Iqbal's conception of a different, sacred, and universalistic time in Islam was, for the most part, superseded by homogeneous, empty time. Because Pakistani nationalism arose out of a discourse of minority rights, the Muslim community was defined in opposition to the Hindu community.[30] Constrained by a discourse of community, the universalistic elements of Iqbal's formulation were mapped exclusively onto Indian Muslims. Under Muhammad Ali Jinnah's leadership, moreover, Pakistani nationalism assumed a discourse of cultural nationalism. It was not only Islam that defined the Pakistani nation but also cultural components, including Indo-Muslim culture and the Urdu language. Following the imperatives of modular forms of nationalism, the ideology of the state became that of one religion, one culture, and one language.

THE CRITIQUE OF PROGRESS

Like Iqbal, Rashed contrasted the empty, homogeneous time of nationalism with other forms of temporality. His most direct description of nation-time came in the poem "Reg-e dīroz" (The Sands of Yesterday, §20). The poem begins by imagining time as space:

> We are the residents of the ruins of love
> raised by the grievous expanse of Time
> a dark Beginning, void of the light of the End!
>
> (lines 1–3)

The experience of time here is precisely that of the river with two unattainable shores in the poem "Another City." If time is a spatial abstraction, then these narrators occupy an intermediate space between two dark eternities, those of *azal*, the eternity at the beginning of time, and *abad*, the eternity at the end of time. Their present space of sorrow contains only love's ruins, and is devoid of any relief or hope for redemption. By love *(muḥabbat)*, the poem means theophany, the revelation of the divine in the world. It refers to the mystical practices of the Sufis, the *ahl-e dil* (people of the heart), who believe that the world was created from love. Where once there was the experience of sacred love and mystical union, there is now only ruin. The "ruins of love" describe time empty of sacred content, in the sense that will permit the imagination of historical progress:

> We, who for centuries have traveled, believe we have reached a shore,
> obtained the reward of our dance of civilization!
>
> (lines 4–5)

The narrators believe their journey through the desert has concluded. They have reached the [ocean's] shore and received the reward of their "dance of civilization": progress and Enlightenment itself.

As the poem moves on, the concept of progress is gradually revealed as problematic. First, it becomes clear that the imagination of historical progress requires the narrators to reject the historical reality of suffering:

> We reside in the hidden chambers of love
> We scoff at tales of being trampled under foot
> We believe we have found a sign of the destination!
>
> (lines 6–8)

The poet highlights the masking of violence that characterizes historical progress; the physical suffering of those who have been "trampled under foot" is rejected as unimportant. In order to maintain their sense of progress (of having "found a sign of the destination"), the narrators must ignore their own history of defeat. Theirs is a laughing denial of death, of literally "being trampled."

By the end of the poem, the notion of progress is fully undone. Rather than having arrived, the enunciators of progress are in fact stuck in the past:

> We are the residents of the ruins of love
> content like a rain-soaked bird in a corner of the past,
> and if ever a sudden tumult should frighten us and we awake
> then the heavy curtain of sleep would remain a barrier to our vision
> We are the residents of the ruins of love!
>
> (lines 9–13)

What the narrators thought was progress was nothing of the sort. No matter how strong the shocks of the present reality, they could not pierce the veil of their delusion. Furthermore, believing they have already arrived, the narrators are no longer able to imagine their future:

> We are the residents of the ruins of love
> We planted trees of dreams in the sands of the past
> The shade was non-existant; we slept under the desire for shade!
>
> (lines 18–20)

The space of history is not neutral territory, but is rather the harsh landscape of the desert. While dreams were planted in the "sands of the past," they never grew to the height that would provide shade, and in their slumber the narrators fail to plant new dream trees.

Despite his insistence on the importance of dreams and on the need for considering the future, Rashed declined to describe in any detail what the future should or will look like. Instead, he decried the absence of dreams in the modern age, while refusing to present any that were not abstract. To advocate any particular dream would be to advocate for an ideological position, which Rashed dismissed as settling for an inevitably corrupt solution. It would also cause his poetry to fall into cliché and limit the effectiveness of his art. He insisted that striving was more important than arriving. So his poems foreground dreams for the future while casting doubt on the certainty of the categories of the present.[31]

The conclusion of "The Sands of Yesterday" exposes its narrators' self-apprehension as false. Conceiving of history as homogeneous, empty time and claiming that they have refined their civilization, the narrators feel they have arrived at a significant milestone of development. They believe, in other words, that they have overcome the losses of their past and reached the height of civilization, moving beyond the past to become modern, or fully civilized. Yet this apparent break with the past is revealed to be nothing more than a continuation of their previous state.

Moreover, what was of value in the past, figured in the poem as the mystical experiences of Sufism, appears inadequately adjusted to the structures of the modern world. The penultimate stanza likens the narrators to Sufis repeating in the darkness the ecstatic phrase "O my God!" *(yā hū)*, from the Arabic *yā huva* (O He!). In an earlier version of the poem, this critique was sharpened through its former title, "Taṣavvuf" (Sufism).[32] These references draw on the mystical understanding of time (*vaqt*), as a withdrawal from the flow of time.[33] "The Sands of Yesterday," through its narrators' misrecognition of their own stasis for progress, makes an analogy to this Sufi withdrawal from the movement of time. The poem likens them to tired, rain-soaked birds stuck in the past and unwilling to move on.[34] All shocks and jolts are repressed. Instead of a meaningful relationship with the present allowing for the possibility of the new, the narrators are instead stuck between the past, which has lost its meaning, and the present, which they cannot meaningfully experience.

This idea of a disconnection between the meanings of the past and those of the present contemporary situation also animates N. M. Rashed's poem "Zamānah ḳhudā hai" (Time Is God, §21) from *Lā = Insān*. The poem takes its cue from the *hadīs̤-e qudsī* on time:

> "Time is God, you should not speak badly of it"
> But you do not see—time is only a rope of thought
> of little value, thin, long
>   the cheap road of separation!
>
> (lines 1–4)

The quotation of the *hadīs̤-e qudsī* here takes the form of a rebuke, as if from a neighborhood imam or a religiously minded elder. The narrator of the poem responds, rejecting this folksy tone and engaging the *hadīs̤-e qudsī* in an unusually abstract manner. He dismisses time as only a "rope of thought." The word used for thought, *ḳhayāl*, connotes "fancy" or "imagination," and nicely undermines the materiality of time before the next lines describe time as thin, long, of little value or substance, and cheap. None of those characteristics corresponds to any usual description of divinity.

In the next stanza, the narrator continues to describe an alternative version of time:

> Those mornings that were millions of years before,
> those evenings that will be millions of years from now
> you do not see them, cannot see them
> though they are present, even now, they are present somewhere,
> but this rope that is stretched before the eyes
> you can see this, and do see this
> for this is that non-existence
> which in becoming being will take a long while
> moments of stars, years of stars!
>
> (lines 5–13)

Time as it is experienced, the present, is the "rope that is stretched before the eyes." The moments of the past and future cannot be seen, even though they exist somewhere in the now. But experience, or what can be seen, is really nonexistence that will require a period of gestation to become being. That period of gestation is very long—the "moments" and "years of stars"—and is measured in an astronomical scale that puts the present in perspective. In other words, the narrator denies our ability to grasp temporal experience.

In an unusual analogy, the poem moves beyond these very abstract pronouncements to elaborate its propositions about time:

> In my courtyard is a young violet plant
> Whenever an airplane passes over its head
> it smiles and waves
> as if that airplane, in its love
> passed by just from the enervating compulsion of its pledge of faithfulness!
> It says with full confidence:
> "Look how to both ends of this very rope
> you and I are bound!
> If there were not this rope, then where in us, in you,
> would the path to our union be found?"
> But it cannot see those causes of separation
> that are stretched from end to end, from the beginning to the end of time
> where this time—the now of time—
> is only a knot!
>
> (lines 14–27)

In this passage, a violet plant—a figure of nature—speaks to an airplane—a figure of modern technology. The violet plant is evidently young and naïve. It does not really grasp how its object of affection, the airplane, is part of a very different domain of existence. The language used to describe the violet plant's affection is reminiscent of the Urdu ghazal. In the ghazal there is a legendary affection of the *bulbul* (nightingale) for the *gul* (rose). Hence, interspecies romance is not entirely without precedent. The violet plant believes that the airplane and it are in love, and that by passing overhead the airplane is keeping its promise of faithfulness—something in the ghazal that is rarely, if ever, fulfilled. But in reading this passage, one is left with the feeling that the young violet plant is in fact mistaking the plane *(ṭ̤ayyārah)* for a bird *(ṭ̤āʾir* or *ṭ̤air)*. It sees the plane as part of nature, its own domain, rather than an unnatural form of modern technology. It finds continuity in a present in which discontinuity reigns.

The narrator counters the violet plant's understanding of modernity as natural with an alternative description of the present. For the violet plant to seek union with the airplane, it must validate and praise the "rope" of time, the present, which binds them together. The narrator, on the other hand, describes the present as merely a "knot" in the cheap string of time. The word used for knot, *gīrah*, like the English "tangle," is a frequent metaphor for a problem or difficulty to be unraveled. The present, the narrator contends, does not epitomize a constant and reliable continuity. The violet plant cannot in fact see the "causes of separation" spread out from end to end of time. The technological modernity represented by the airplane is a symbol not of continuity but of change. Where the violet plant sees union, then, the narrator instead sees the many possibilities of separation.

In this poem, Rashed takes an Islamic discourse on time, represented by the *hadīs̤-e qudsī*, and, through the love story of the airplane and the violet plant, replaces it with a retelling of Urdu poetic tradition. He uses religion here in the service of literature. In the process, he recasts the role of separation and disconnection of human or divine love in the ghazal as the separation and disconnection of modernity itself. The poem concludes that the reason for the contemporary experience of disconnection is that modernity is not natural. Modernity in general, but especially as represented by technological change, has disrupted time to the point where teleological understandings of time are impossible. If the present is not a natural outgrowth of history, then neither are the social configurations of modernity, including the nation, inevitable developments in time. In this way, Rashed revives the questions of temporality raised by Iqbal. But while Iqbal understood Islam as providing a unity of spirit and matter, and thus of history and nature, Rashed's late poetry unravels this unity by separating history and nature, continuity and change.

PAKISTAN'S NOW

N. M. Rashed composed many of his poems reflecting on the temporality of a collective after the 1965 India-Pakistan War, at a moment characterized by an increasing solidification of the discourse of Pakistani cultural nationalism. C. M. Naim has argued that the 1965 war between India and Pakistan appeared to further separate the Urdu literary community, already partitioned between two nations.[35] Pakistan was itself increasingly divided, since the divisions between West Pakistan and East Pakistan were especially evident. These would culminate in the mass-murderous war of Bangladesh's secession in 1971. This period was marked by very serious discussions of the meaning of Pakistan and its historical trajectory.

Rashed opposed the formulation of "one nation, one religion, and one culture," which even many members of the "progressive" Left espoused.[36] Rashed wrote a response letter to an editorial espousing that formulation in the Karachi-based journal *Nayā Daur*, edited by Jamīl Jālibī. The anonymous editorial argued that Pakistan was in serious need of "correct thinking" *(fikr-e ṣaḥīḥ)*, which it defined as knowing "the source of something's creation" *(manshā-e taḳhliq)* and not stopping it from reaching its "purpose of creation" *(maqṣad-e taḳhlīq)*, or its logical or teleological end.[37] For the author, that meant that the nation should rest on its three pillars: Islam, Indo-Muslim history and culture, and Urdu.[38]

In his 1967 letter in response, N. M. Rashed attacked both the editorial's logic and its conclusions.[39] No Pakistani, Rashed argued, could possibly deny the reason for Pakistan's creation, since it was part of his own personal memory. However, Rashed took exception to the claim that the purpose of Pakistan was fully contained within its beginning. To do so, he writes, is "to take a restricted reason for creation, which was presented to Indian Muslims in the form of a few important but contingent, or temporary, slogans *(vaqtī na're)*, and to give them the position of an eternal dogma *(ek azalī aur abadī uṣūl)*." To do so, he argues, is to "forever bind Pakistan's future to those slogans which, after fulfilling their heavenly political necessity, should have become a part of history—as if after coming into existence Pakistan was not capable of advancing further and attaining new growth in the light of its new experiences and necessities."[40]

This statement expresses in prose the criticism of teleology that characterizes much of Rashed's late poetry. Instead of maintaining continuity with the past, he argues that Pakistan should focus on its present composition: its soil (or folk culture), the moral standards provided by the Arabs through Islam, the aesthetic of Iran, and the institutions and technologies of the West. In response to the editorial's privileging of Urdu and Indo-Muslim culture, Rashed offers what can be seen as the response of a Persian- and English-educated Punjabi, who happens to write in Urdu. But much more than an ethnic response, Rashed offers a modernist one. The four elements he mentions are inherently in conflict. It is through this conflict that Rashed promotes an aesthetic that privileges disruptions, offering the possibility of something entirely new and more appropriate for the present and future. Rashed recommends an incorporative aesthetics of experience. This experience is to be based on the contemporary elements of Pakistan, not on a teleological trajectory of Islam, Indo-Muslim culture, and Urdu. Much of Rashed's later poetry would reflect on the absence of this rich experience of the present, and the barriers to a more productive relationship with experience.

Rashed's poem "Afsānah-e shahr" (Legend of the City, §22) gives voice to this concern by describing a collective as a city blindly following a "legend" of the past. The entire populace *(shahr ke shahr)* of "beguiled but simple travelers" has been deceived. A "thief" has stolen from them "love's defiant cry" and would have them instead contemplate "in a dream what lies behind the closed door." Then, the "unexpected trembling of an errant drop" of water in the "desert" of their hearts claims that it will show them the "mirage of a smile on the morning's lips!" (lines 1–6). In a private letter, Rashed identified this poem as "like the story of Pakistan," adding, "or of every newly independent country." The description of the "thief" addresses the country's creation, he writes, and the "mirage of a smile," the efforts toward fresh "revolution" and reform.[41] "Love's defiant cry" mentioned here—that which is stolen—signifies the possibility of revolutionary and progressive social formations. Its loss corresponds to the "hearts' ruins" that Rashed describes in "The Lordship of Nimrod" (§15.28), a poem addressed to Iqbal and in critique of an early independent Pakistan. As this later poem was written in 1968, the "mirage of a smile," in the context of Rashed's comments, can be read as a condemnation of General Ayyub Khan's reforms of that year, which were part of his celebration of the "Great Decade" of his rule.[42] The "legend" of the city, or in this case presumably the history of the nation, is a deceitful ideology, lacking in both truthfulness and conviction.

The second stanza of the poem presents a focused critique of the temporal understandings of this "legend." It depicts this city as suffering from its adherence to the path laid out in the past, instead of seizing the possibilities of the present:

> The city and its legend, those limping feet of worn-out longing
> that still move on the stolen and twisted lines of legend
> like those prisoners who, even if the clinking of the chain of their nerves
>   and fibers
> stopped, would cry out: "Where?
>   Now where should we go?
> Where should we go now in the winter of fresh and unseen sights?"
> Like those prisoners for whom the valueless bars of time
> are never cold or warm, and never hard or soft
> They neither welcome their release, nor feel shame at their imprisonment!
>
> (lines 7–15)

The prisoners cannot evaluate the "bars of time" that imprison them, for they appear to have no stable attributes. Even as the prisoners acknowledge the possibility of change, the positive aspect of history characterized by the occurrence of the new ("the winter of fresh and unseen sights"), they are unable to advance with conviction in any direction. They appear, the poem concludes, like "those souls that / seek no other union except for on the bridge." The phrase "on the bridge" *(sar-e pul)* invokes the expression "friends on the bridge" *(yārān-e sar-e pul),* an idiom for temporary companions meeting in a place of transition. In this poem, when the travelers "seek no other union" than "on the bridge" and "do not even long to cross the bridge," they are unwilling to keep their promises, form more binding relationships with each other, or move forward in new directions (lines 16–19). The poem criticizes an unwillingness to move beyond the accumulation of structures and relations that mark the present in order to envision a new future. The "legend" of the city is a crippling ideology that precludes more revolutionary and spontaneous possibilities.

This poem, like Rashed's commentary on Pakistani culture, identifies as a fundamental problem an inability to live freely in the present. In his discussion of the nation's culture he pointed to the need to acknowledge and to value the contemporary composition of the nation. In this poem, he looks to the need to overcome a historical trajectory defined in the past and, instead, to seek out a more fulfilling and authentic future, not one based on "slogans" or "dogma." His poem, like his oeuvre overall, calls for both free expression and new possibilities instead of conformity and adherence to the traditions or historical movements of the past.

DEATH AND HISTORY

Rashed explains why people conform to oppressive ideologies and are unwilling to seize the possibilities of the present, as the inevitable result of the fear of death. In Rashed's late poetry, the fear of death is a subjective and psychological reason for the compulsion to adhere to teleological understandings, including progress. To quote the poem discussed above, this fear leads people to keep following the same "stolen and twisted lines of legend," instead of grappling with their contemporary moment. In Rashed's work, to embrace death is to accept life in this world. Death is transformed from a negative presence to a source of meaning in human life. The role played by death in Rashed's poetry shows how closely the writer grappled with then-prevalent elements of radical post-Freudian psychoanalysis, even as he invoked Urdu literary tradition.

The poem "Yih k͟halā pur nah huʾā" (This Void Was Not Filled, §23) from *Gumāñ kā mumkin* addresses the absence of death as a form of repression, creating a mental vacuum and preventing a more fulfilled experience of life. It describes an "empty" mind. That mind remains "an emptiness unfilled" by "light," "song," or "even by lost perfume." A "comforting word," a "smile," or even a "sigh" of passion cannot breach it. It remains just "a nothingness in constant tremor" and "in mourning of useless exertion" (lines 1–10). Like the "prisoners" in the previous poem, or the "rain-soaked birds" of "The Sands of Yesterday" (§20.9–12), this mind has no rich experience of time. It is merely a negation *(nafī)* with no positive sign of life *(zindagī)* or being *(vujūd).*

The poem goes on to link this mind with a collective. The narrator asks why "we who are unfulfilled, who have known sorrow" should not fill this void with "the picture of a minaret / or with the buzzing of color / or with the fragrance of dreams" so that "death would remain away / far away from us" (lines 16–20). The "picture of a minaret" serves as a sign of religion. The narrator identifies this, and other potential sources of fulfillment, as the approach of a "drunken beggar *(sar-mast gadā)* / asleep on this doorstep" (lines

14–15), who is most likely a Sufi dervish or fakir.[43] And so these are not really viable alternatives, for in Rashed's poetry the Sufi's search for *fanā*, or mystical extinction, cannot counter negativity. It lacks positive affirmation, understood as a union of internal passion with external, social transformation. For the "voice" of the dervish, Rashed writes in another poem, is that of "the poverty *(faqr)* which is the bass and treble of death!"[44] Mysticism, this passage contends, is a form of escapism, a turning away from the transformation of the present. The experience of this mysticism is described in a synesthetic manner, as a physical "minaret" takes the form of a "picture," then "color," that of a "buzzing" sound, and finally "dreams" that of a "fragrance" (lines 16–18). This blurring of senses suggests a form of self-delusion, and a distance from reality.

Instead of religion or mysticism, the narrator suggests that the only way to fill this void is to accept the finality of death. The poem concludes:

> No, we know,
>   we who are unfulfilled, who have known sorrow
> we know the emptiness is the absence of death
> Why should we make it "body" with light or song
>   or with a comforting word
> and then accept death without a second thought?
> Why should we open the door to new celebrations
>   and begin the dawn of fulfillment?
>
> (lines 21–28)

The denial of death erodes experience and makes it impossible to live in the present, the poem claims. The acceptance of death signifies an embrace of bodily, this-worldly life. The message of this poem is in line with Rashed's other condemnations of transcendence, including his preference for allegory over the symbol. The poem argues that it is necessary to restore to the fabric of experience the body and the cycles of the body, including death. In this way, the poem calls for a return to the natural cycle of human life as a means to lessen the effects of repression and to open the possibility of a more liberated subjectivity—a mind that is not empty.

"In Search," (§24) the next poem in *Gumāñ kā mumkin*, takes this reflection on the subjective effects of the repression of death a step further by linking it more explicitly to the search for historical continuity. The poem begins with a reflection on the difference between human and natural experiences of time. Taking up the "rose and jasmine" as elements of nature, the narrator reflects that despite the beauty or perfection of their "body's form," they are still "unaware of tomorrow/today *(kal).*" Unlike humankind, they have no fear of an "inevitable death" (lines 1–6). Addressing the human world, the narrator continues,

> In the absurd search for our history
> we are overcome!
> We do not reveal
> the hidden depths of our beings,
> We do not express our desires!
> This history is not mine and is not yours
> This history is a flowing crowd
> It is the history of this flowing crowd
> that is the cry
> repeated in our "You" and "I"
> repeated in the being of our civilization!
>
> (lines 7–17)

The narrator states that "we" cannot find our past, for we are unable to understand the meaning of our own existence, or even to give voice to our desires, presumably because of the repression that causes the mind's vacuity. As in Freud, this problem of repression—of not speaking our longings—is fundamentally social. Instead of an individual, personal voice, history provides only a "flowing crowd," and a social and civilizational history of repression. It structures the formation of subjectivity—as the poem emphasizes through the repetition *(takrār)* of " 'You' and 'I' " *(man-o-tū).*

In this poem, civilization and history appear to be opposed to the longings and desires of the individual. As the poem goes on, the desire to follow the trajectory of history is defined as the fear of death. The reason for "moving in the footprints of this flowing crowd" is to escape the fate of "lying alone in the darkness of night." The real goal of what "we" perceive as "advancing," or progress, is "not to live / not to remain more alive" (lines 19–25). Instead, the narrator concludes,

> We are advancing to escape from some defect,
> from the clutches of the highwayman of death,
> for the sake of separation!
> We are advancing because we fear some individual
> who behind the broken windows of the inner world
> laughs mischievously—
>
> (lines 26–31)

To follow the footprints of the crowd is to avoid the "separation" *(furqat)* of the finite from the infinite, which is fundamental to human life. To overcome separation by joining the "flowing crowd" is dismissed as the denial of one's nature as a separate, individual self *(fard)*. It is this individual nature that remains hidden and unknown behind "the broken windows of the inner world *(bāṭin)*." To join the historical trajectory of the past is to deny the possibilities of the individual and to conform to the repressive will of the collective, which would deny individual desires and prevent self-knowledge.

This poem very clearly invokes literary tradition in order to mark its departure from it. The poem describes the "history" of the "flowing crowd" as the "the cry / repeated in our 'You' and 'I' / repeated in the being of our civilization" (lines 15–17). The phrase " 'You' and 'I' " here is the Persian *man-o-tū*, a phrase commonly used in Sufi understandings of selfhood. Sufis seek to overcome that opposition, while Rashed's poem maintains it. The Persian poet Hafiz, for example, tells the "self-serving (lit. self-seeing) *zāhid* (ascetic)" that the "secret of this [mystical] veil is hidden and will be hidden" from the "eyes of 'You' and 'I.' "[45] Hafiz condemns the *zāhid*'s self-interest, since he merely aims to help himself into paradise through his austerities. Yet Hafiz's verse also denies the separation of the inner self from the divine. Muhammad Iqbal would later take up this phrase to argue that the self, or *ḳhvudī*, is "born in 'You' and 'I' " and yet "free from 'You' and 'I.' "[46] In another verse he describes how his *sāqī* (wine bearer) "destroyed the world of 'You' and 'I,' " having served him the wine of the expression of divine unity.[47] In both Hafiz and Iqbal, perceptions of " 'You' and 'I' " are negated in states of divine intoxication.

Rashed's poem describes separation as the wellspring of life and creative activity. Separation should be embraced, not feared. The poem opposes the loss of selfhood in a Sufi mystical extinction as much as the loss of individuality in the crowd. Both are betrayals of the self. For Rashed, individual experience is crucial to the expansion of the possibilities of life. As we saw in his comments on Pakistani national culture, to stay on a predetermined historical trajectory and to maintain a historical continuity is to oppose the creative possibilities of life. Continuity and repetition, he argues, are aligned with death.

Rashed's reflections on death in his late poetry are informed by his reading of the radical psychoanalysis of Norman O. Brown, especially his 1959 *Life Against Death: The Psychoanalytical Meaning of History*.[48] Along with Herbert Marcuse's *Eros and Civilization*, Brown's work was a staple of the

New Left and counterculture movements in the 1960s.[49] As mentioned earlier, "death" is a universal theme of modernist poetry, particularly the currents of modernism influenced by Freudianism. From his earliest work, Rashed found in Freudianism a means to critique Urdu literary tradition as well as the work of Iqbal. His engagement with Brown in his poetry and in his prose writing is an extension of this line of critique.

Rashed's specific engagement with Norman O. Brown can be substantiated textually through a prose piece he wrote on the poet Mirzā Ġhālib titled "Ġhālib hamāre zamāne meñ" (Ghalib in Our Age). Later described as a radio address, the text was first published in 1970, and was most likely written for the occasion of Ghalib's birth centenary in 1969.[50] Rashed quotes (without attribution) large portions of Brown's text in his assessment of the Urdu poet.[51] He adopts Brown's ideas of repression, universal neurosis, the reality and pleasure principles, narcissism, and instinctual freedom to claim that Ghalib's unique combination of "inner-looking" and "outer-looking" anticipated the Freudian concept of the unconscious *(lā-shuʿūr)*. By seeking a balance between the reality and pleasure principles, Rashed claims, Ghalib held open the possibility of a freedom from neurosis. Ghalib's poetry also attempts to balance the pleasure and reality principles—"the emotion of human love" and the "experience of reality"—in a "field of instinctual freedom." In Rashed's words, Ghalib's poetry opposes the "closing of any doors on the completion of human desires" and looks "doubtfully at fundamental religious principles and established principles of morality." Rashed argues that Ghalib seeks a lessening of repression through a transformation of Eros *(żauq-e ḥayāt)*.[52] While Rashed's description of Ghalib is interesting in its own right, it is perhaps best read as a statement of his own poetic project and his understanding of modernism as a site for critique.

Rashed's late poems further explore Norman Brown's radical psychoanalysis by adopting, in a surprisingly straightforward manner, his notion of history as a "forward-moving dialectic of neurosis," a transformation of the "the timeless instinctual compulsion to repeat." To see "history as neurosis," Brown explains, is "[t]o see how man separated from nature, and separated out the instincts."[53] History is neurosis, in other words, because, by definition, repression separates man's existence from his essence, by which Brown means man's instincts or drives.

Rashed's "This Void Was Not Filled" reflects Brown's injunction to overcome history/repression. The problem of the repressed mind, the poem states, is that it is not "body," for the mind lives in the "absence of death."

Accepting "death" would "open the door to new celebrations" and "begin the dawn of fulfillment" (§23.23–28). As Brown writes, "only an unrepressed humanity, strong enough to live-and-die, could let Eros seek union and let death keep separateness."[54] Rashed finds confirmation of his long-standing promotion of embodiment in Brown's argument that "life not repressed—organic life below man and human life if repression were overcome—is not in historical time." This other state, Brown imagines, would be the "mode of unrepressed bodies," for "psychoanalysis comes to remind us that we are bodies, that repression is of the body, and that perfection would be the realm of Absolute Body."[55] Rashed calls in "This Void Was Not Filled" to return the empty mind to the "body," in order to overcome its fear of death. This poem is certainly consonant with Brown's thought, although it does not plot his theories in a systematic manner.

Rashed's "In Search" (§24), on the other hand, contains nearly exact translations of parts of Brown's text. That poem, also described above, characterizes humankind as plagued by a fear of death. It represents the search for history as a futile attempt to overcome the fear of death and of individuality by following the history of the crowd. A number of lines in Rashed's poem describe that "advancing" crowd by adopting the words and imagery of a paragraph in Brown's text. I quote that paragraph in full here, bracketing the corresponding lines of the poem in italics:

> The essential point in the Freudian diagnosis of human sociability was seen by Róheim: men huddle into hordes as a substitute for parents, to save themselves from independence, from "being left alone in the dark" [c.f. *we are advancing / so that we do not stay / lying alone in the darkness of night*, lines 20–22]. Society was not constructed, as Aristotle says, for the sake of life and more life, but from defect, from death and the flight from death, from fear of separation and fear of individuality [c.f. *We are advancing / not to live, not remain more alive / We are advancing to escape from some defect / from the clutches of the highwayman of death / for the sake of separation!*, lines 26–28]. Thus Freud derives fear of "separation and expulsion from the horde" from castration anxiety, and castration anxiety from the fear of separation from the mother and the fear of death. Hence there are no social groups without a religion of their own immortality, and history-making is always the quest for group-immortality. Only an unrepressed humanity, strong enough to live-and-die, could let Eros seek union and let death keep separateness.[56]

It should be clear that Rashed's poem takes much of its content and even its imagery from this significant paragraph of Brown's text, as did his essay on

Ghalib. The final line of Brown's paragraph, also quoted above, finds a means to embrace Eros and bodily life in overcoming the fear of death.

In order to engage with this post-Freudian discourse, Rashed inverted the terms of Urdu literary tradition, particularly those drawn from Sufism. There are certainly continuities here with his earlier works in *Māvarā*, which criticize the ghazal's focus on the sacred by invoking corporeal desire and sexual love. When he explores similar themes across several of his late poems, he employs much more sophisticated terms. Rashed links the emptiness of experience, the "negativity" caused by the fear of death, to mystical extinction *(fanā)* in search of union. As he describes in "Sands of Yesterday" (§20), the denial of death and suffering in the concept of progress can be found in the unity of the Sufi calls of *yā hū*. The possibilities of the individual *(fard)* are contrasted with the conformity to the crowd or the escapism of the dervish and celebrated in "This Void Was Not Filled" (§23). Furthermore, in "Time Is God" (§21), he characterizes the present as a moment of separation, not of union with a historical or spiritual movement. Death, he argues, makes possible "life," the experience of separation. The denial of death, through the search for perpetual historical continuity, is also the denial of the possibility of change or the positive, creative aspect of life.

THE POSSIBILITY OF SUPPOSITION

As the previous poems suggest, the understanding of temporality for which Rashed advocates in his poetry correlates with his preference for allegory over symbol. Instead of the certainty of the transcendent meanings of symbols, he focuses on the transformative power of the doubt and skepticism that is a feature of allegory. The title work of his final volume, "Gumāñ kā mumkin: jo tū hai, maiñ hūñ" (The Possibility of Supposition: That You Are, I Am, §25), makes this point most firmly. It does so by returning to the imagery of horizontality and verticality discussed at the beginning of this chapter.

The poem's narrator is a traveler over the "lake of time." Like other humans, he is carried across the lake by waves of time, "parallel to the horizon." On the other side of the "lake of time" is the "munificent sun," or the domain of nature and prehistory, which cannot hear the narrator's "faint voice." The sun lends its attributes to natural objects: its "roundness" and "smoothness" to the "cold stone," and its "generous profusion" to "flowing water." The sun recognizes them, for their existence is self-evident. Though the narrator has "memories [like the cold stone] of the age of sand and wind," or of his own history as a natural thing, his rationality forces him to imagine himself as his "own proof" and his "own answer" (lines 1–16). And so self-understanding—that which was "hidden in darkness" in "Another City" (§19.1)—emerges as the narrator's most pressing concern.

As an allegory of subjective experience, the narrative of the poem is reminiscent of the storytelling practices of the Urdu *dāstān*, Sufi narratives of mystical experience, and Iqbal's *Jāved-nāmah*, a Dante-like tale of travel through the celestial spheres into the divine presence.[57] In the next section, the narrator leaves the lake by following a group of "celestial travelers" in a vertical movement out of the flow of time. Those "moving parallel to the horizon," he explains, are brought across by "time-waves." Those like him, who crave a "celestial" journey, hear the murmuring of an underworld voice that tells them what all the other "mariners" fear: those moving horizontally, parallel to the horizon, will eventually be drowned by the waves of time. That voice belongs to a "thief of verticality" hidden in the lake, whose "curls dangle from the roof of the horizon." The "thief," who knows the "secrets of the domes," explains that he has been waiting for the travelers since the beginning of time. His companions—"trees, minarets, towers, ladders"—all move "parallel" to him. He is the "final halting place of all airplanes," and the "shore" of every "mariner," ready to place them "into the embrace of their End." While all fear his voice, those who long for a celestial journey descend with the "rope of this verticality alone" and, in doing so, are "advancing on the heights." Traveling vertically, in a descent that becomes an ascent, the narrator finally arrives on a shore where "the footprint of God has found refuge / where the weak eyes of God / have now escaped to safety." Although they are absent from the lake of time, signs of the divine appear on this other shore, outside of the flow of time (lines 20–49).

Arriving on that shore, which is presumably near the divine presence, the narrator, still concerned with self-understanding, wonders if he might have chosen the wrong road. Why, he thinks, did he "choose that road / on which there is not the supposition *(gumāñ)* of union *(viṣāl)* with myself?" (lines 53–54). For while the path outside of time leads him to a place where he would attain the Sufi's desired union *(viṣāl)* with the divine and therefore self-extinction (*fanā*), what the narrator truly desires is union with his self. That would give him the understanding of his own essence that he craves. The path of extinction stops at the "edge of the heart's uncertainty *(ib'hām)*."

Ahead of (or greater than) that destination, the narrator explains, is the "possibility of supposition / that you are, I am" (lines 55–58).

A significant feature of this poem is the ambiguity of this title phrase, the "possibility of supposition," which is repeated throughout the poem. While I have translated the word *gumāñ* as "supposition," it can also mean doubt, conjecture, and imagination. The latter phrase, *jo tū hai maiñ hūñ*, can mean either "if you are, I am" or "which you are [and] I am." The poem does not specify with whom the narrator is speaking, though at one point (line 97, *tū jāntī hai*) this "you" is marked as grammatically feminine. This could suggest that the narrator is addressing a female companion—not at all an uncommon rhetorical frame for Rashed's poetry. However, another possibility arises from the fact that the gender of the most common Urdu words for essence, self, and soul *(żāt, k͟hvudī, rūḥ)* is feminine. In this case, we can read the clause as the narrator's attempt to find the "answer" to his own existence by knowing his own internal essence. The poem strongly suggests this reading, as the narrator declares that the reason he has proceeded on this journey was in "hope of finding you (of finding myself)," in search of "one possibility," "a face," and "such a picture," "that you are, I am" (lines 61–67).

As the poem goes on, the narrator reflects on his experience and expresses skepticism at the certainty of any given solutions. Recounting a long life, he lists destinations passed in this pursuit—gardens, statues, love affairs, religious institutions, and so on—that were meant to answer the question of existence (lines 68–83). At the end, they all proved to be nothing more than "their own negation" (line 94):

> Answers, assuming the form of history,
>   only repeat themselves—
> "We are the answers—we are the answers—
> we are certain that we are the answers—"
> how they repeat certainty with such certainty!
>
> (lines 89–93)

Neither the narrator's search outside of time nor "history" provides any real answers. The past merely brings claims of certainty. Certainty *(yaqīn),* here and elsewhere in Rashed's poetry, is the opposite of the supposition and doubt *(gumāñ)* that the poem foregrounds. By focusing on the most fundamental forms of doubt, this poem is similar to Rashed's ruminations on the distance between word and meaning discussed in the previous chapter, and to his skepticism of transcendentally grounded understandings. Rashed's narrator here is clearly opposed to Iqbal's hero, the *mard-e momin* (man of faith), who has removed all doubt.

Skeptical of the answers of history and uncertain about the journey out of time, the narrator considers his dilemma using yet another allegory, a reflection on the logs *(kunde)* flowing on the surface of the river of time. "They know," he explains, that "this is an event [or accident] from which / for them (for anyone) / there is no asylum!" The logs cannot "become trees again," he explains, as "before the logs all the roads of return / are closed." They also cannot turn into "crocodiles," or become something they are not. However, there are numerous possible futures for the logs: "ghats / that have always opened their embrace," "ships / that are not yet even conceived by shipbuilders," "pages on which black words will be printed," "books / that have no readers, nor ever will," blank "painters' canvases" on which "the colors of tears would fall" and "the future fill them / with the form of their dream" (lines 97–124). Each of these future forms of the log is, noticeably, a product of human action or creativity.

The conclusion of the poem makes clear the significance of this final allegory, as well as of the poem on the whole. The narrator repeats the lines, "before the poor logs all roads of return / are closed" (lines 125–26), but adds:

> Those roads of imagined eternity *(baqā-e mauhūm)* are still open now
> ahead of them is the possibility of supposition—
> the possibility of supposition that you are, I am!
>   that you are, I am!
>
> (lines 127–30)

Unlike previously in the poem, there is a comma in this final line (*jo tū hai, maiñ hūñ*) that suggests a reading of "which you are, and I am" (rather than "if you are, I am"). In other words, both the addressee, presumably the narrator's self or soul, and the narrator himself are the "possibility of supposition." Not only can they not be defined with any certainty, they are themselves the origin of doubt and speculation. In Islamic thought, there is a distinction between the *baqā* (eternal) and the *fanā* (transitory). As we have seen, Rashed concentrates in his poetry on the qualities of temporal, transitory life (*fanā*), such as the body and self. The unusual phrase in these lines, *baqā-e mauhūm* (imagined/supposed/imaginary duration/perpetuity/eternity), stresses the significance of imagination *(vahm*, the Arabic root of *mauhūm)* in the future, where the meaning of his existence that the narrator seeks may, perhaps, be found.

Instead of maintaining structures of the past or seeking a mystical, self-effacing union, the narrator focuses on the possibilities of the present and future, especially by casting doubt on existing structures. The repetition of the line about the logs' inability to "return" suggests, when applied to human life, the impossibility of returning to a previous state, of resuming participation in an unadulterated cultural, religious, traditional, or national essence. Instead of annihilating the self, as in Sufism, or following an already prescribed historical trajectory, the narrator calls for a continued openness to the present, a distrust of its institutions, and an exploration of the self through creativity.

"The Possibility of Supposition," like Rashed's oeuvre on the whole, explores the possibilities of literature to offer a this-worldly critique. As should be obvious from this poem, that critique does not involve a kneejerk rejection of religious meanings so much as it necessitates looking at all present and traditional structures with a degree of suspicion. In rejecting teleology, Rashed's poetry leaves the meaning of "human" open-ended, although it is bounded by death. On principle, his poetry accepts no fixed answers grounded in an essence established in the past or outside of time. To do so would be to slip into ideology. Instead, it focuses on the material suffering of this world and the creation within it of new possibilities and uncertainties. Separation rather than union is the stuff of life, and suspicion rather than certainty is the proper ground for creative expression.

Conclusion

HASAN THE POTTER

A BOOK ABOUT N. M. RASHED'S WORK would be incomplete without a discussion of "Ḥasan Kūzahgar" (Hasan the Potter, §26–§29), a long poem in four parts that was split across N. M. Rashed's final two volumes. Many critics consider it to be one the greatest statements about love and creativity in Urdu poetry, the masterpiece of Rashed's late period, and among the finest free-verse poems in the language. The poem is a monologue in which the potter Ḥasan addresses the mesmerizing Jahāñzād (literally "daughter of the world"). Each section is set in a different time and place, and each is a variation on a single theme. As such, it resembles a pot, being made and remade. Altogether, the poem narrates Hasan's transformation.

The poem is exemplary of Rashed's work, for it draws on a rich genealogy of thought, including both Urdu sources and global modernism. It addresses a transnational Urdu literary community while at the same time critiquing the multifaceted "tradition" in which it shares. The potter is a recurring figure in both religious and literary tradition. In the Quran, as in the Hebrew Bible and the New Testament, human life is described as a creation from clay and water. "The potter's wheel," explains M. A. R. Habib, is "the cycle of existence, and God, the potter, has the power to make and unmake Man, his earthen vessel." Persian poetry, particularly the work of Omar Khayyam, also adopts this imagery.[1] In Sufi interpretation, a human being is formed like a clay wine cup, which is a vessel for the wine of divine love or knowledge. Rashed's poem builds on this history, but adds to it elements of the Urdu ghazal, Freudianism, and Bergsonism until ultimately the poem amounts to a secular and cosmopolitan critique of ideology and representation. "Ḥasan Kūzahgar" encapsulates the concerns developed throughout the oeuvre of N. M. Rashed, who sought to be a universal modernist in Urdu and consistently adopted an iconoclastic position in his poetry. This conclusion will reexamine the themes of Rashed's poetry through a reading of this emblematic poem.

EMBODIMENT

N. M. Rashed's earliest modernist poetry criticized literary tradition for failing to properly represent embodied, earthly love. *Māvarā* (The Beyond), his first volume, mocks "Platonic" or otherworldly love. Instead of expressing desire for an ambiguous or divine beloved, as frequently occurs in the ghazal, Rashed's early free-verse poems represent very human (and exclusively heterosexual) couplings. At that point in his career, he emphasized the need for "erotic thoughts" in literature as an expression of selfhood outside the boundaries of realism. Early Muslim literary reformers and some contemporary "progressive" writers saw realism as the means to move beyond what they presumed was the escapism and decadence of earlier Urdu poetry. Rashed rejected this argument and instead stressed the need to channel the repressed forces of the unconscious in poetry. His poetry of the period employs a self-consciously Freudian dichotomy between the pleasure principle and the reality principle—his characters appear to be neurotics turning away from reality. Although certain contemporary critics radically misunderstood his project, condemning him for representing his own psychological disorder, Rashed in fact anticipates the work of Frantz Fanon by locating the source of the characters' neurosis in their social situation rather than in a purely individual condition. Those poems, which are clearly situated in late colonial British India, contain an anticolonial critique as well as a challenge to literary tradition.

The first section (§26) of the much later "Hasan the Potter" renews the critique of literary tradition first articulated in *Māvarā*, focusing, as he did in that volume, on the ghazal. In the first lines of the poem, Hasan announces his presence:

> Jahanzad, in the alley below in front of your door
> It is I, love-struck Hasan the Potter
>
> (lines 1–2)

The "alleyway" in front of the "door" is the typical locale of the *'āshiq*, the lover in the ghazal. Hasan also describes himself as "love-struck" (*sokhtah sar*, literally "having a burnt head"), one of many expressions for the devastation wrought by love on the ghazal lover's social and physical life. Formally, the connection between Hasan and the *'āshiq* is solidified by the fact that these first lines make up a *shĕ'r*, the basic couplet of the ghazal and *maśnavī*.[2]

In this first section of the poem, Hasan tells the tale of how for nine years his love for Jahanzad had destroyed his creativity and livelihood. He had been a potter both in name and in fact, he says, able to "shape the flow of dreams into pots with clay and water" (line 28). Then, to paraphrase the poem, nine years ago on a dreamy night in Baghdad, he was transformed by a luster he saw in the gaze of the then-innocent but knowing Jahanzad. His body and soul traveled through clouds and moonlight, and that night became the amber in which Hasan's very being became stuck. He drowned in a wave of a river of ecstasy and never resurfaced (lines 30–43).

Like the characters of *Māvarā*, who turn away from "reality," unable to face the conditions of late colonialism, Hasan, a sign of literary tradition, turns away from reality and an enriching experience of time. For during this period of nine years, Rashed writes, time passed over Hasan as over a "buried city" *(shahr-e madfūn)* (line 18). He abandoned his pots. The clay, the scent of which used to transport him, stiffened into stone. The goblets, cups, flasks, pitchers, lanterns, and flowerpots that were the expression of his art, as well as his meager means of livelihood, lay in fragments. Hasan, his feet stuck in mud, dust in his disheveled hair, sat naked next to his potter's wheel with his head on his knees in despair like some phantasmal, grief-stricken god (lines 8–27). During this period of nine years, Hasan's wretched wife of "burnt fortune" *(soḳhtah baḳht)* came to him daily, shook him by the shoulder, and told him to look at his dilapidating house and his starving children. All were suffering from the suspension of the potter's art. "Love," she would say, "is the game of the rich." But Hasan remained the ecstatic dweller in the ruins of that imaginary city where there is no voice, no motion, no shadow of a bird in flight, not even a sign of life. Describing himself, Hasan likens time to a potter's wheel, molding and unmolding men like pots and jugs. In the mold of suffering, he was nothing but a heap of dust without a trace of moisture (lines 44–63).

The conclusion of part one suggests that Hasan catches a glimpse of freedom from the bondage of his desire for Jahanzad. For the morning upon which he speaks, Hasan saw Jahanzad again, and her glances spoke once more. He felt the faint trembling of moisture in the heap of dust of his being, which would, perhaps, turn his dust into clay. Just as her gaze had captivated him nine years earlier, now her eyes speak to him again. If he could get her blessing, he would turn again to his pots; he would become again that potter whose works of clay were the delicacy and illumination of every palace and street, city and village. He imagines a future in which through his art, through clay, water, color, and glaze, he will again produce the sparks that illumine the ruins of hearts (lines 77–95).

Hasan's transformation—from potter to dust and back—shows the transformation of subjectivity called for by Rashed's poetry on the whole. Put into the Freudian terms that structured Rashed's thought, this new subject would have rich experiences uninhibited by neurosis and exhibit creativity, rather than a Sufi-like withdrawal from the world of time and space. Many critics have read this section as a straightforward allegory of "Eastern" civilization. Instead of mystical withdrawal or seeking the beyond, the poem instead emphasizes the need for a creative and productive relationship with individual experience. By declaring his presence, Hasan begins to transform himself from a stereotypically devastated lover into a creative individual.

POSITION WITHOUT IDENTITY

The discussion of "Irān meñ ajnabī" (A Stranger in Iran) in chapter 2 showed how, contrary to its critical reception at the time, in that poem "Asia" functions as a position without identity. Instead of a transcendent or cultural essence, what binds Asia together is a common experience of imperial domination. That experience, which Rashed sees linking India and Iran, can be shared but never fully possessed. Rashed offered this mode of solidarity as an alternative to the two ideologies most prevalent in Urdu literary discourse, namely Soviet-sympathizing progressivism and the traditionalism of the "auratic critics" who sought to reestablish a "metaphysical tradition" disrupted by modernity. Rashed opposed both, for in his eyes both communism and traditionalism sought to efface individual experience. He opposes these ideologies through representations of historically contingent experiences of Iran, each in the form of a poetic "fragment" *(qiṭ'ah)*. The *qiṭ'ah* highlight the individual experience of the narrator, who confronts various forms of difference in his daily life in wartime Tehran.

Those small events form the first step in the poet's critique of ideology, which expands and deepens across his career. In *Māvarā*, Rashed opposed "realism" for failing to account for the psychic life of the individual. In "Īrān meñ ajnabī," which was written after Partition, the poet adds to this opposition a distrust of established modes of belonging, including both nationalism and communism, which he sees as equivalent to the imperialism recently defeated by the countries of Asia. Rashed dismisses both nationalism and communism as exclusionary mythologies that ignore the individual's suffering and stifle his creative potential. In "Īrān meñ ajnabī," Rashed begins to articulate an alternative function for literature. Instead of representing collective experience, whether of a nation, a class, or a civilization, literature becomes for Rashed a site for the critique of forces opposed to individual experience, generating skepticism toward any preordained solutions.

Urdu literary criticism, whether informed by a progressive or a traditionalist point of view, uses the familiar terms of Sufi exegesis that identify an "internal" *(bāṭinī)* and an "external" *(ẓāhir)* meaning. By this Sufi logic, the wine drinking in a ghazal might on a deeper level mean divine intoxication, for example. To some progressives, the "internal" meanings of the Urdu ghazal appeared as a form of mystical withdrawal and escapism, and its "external" metaphorical forms as merely catering to the decadent desires of the feudal aristocracy. They condemned literary tradition (as well as modernists and traditionalists) for failing to focus on the social conditions of collective life. Progressive realists expressed their own concern as being with the "external" world of the collective, rather than with the "internal" world of the individual soul. Many progressive critics also condemned as "internal" the personal "unconscious" of modernism as well. They interpreted it as a form of European bourgeois filth, imbibed by "regressive" Urdu modernists following the West. They demanded a more rational and less sexual subject, much along the lines of the earlier Muslim literary reformers.

Traditionalists, on the other hand, privileged "internal" and metaphysical meaning over the "external" focus of many progressives. They aimed to restore Urdu literature to its own earlier "metaphysical" tradition, which they understood as Sufism. For them, earlier Muslim reformers, progressives, and literary modernists had departed from that tradition *(rivāyat)* in their eagerness to follow the West. With the progressive realists, traditionalists criticized modernists like Rashed for focusing on an individuated self and a personal unconscious. However, they added that in doing so modernists showed their own ignorance of deeper metaphysical and spiritual meanings. Traditionalists aimed to revive a form of collective life less marred by individuated selves, a life which some argued was present during periods of "Muslim" rule in India before the rise of "Western" modernity under "British" rule.

In "Īrān meñ ajnabī," Rashed rejects traditionalism and progressivism as mirror images of one another. At one point in the poem, he describes Soviet sympathizers as espousing a sort of Russian "pantheism" *(hamah-ūst)*. A phrase that means literally "all is He," *hamah-ūst* is used to describe a Sufi experience of unity with the divine that is frequently considered heretical. By making this analogy, Rashed criticizes advocates of Soviet communism as rejecting all other explanations and withdrawing from a perspective that would see the Soviet Union as an imperialist power. Rashed further criticizes the traditionalist perspective for failing to appreciate the possibilities of individual experience. He does the same for the progressive approach, which, in his view, focuses on reason over passion and thereby rejects the creative potential of psychic life. To Rashed, both of these most prominent perspectives on literature appear to be ideologies that resist and suppress doubt and that disparage individual experience.

In "Ḥasan Kūzahgar 2" (§27), Rashed returns to the relation of the "internal" and the "external," but traditionalism is the focus of his critique. Having seen Jahanzad in Baghdad, Hasan now has returned to his "pots" and his dilapidated "hut," in what is perhaps a village outside the city (lines 11–12, 70–71). The poem records his continuing thoughts about the pleasure of the night he spent with her, and he implies that she has broken other individuals, as well (lines 4–9). Back in his home, Hasan plays a "game of simple love" with his wife—sometimes laughing, sometimes crying (line 51–56). He does not have the strength for the love that Jahanzad wants, which is presumably the maddening world-renunciation of the ghazal lover. Although Hasan longs for Jahanzad, he also desires "things" and worldly "wealth" (lines 82–83). By the middle of this section, Hasan appears to have come to terms with "external" reality, even if he does not find it entirely fulfilling.

Reflecting on the "inner" meaning of his love, Hasan describes his perception of Jahanzad as a mirror of his own self. This description inverts a convention of Sufi poetry, in which the lover's self is effaced to the point that his heart becomes a mirror of the (divine) beloved. Hasan declares, "Every love is a question for which except for the lover / there is no other answer" (lines 88–89). He finds the reward of love, especially in its unrequited form, to be a greater expression and experience of the lover's self. That night in Baghdad, Hasan heard a voice from the corner of his *bāṭin* (inner being). He found that same voice "on the shore of the icy centuries of [his] art," which is also the shore of the ocean of Jahanzad's eyes. This ocean was both the mirror of his *żāt* (his self) and the mirror of the faces of his pots, being made and unmade. This ocean, he declares, is the mirror of every art, and of every lover of art (lines 91–102).

The relationship between the "internal" and the "external" described by Hasan recurs throughout Rashed's poetry, and it becomes the means by which he provides an alternative model for the self and a critique of transcendence. Hasan neither privileges an "internal," spiritual meaning nor does he focus on the "external" alone. Instead of seeking a transcendent beloved and erasing the self, as in Sufism, Hasan declares that what the lover finds through love is himself. Although Rashed's poem uses terms that in literary tradition are used for the spiritual essence of the individual, Hasan describes a self more familiar from psychoanalysis. Here, *bāṭin* or the "internal" is transformed into the unconscious. There are elements of mystery and revelation, certainly, but they do not point to a transcendent higher reality beyond the human self, as alleged by traditionalism. Instead, they signify hidden layers of individuated human selfhood. This emphasis on the internal is itself a critique of the rational, reality-focused subject frequently found in progressivism. Hasan's perspective here mirrors Rashed's approach to modernism on the whole, as a synthesis of the external and the internal.

ALLEGORY AND COLLECTIVITY

Rashed's later poetry traced this critique of prevailing literary discourse to the fundamentals of language and poetic form. He rejected both socialist progressivism and traditionalism as false certainties built upon false unities that were expressed most perfectly in poetic symbols. Symbols, Rashed finds, depend on a presumed unity of word and meaning for their power. The modernist form of allegory that Rashed favored in his late poetry makes that disunity apparent. In his earliest postcolonial works, Rashed presented the separation of word and meaning as a constitutive element of language. He therefore opposed claims to their unity—especially those that would unite divine and human will, as in the poetry of Muḥammad Iqbāl. In a reading of "Heart, My Old Desert-Wandering Heart" (§18), the third chapter explains how Rashed's modernist allegories work both "vertically," through the use of metaphor, and "horizontally," through narrative. This chapter marks a shift in Rashed's poems away from narrative elements taken from the author's personal experience, whether as a late colonial subject or an Indian soldier in Iran, and toward reworkings of the conventional subject matter of the Urdu literary tradition, as seen in "Hasan the Potter." Rashed's later poems frequently seize elements from the variegated tradition of the Urdu literary community and, through unusual juxtapositions and narrative configurations, repurpose them in a way that challenges traditional understandings. By exploring the implications of this technique for creating meaning without resorting to ideology, Rashed's late poetry considers the possibility of alternative forms of collectivity that do not rely on transcendent forms of unity or the eradication of individual experience. His poetry in this way becomes a cosmopolitan and secular site for a critique of contemporary life. It remains open to a diverse range of possibilities and does not bear any certainty in transcendent meanings.

"Hasan the Potter 3" (§28), like the poem as a whole, works as modernist allegory. Through this narrative monologue, Hasan continues to reveal his transformation into a creative individual in a way that resonates with a number of aspects of the cosmopolitan tradition that Rashed's poetry invokes. Hasan begins by remembering swimming with Jahanzad in the pool of a caravansary in Aleppo, Syria. There they swam all night locked in each other's arms. They swam against the "decline of age," and with a "joyous fear" like that of water "swim[ming] in tears" (lines 1–10). Jahanzad broke the silence, asking Hasan if the "thirst of his soul" had drawn him there, as well (lines 11–12).

Hasan then reflects on the relationship between the body and soul, wondering if he left his body there in Aleppo. He declares that, no, that would not be possible. For he has no concept of the "duality" *(dū'ī)* of the body and soul. Moreover, he declares that before everything else he must be himself. There must be the experience of selfhood—of separateness—for them both to exist. "Before everything I am myself!" he exclaims, and "If I am alive then how can I deceive 'myself'?" (lines 24–25). As part of this desire for honesty, he feels forced to admit that he simply cannot understand Jahanzad. She remains for him a "riddle" that he cannot "'unravel'" (lines 26–30).[3]

Next, Hasan wonders about a rival for Jahanzad's attentions named Labīb, whose name she repeated throughout the night. Labīb had a more fervid physical relationship with Jahanzad—tearing at her lips and pulling at her hair—in a way that Hasan never could (lines 35–38). Hasan explains that his own affection, by contrast, involves his inner self perhaps even more than this body. Using imagery that draws on literary tradition's likening of the human body to a clay vessel, Hasan explains that his relation with Jahanzad, unlike Labib's, was not one of the "union of water and clay." It involves something more—presumably his inner self or soul—since the "being of man always remained outside of water and clay" (lines 42–43).

Hasan continues to relate the "triangle" he forms with Jahanzad and Labib to his own artistic practice, and to describe his process of artistic creation. Theirs is an "ancient triangle." Hasan offers to break it, but then retracts the offer. For the spell of the potters wheel, he claims, is the "same as that of the ancient triangle" (lines 48, 52). Hasan asserts that their rivalry for Jahanzad—the desire for the pleasure of her attention—serves as a catalyst for his art. He proceeds to describe the process of his creativity. As he makes his pots, the attributes of Jahanzad wash him away and spill out as his inner nature. Hasan now craves that experience, above all others. He has moved beyond his desire for the "pool at the caravansary in Aleppo" or that "Tigris of tears" that preoccupied him for nine years. Instead, he waits for those moments of "timeless time" *(zamān-e be-zamān)* from which his creativity flows (lines 78, 74, 81).

Beginning with Hasan's discussion of duality, this poem contains vertical levels of meaning that invoke and critique literary tradition, and especially ideas of the extinction of the self in the search for a transcendent meaning. Against the self-extinguishing of Sufism, Hasan declares that even in his experience of union with Jahanzad his own self must remain intact. For them both even to "exist," he must first be "himself." Hasan also insists that both body and soul are connected. This position counters approaches that would privilege transcendent inner meaning and those that would focus only on the world of bodies and external forces—the positions of traditionalism and progressivism, crudely construed. What Rashed proposes in his description of Hasan's creative practice is a different relationship between the inner and outer. This relationship does not claim a unity between an inner or transcendent meaning and an external form, as in the symbol. Rather, it emphasizes the uncertainty and impossibility of that connection through an allegorical discussion of artistic creation.

A second vertical level on which this allegory works is Freudian, for this section can be read as a description of sublimation. It is therefore worth retelling the transformation of Hasan in the language of psychoanalysis. In the first section, a neurotic Hasan reports having withdrawn from the world and time on account of his desire for Jahanzad. In the second, he sees her as a mirror of himself. This suggests that she is most meaningful to him as the cathexis of his own libidinal energy. She reflects the oceanic depth of his unconscious. In this third section, Hasan is finally able to sublimate his libidinal energy productively into his art practice. Hasan surrenders the possibility of their physical union and describes his preference for experiencing moments of creativity. He must wait for those moments, however, as his art is less a subjective or heroic act of will than a surrendering to an experience of the self.

Finally, the description of the experience of "timeless time" as the source of Hasan's creativity shows the multiple layers of the "tradition" from which Rashed's poetry draws. Freud described the unconscious as timeless. The post-Freudian psychoanalysis of Norman O. Brown, which Rashed found particularly useful, developed this point further as a critique of history. Yet the poet's phrase, "timeless time," also invokes Sufi ideas of a time outside of serial time, as well as Iqbal's critique of these ideas described in chapter 4. "Timeless time" is a figure for what Henri Bergson describes as the intuition of duration—leaving serial time and entering into the continuous flow of past, present, and future. In an unpublished note on this poem, Rashed made this relation to Bergson more explicit, describing the message of the poem with reference to the philosopher's concept of élan vital: "Love is no doubt important to the artist; but his art and his means of livelihood are even more important. Even in its great intensity, love is meaningless in the end unless it turns into an *élan vital* for the artist and leads him to still better creativity."[4]

Throughout this poem, the representation of artistic practice resists the transcendent unity of the symbol, even as it describes a profound experience. For Hasan appears to have experienced the timelessness of the unconscious and channeled that experience into his artwork. Importantly, he makes no claims to the unity of his artwork with a transcendent or sacred realm, however. It is the attributes of a very human Jahanzad, filtered through his own inner being, that become the work of art. Hasan sublimates his desire for a physical union with her into his art, as he waits for moments of a profound experience of the self. This experience of creativity, not a union with the sacred, is for Hasan the limit of his own "mystic knowledge" (line 68).

TEMPORALITY

Many critics have compared N. M. Rashed's "Ḥasan Kūzahgar" to Muhammad Iqbal's renowned Urdu poem, "Masjid-e qurṭabah," Iqbal's poetic meditation on art, modernity, and the Muslim community. The poem is a response to the Great Mosque of Cordoba, Spain, an artifact of Muslim expansion into Europe that Iqbal visited on his return from the second session of the Round Table Conference in 1931. The poem begins with a reflection on the transience of the world in the "succession of day and night." "Temporal and transient are all works of art," Iqbal writes, "the work of the world is without permanence, the work of the world is without permanence!" All things, he explains, are subject to annihilation *(fanā)*. For Iqbal, however, the "man of God" *(mard-e k̤hudā)*, through his passion *('ishq)*, is able to create a work of art that is eternal, moving beyond time's "extinction" *(fanā)*.[5] Critic Ḥamīd Nasīm explains that for Iqbal the Great Mosque at Cordoba is a "living, eternal symbol" *(zindah jāvidān simbal)*, and "the message of eternal life of the resolute and skilled Mosque builders." Rashed's poem, he argues, has the opposite effect: it is "a sorrowful poem" like a "Greek tragedy."[6] But where Ḥamīd Nasīm sees sorrow, there is more properly doubt and mistrust, the sensibility that emerges out of Rashed's critique of the symbol and his move to allegory.

Chapter 4 shows how Rashed's late poems critique the understanding of time in Iqbal's poetry wherein, as in "Masjid-e Qurt̤abah," the logic of the symbol reigns. Iqbal took up aspects of Henri Bergson's vitalist philosophy, particularly its distinction between serial time and duration. Iqbal also translated Bergson's intuition, or the perception of duration, into the familiar terms of the perception of the heart rather than the intellect, or of passion rather than reason. He criticized Bergson for being too atheistic, however, and for not realizing that a self must sustain duration. For Iqbal, that self is the divine essence *(żāt)*. Hence in "Masjid-e Qurt̤abah," Iqbal explains the relationship between serial time and duration as follows: "the chain of day and night, the two-colored silken thread / from which the divine essence *(żāt)* makes its coat of attributes *(ṣifāt)*."[7] Iqbal argues that it is possible for thought, through a "deeper movement," to experience an "immanent Infinite" in its "self-unfolding movement." That "ultimate Reality" is, he explains, "pure duration."[8] This is consonant with the well-known *hadīs̤-e qudsī*, "time is God."

Iqbal argues that the Muslim understanding of history is as a "continuous, collective movement." He criticized Sufi esoteric understandings of time as an escape from the confinement of seriality by emphasizing the movement of both a human collective and of the "immanent Infinite."[9] Iqbal's hero, the *mard-e momin* (man of faith) or *mard-e k̤hudā* (man of God), is able to act in accordance with divine will, understood as the force of love. In

"Masjid-e qurtabah," the Great Mosque of Cordoba is a symbol in the temporal world of unity with the eternal. "There is though in this form [of the Mosque] the color of eternal stability," he writes, "that a man of God *(mard-e ḳhudā)* completed."[10] Love provides that stability. Iqbal continues, "O Mosque of Cordoba! Your being is from love / love entirely eternal in which there is no past."[11] Iqbal's poem celebrates the man of faith *(mard-e momin)* for his ability to partake of the "attributes" of God. "The hand of Allah is the hand of the man of faith," Iqbal writes.[12]

As explained in chapter 4, Iqbal is important for Rashed, in part, because of his position as the "spiritual father" of Pakistan. In 1930, for the first time publically in the Muslim League, Iqbal called for a "consolidated North-West Indian Muslim State."[13] However, that famous speech in the genealogy of Pakistan approached Muslim nationhood as fundamentally opposed to the nationalism of Europe. Iqbal opposed the serial understandings of time commonly foundational to nationalism, as well as its attachment to territory and commitment to formal secularism exemplified by the separation of church and state. The universality of the "Muslim" community contradicts all three of these principles of nationalism. Conceiving of "matter" as "spirit realizing itself in space and time," Iqbal explains that to the Muslim, "God and the universe, spirit and matter, Church and State, are organic to each other."[14] Following the logic of colonial difference, however, this unique perspective became that of the Indian Muslim's national genius, and Iqbal became a founding philosopher for Indo-Muslim nationalism. The inner, spiritual understanding of community provided by his thought became central to Pakistani nationalism.

Chapter 4 examined N. M. Rashed's poetic exploration of "time" formed as a critique of Iqbal, as well as other elements of literary tradition, through the allegorical technique explained above. Like Iqbal, Rashed critiqued the "homogenous, empty time" characteristic of nationalism and progress. He criticized understandings of "progress" for masking violence and tales of defeat. He disrupted Iqbal's sense of historical unity by highlighting the causes of "separation" and the unnaturalness of the contemporary, technological moment. In the process, Rashed placed history and nature, and change and continuity, in opposition to one another. Where Iqbal sought an "immanent Infinite," defined as an experience of God as pure duration, and civilizational continuity with divine will, Rashed emphasized the limitations of civilizational "progress" and focused on the possibilities of a more meaningful and productive experience of the "now." Throughout, Rashed employed an allegorical technique, grasping and repurposing elements from the Urdu ghazal, religious tradition, and the poetry of Iqbal himself.

In prose writings and in poetry, Rashed consistently criticized the discourses of Pakistani cultural nationalism that bound the nation to a particular teleology. He opposed the centripetal discourse of "Islam, Indo-Muslim culture, and Urdu," which suggested that Pakistan had a predetermined "purpose for creation" with a specific end in mind. In prose written after the 1965 India-Pakistan War, when Pakistani cultural nationalism found renewed emphasis, Rashed championed a more inclusive, though inherently conflicting, set of elements as the basis for the nation: folk culture, Persian aesthetics, Western institutions, and Arab ethics. Through this modernist montage, he suggested, Pakistan could find an approach to the present that was new and appropriate to its situation, as well as more in tune with its composite history. In poetry, he voiced these concerns as a need to break with the "legend" of the past, or with ideological myths that are used deceitfully, so as to move forward in new directions and overcome forms of social and ideological oppression. Instead of continuity, then, Rashed's poetry emphasizes both the need for, and the possibility of, change.

A particular concern of Rashed's late poetry is death. Chapter 4 argues that Rashed's poetry participates in a global modernist discourse, and shows that his concern with death in particular involves post-Freudian psychoanalytical understandings, particularly those associated with Norman O. Brown. Rashed's poems charge that people seek historical continuity and fail to embrace the revolutionary possibilities of the present because they live in fear of death. Embracing death in his poetry means privileging this-worldly life over a spiritual beyond. His poetry visualizes the fear of death as the source of a negation in the form of a mental repression opposed to life. He opposes the Sufi search for *fanā*, or mystical extinction, as did Iqbal. Unlike Iqbal, however, he also opposes claims to unity with a spiritual mission or a collective historical movement. The search for unity, Rashed argues, seeks to ignore or overcome the problem of individual existence by obliterating the self in the collective life of the "crowd." He instead calls for self-knowledge and an embrace of transitory, human, corporeal life. He inverts the common Sufi desire for "unity" with a call for self-knowledge and an acceptance of "separation."

Rashed's poetry ends with a call for doubt *(gumāñ)* rather than certainty *(yaqīñ)*. He conveys this call through a narrative voice that serves as an antithesis to Iqbal's man of faith *(mard-e momin)*. In "Masjid-e Qurṭabah" Iqbal writes that what drives his hero is certainty: "The man of God's certainty *(yaqīñ)* is the center point of the compass of Truth / and this world is entirely superstition, magic, and illusion."[15] The narrator of Rashed's poem "Gumāñ kā mumkin" (The Possibility of Suspicion, §25) starts out on a Sufi quest, leaving the "lake of time" and approaching the divine presence. However, Rashed's narrator recoils. For such a journey, where the "ambiguity of the heart" dissolves, provides no answers to his own questions about finite and transitory life. In that journey, all previous "answers" appear as merely claims to certainty. He finds instead that the nature of the self can only be known and experienced in this world, and he turns his attention to the realm of human life. Instead of privileging a spiritual world beyond, Rashed's poem keeps its focus in the realm of individual experience, of both the inner self and outer world.

The fourth and final section of "Ḥasan the Potter" (§29) celebrates and elevates the role of individual experience and creativity against ideology or representation. It does so, in part, by considering the passage of historical time. Hasan begins his final monologue to Jahanzad by describing the discovery of the shards of his pottery in a "buried city" a thousand years in the future. Each broken piece is like the "memory" of their "ruined city" (lines 1–4). He introduces another young potter in that future city, also named Hasan, who falls in love and shapes pots. Hasan imagines "a crowd of past-worshipers" descending on the "corpses" of his pots. These are people who never perceived the depths of a wine "cup" or "goblet." How, he muses, could they "know of the rainbow" from which his "colors" came, "from which of the butterflies' wings," "from which beauty," "from what self," or "from what features" he shaped the pots—or even the young potter his own pots (lines 17–33)?

Much has been made by critics of Rashed's landscape in this poem. Tabassum Kāshmīrī likens it to "One Thousand and One Nights" and argues that Rashed's geographical imagination is more closely linked to "West Asia" than to the author's own homeland. He notes that although Rashed stated in prose and in poetry that he had no interest in the past, a poem like this one shows how Rashed draws on his "civilizational unconscious."[16] Fateh Muhammad Malik adds that this is part of Rashed's "revolutionary political consciousness." Drawing on Rashed's family's Sufi devotion and his brief political participation with the Khaksar movement, Malik states that Rashed dreamed of a new life for Islam—and speculates that he most likely hid his commitments because of his employment with the United Nations. For Malik, the poem's setting in Baghdad depicts a time of the lost empire of Islam, and the poem reflects Rashed's hope to restore anew the worldwide civilization of Islam.[17]

However, the archaic landscape of the poem is better understood as a commentary on the function of art and a critique of contemporary "civilization." The future city of the young potter is presumably the contemporary world, as Hasan imagines archeologists examining his own pots in a future that is the poem's present. If they wish, he meditates, they will find the "civilization" *(tahżīb)* of these "shards," but "how will they find Hasan the Potter" (line 61–62)? In other words, they will read Hasan's art as representative of his moment of history, but his own experience will still have been lost. These future people, he goes on, have never looked into a "wine cup" *(jām)* or "goblet" *(mīnā)*—both Urdu words that are arcane in contemporary speech though common enough in the ghazal (line 21). Both are associated with the wine of divine intoxication, and they are signs of the experience of passion *(ʿishq)* rather than reason *(ʿaql)*.

The fact that the future people have never looked inside those vessels signals the inadequacy of contemporary experiences of the self—a topic that Rashed addressed in a number of poems. Hasan criticizes these future people for denying the passionate, irrational, and corporeal components of creativity and desire. He explains that these "innocent savages," who are "in search of some unattainable grandeur," are "disheveled by their very own stature" (lines 38–39). This passage invokes a Freudian understanding of civilization and modernity as a product of repression, critiquing the belief in progress. These people, he implies, deny the true nature of their embodied state, and therefore lack access to their own unconscious desires. The future people know nothing, Hasan continues, of the "evil spirit" *(āseb)* inside him and the young potter that drives their creativity forward. The same spirit awakens both of them. It tells them that it is a day to rejoice, as the "pain of prophecy" has reached the "thirstiness of [their] cup and goblet" (lines 40–44). The statement draws on the Persian and Urdu literary convention of the human being as a wine cup that can hold the intoxication of divine love or knowledge.

The "pain of prophecy" experienced by the potter is the experience of creativity, which reveals the human self. To the future people, the "corpses" of his pots might seem like the "et cetera, et cetera of some tale of annihilation," destroyed in the march of progress. For "us," Hasan declares, they are "our calls to prayer" and "our signs of searching" (lines 81–83). The art objects perceive human nature in excess of their artists' self-knowledge. At the conclusion of the poem, the pots themselves speak, declaring that "we are watching you," and that "we comprehend your pain." They are "eyes that are open inside" of humankind. They understand the knowledge of the "secret of every beauty." They partake also of universal creativity. For they are like the "stolen kiss" when "one face" bent down, like a tree, and placed a "flower petal," or heart, in the "chest of every man" (lines 88–92). Hasan describes his human creativity as partaking in a universal creativity, in a way reminiscent of Bergsonism. Consistent with Bergson and opposed to Iqbal, creativity in the poem is not directed toward any particular teleological end. Unlike Iqbal's man of faith or man of god, Hasan proposes no unity with divine will. Art is a means for understanding the self rather than knowing the beyond, despite the profound and depersonalized experience of creativity.

"Hasan the Potter" exemplifies N. M. Rashed's understanding of the role of literary creativity. The image of the potter, molding the art object with his hands, stresses the individual and corporeal act of creation, as the pot carries the traces of an individual's touches and caresses. "Ḥasan Kūzagar" maintains the connection between art and a purely individual experience driven by desire—a connection that Rashed advocated for consistently throughout his literary career. It employs a modernist form of allegory in order to poise the poet's concept of creativity as a critique of the tradition of thought in Urdu letters, focusing on Iqbal as the most significant of the poet's predecessors. This poem, like Rashed's late oeuvre as a whole, advocates the new and vital role for modernism as mode of critique, within the context of a multifaceted tradition.

CONCLUSION

In Urdu literary history, modernism has typically been read as a rejection of politics. As such, it appears as the "other" of progressive literature—focused on individual psychology rather than society, and on literature rather than life. In the postcolonial period, modernism *(jadīdiyat)* also came to mean secular rationality emitting from the West, which was dismissed as fundamentally incompatible with a tradition built upon Islamic civilizational history. Counterintuitively, modernism later became associated with the traditionalist approach, because former advocates of *jadīdiyat*, especially

Muḥammad Ḥasan ʿAskarī and his circle, advocated a return to traditionalism. This book has argued against both of these negative definitions of modernism in favor of an aesthetic approach that privileges the category of experience in all its uncertainty.

Progressive criticism's slogan, by which it opposes modernism's alleged "adab barā-e adab" (literature for literature's sake) with "adab barā-e zindagī" (literature for life's sake), is clearly much too superficial to be useful. Rashed's poetry is deeply invested in the category of "life" and is engaged in a complex relationship with Bergsonian vitalism, especially as reinterpreted by Muhammad Iqbal. Yet, insofar as Rashed advocated literature as a position from which to criticize ideology, the label of "literature for literature's sake" is certainly appropriate. For Rashed, literature is a space for a critical discourse that is secular and anti-identitarian, opposed to both religious understanding and to the naturalization of national identity. Rashed is less tolerant of nationalism than religious thought, however. His poetry is much too deeply invested in Islamic discourse to be considered a visceral rejection of religion. Yet it is also deliberately iconoclastic, announcing its freedom from the religious understandings that pervade the multifaceted tradition of Urdu literature.

Rashed's poetry defines modernism as a site for the articulation of a this-worldly subjectivity. In the first instance, this manifested itself as a rejection of the self-effacing *ʿāshiq* (lover) of the Urdu ghazal. In place of self-extinction through mystical union, Rashed's poetry emphasized desire in this world. He initially saw this emphasis as a simple acknowledgement of sexual desire and of the importance of that desire in everyday life. The "realism" of sex and its unconscious effects not only challenged the ghazal tradition, but also newer forms, like the "natural" poetry of Muslim reform as well as the chaste romanticism of the 1930s. Later, Rashed pivoted away from these objects of critique and focused squarely on the thought of Muhammad Iqbal. For while Iqbal similarly disapproved of the otherworldly focus of Sufism, Rashed took issue with Iqbal's notion of *k̲h̲vudī*, or selfhood, for its grounding in metaphysical reality and disavowal of psychoanalytical understandings of desire.

Rashed's commitment to an uncompromisingly individual notion of subjectivity became his touchstone for the evaluation of ideologies of literary production. Rashed understood the focus of many progressives on socialist realism as a form of ideological regimentation—one that hindered the exploration of the psychic life of the individual and that subsumed the individual into the collective. Similarly, Rashed also criticized religious approaches to literature for denying the individual for the sake of transcendent experience. Rashed continued to foreground individual experience, even as he acknowledged that such experience involved both the external and the internal world. There are certainly experiences of great depth and of the impersonal in his poetry, as there are in the process of creativity described by Hasan the Potter, and these appear to be similar to the mystical journeys of Sufism. Yet for Rashed these experiences reside in the timelessness of the unconscious self, not in the beyond. There is no underlying sense of a higher "reality" in his poetry.

Indeed, such claims to metaphysical experiences are anathema to the poet, for he sees them as taking the form of an ideological reification that is used to justify domination in this world. Rashed concentrates on Iqbal's poetry because of its afterlife in Pakistani nationalism. While becoming and aspiration are central themes of Iqbal's poetry, Rashed also identifies in it a problematically teleological sense of continuity and of certainty. Rashed's immanent critique of Iqbal's thought anticipated the transformation of his legacy under the Islamist regime of Zia-ul-Haq, and it remains an important line of thought in cultural debates in Pakistan.

In his modernist writing, Rashed marshals doubt in opposition to the certainties of metaphysics and political ideology. He explores this most fully in his critique of the symbol and promotion of modernist allegory. He continually opposed the imperialism of the West, while refusing to uphold the East or Islam as its spiritual other. Instead, Rashed remained deeply critical of civilizational claims on the whole, regardless of their origin. Drawing on a Freudian notion of civilization as repression, Rashed boldly challenged the encompassing importance of Islam. There is still much to be gained from an understanding of his formally challenging and fiercely anti-ideological poetry.

APPENDIX

Poems in Transliteration and Translation

§1. BĀDAL (SĀNEṬ)

chhāʾe huʾe haiñ chār t̤araf pārah-hā-e abr
āġhosh meñ liʾe huʾe dunyā-e āb-o-rang
mere liʾe hai un kī garaj meñ sarod-e chang
paiġhām-e imbisāt̤ hai mujh ko ṣadā-e abr
uṭṭhī hai halke halke saroñ meñ navā-e abr
aur qat̤r-hā-e āb bajāte haiñ jaltarang
gahrāʾiyoñ meñ rūḥ kī jāgī hai har umang
dil meñ utar rahe haiñ mire naġhmah-hā-e abr
muddat se luṭ chuke the tamannā ke bār-o-barg
chhāyā huʾā thā rūḥ pah goyā sukūt-e marg
chhūṛā hai āj zīst ko ḳhvāb-e jamūd ne
un bādaloñ se tāzah huʾī hai ḥayāt phir
mere liye javān hai yih kāʾināt phir
shādāb kar diyā hai dil un ke sarod ne!

§2. EK DIN—LĀRINS BĀĠH MEÑ (EK KAIFIYAT)

baiṭhā huʾā hūñ ṣubḥ se lārins bāġh meñ
afkār kā hujūm hai mere dimāġh meñ
chhāyā huʾā hai chār t̤araf bāġh meñ sukūt
tanhāʾiyoñ kī gaud meñ leṭā huʾā hūñ maiñ
ashjār bār bār ḍarāte haiñ ban-ke bhūt
jab dekhtā hūñ un kī t̤araf kāñptā hūñ maiñ
baiṭhā huʾā hūñ ṣubḥ se lārins bāġh meñ!

lārins bāġh! kaif-o-lat̤āfat ke ḳhuld-zār
vuh mausam-e nashāt̤! vuh ayyām-e nau-bahār
bhūle huʾe manāz̤ir-e rangīñ bahār ke
afkār ban-ke rūḥ meñ merī utar gaʾe
vuh mast gīt mausam-e ʿishrat-fashār ke
gahrāʾiyoñ ko dil kī ġham ābād kar gaʾe
lārins bāġh! kaif-o-lat̤āfat ke ḳhuld-zār

hai āsmāñ pah kālī ghaṭāʾoñ kā izhdihām
hone lagī hai vaqt se pahle hī āj shām
dunyā kī āñkh nīñd se jis vaqt jhuk gaʾī
jab kāʾināt kho gaʾī asrār-e ḳhvāb meñ
sīne meñ jū-e ashk hai mere rukī huʾī

§1. CLOUD (SONNET)

Bits of cloud spread in all directions,
embracing the world of luster and color
For me, their thunder plays the lute's melody
For me, the clouds sound a message of joy
The cloud's voice has lightly risen in pitch,
and drops of water play musical water-chimes
In the depths of my soul, every longing has awoken
The songs of the clouds are descending into my heart
I'd long been robbed of longing's leaves and fruit,
and my soul been left with the quiet of death
Listless sleep today abandoned my being
Those clouds renewed my very being
For me, the universe is young again
Their song has made my heart feel fresh!

§2. ONE DAY IN LAWRENCE GARDEN (AN IMPRESSION)

I have been sitting in Lawrence Garden since dawn
A swarm of thoughts in my mind
        Silence is spread in all directions in the garden
        I am lying in the lap of solitude
Trees, becoming ghosts, frighten me again and again
As I look at them I tremble
    I have been sitting in Lawrence Garden since dawn!

Lawrence Garden! Paradise of intoxication and elegance
That climate of joy! Those days of early spring
        Forgotten, colorful sights of spring
        have become ideas and descended into my soul
Those drunken songs of the pleasure-scattering season
filled the depths of my heart with pain
    Lawrence Garden! Paradise of intoxication and elegance!

There is a throng of black clouds in the sky
Evening has begun even before its time
        when the eye of the world drooped with sleep
        when the universe was lost in the secrets of dreams
In my chest a river of tears is dammed

jā-kar use bahāʾūñgā kunj-e gulāb meñ
hai āsmāñ pah kālī ghaṭāʾoñ kā izhdihām
afkār kā hujūm hai mere dimāġh meñ
baiṭhā huʾā hūñ ṣubḥ se lārins bāġh meñ!

§3. SITĀRE (SĀNEṬ)

nikal-kar jū-e naġhmah ḳhuld-zār-e māh-o-anjam se
faẓā kī vusʿatoñ meñ hai ravāñ āhistah āhistah
bah sū-e nauḥah-ābād-e jahāñ āhistah āhistah
nikal-kar ā rahī hai ik gulistān-e tarannum se!
sitāre apne mīṭhe mad bhare halke tabassum se
kiye jāte haiñ fit̤rat ko javāñ āhistah āhistah
sunāte haiñ use ik dāstāñ āhistah āhistah
diyār-e zindagī mad-hosh hai un ke takallum se
yihī ʿādat hai roz-e avvalīñ se un sitāroñ kī
chamakte haiñ kih dunyā meñ masarrat kī ḥukūmat ho

chamakte haiñ kih insāñ fikr-e hastī ko bhulā ḍāle
liye hai yih tamannā har kiran un nūr pāroñ kī
kabhī yih ḳhāk-dāñ gahvārah-e ḥusn-o-lat̤āfat ho

kabhī insān apnī gum-shudah jannat ko phir pā le!

§4. VĀDĪ-E PINHĀÑ

vaqt ke daryā meñ uṭṭhī thī abhī pahlī hī lahr
chand insānoñ ne lī ik vādī-e pinhāñ kī rāh
mil gaʾī un ko vahāñ
āġhosh-e rāḥat meñ panāh
kar liyā taʿmīr ik mausīqī-o-ʿishrat kā shahr,
mashriq-o-maġhrib ke pār
zindagī aur maut kī farsūdah shah-rāhoñ se dūr
jis jagah se āsmāñ kā qāfilah letā hai nūr
jis jagah har ṣubḥ ko miltā hai īmā-e z̤ahūr
aur bune jāte haiñ rātoñ ke liye ḳhvāboñ ke jāl
sīkhtī hai jis jagah pardāz ḥūr
aur farishtoñ ko jahāñ miltā hai āhang-e surūr
ġham naṣīb ahrīmanoñ ko giryah-o-āh-o-fiġhāñ!

I will go into the rose garden and let it flow
A throng of black clouds in the sky
A swarm of thoughts in my mind
I have been sitting in Lawrence Garden since dawn!

§3. STARS (SONNET)

Leaving the paradise of the moon and stars, the river of song
is traveling in the openness of space—slowly, slowly
toward the world's abode of lamentation—slowly, slowly
Leaving a garden of song, it is coming!
Stars, with their sweet, intoxicated, light smiles,
are making nature young—slowly, slowly
are telling her a story—slowly, slowly
The domain of life is intoxicated by their words
Since the first day this has been the habit of the stars
They are shining, so that in the world there might be the rule of delight
They are shining, so that man might forget his life's worries
Every single beam of light carries the desire
that someday this world of dust will become a cradle of beauty and elegance,
that someday man will regain his lost paradise!

§4. HIDDEN VALLEY

The very first wave in the river of time had just risen
when a few humans started on the road to a hidden valley
There they found
sanctuary in the embrace of ease
They built a city of music and mirth,
beyond the East and West,
far from the worn highways of life and death,
a place from which the caravan of the heavens takes light,
from which every morning is given the hint to rise,
where nets of dreams are woven for the night,
and where houris learn to fly,
and angels find their beautiful melodies,
and devils are destined for grief, weeping and wailing and sighing!

kāsh batlā de koʾī
mujh ko bhī is vādī-e pinhāñ kī rāh
mujh ko ab tak justajū hai
zindagī ke tāzah jolāñ-gāh kī
kaisī bezārī sī hai
zindagī ke kuhnah āhang-e musalsal se mujhe
sar-zamīn-e zīst kī afsurdah maḥfil se mujhe
dekh le ik bār kāsh
us jahāñ kā manz̤ir-e rangīñ nigāh
jis jagah hai qahqahoñ kā ik darak̲hshandah vufūr
jis jagah se āsmāñ kā qāfilah letā hai nūr
jis kī rifʿat dekh-kar k̲hvud himmat-e yazdāñ hai chūr
jis jagah hai vaqt ik tāzah surūr
zindagī kā pairahan hai tār tār!
jis jagah ahrīmanoñ kā bhī nahīñ kuchh ik̲htiyār
mashriq-o-maġhrib ke pār!

§5. GUNĀH AUR MUḤABBAT

gunāh:

gunāh ke tund-o-tez shŏʿloñ se rūḥ merī bhaṛak rahī thī
havas kī sunsān vādiyoñ meñ mirī javānī bhaṭak rahī thī
mirī javānī ke din guzarte the vaḥshat-ālūd ʿishratoñ meñ
mirī javānī ke mai-kadoñ meñ gunāh kī mai chhalak rahī thī
mire ḥarīm-e gunāh meñ ʿishq devatā kā guzar nahīñ thā
mire fareb-e vafā ke ṣaḥrā meñ ḥūr-e ʿiṣmat bhaṭak rahī thī
mujhe k̲has-e nā-tavāñ ke mānind żauq-e ʿiṣyāñ bahā rahā thā
gunāh kī mauj-e fitnah sāmāñ uṭhā uṭhā-kar paṭak rahī thī
shabāb ke avvalīñ dinoñ meñ tabāh-o-afsurdah ho chuke the
mire gulistāñ ke phūl, jin se faẓā-e t̤iflī mahak rahī thī

ġharaẓ javānī meñ ahriman ke t̤arab kā sāmān ban gayā maiñ
gunah kī ālāʾishoñ meñ luthṛā huʾā ik insān ban gayā maiñ

muḥabbat:

aur ab kih terī muḥabbat-e sar-madī kā bādah-gusār hūñ maiñ
havas-parastī kī lażżat-e be-s̤abāt se sharm-sār hūñ maiñ
mirī bahīmānah k̲hvāhishoñ ne farār kī rāh lī hai dil se
aur un ke badle ik ārzū-e salīm se ham-kinār hūñ maiñ

If only someone could also show me
the way to this hidden valley
I am still searching
for a fresh arena of life
How fed up
I am with the ancient, perpetual melody of life,
with the melancholy company of life's earth
If only I could see just once
the colorful vision of that world,
where there is a refulgent abundance of laughter,
that place from which the caravan of the heavens takes light,
and seeing whose height, even God's courage fails
that place where time is a new delight,
and the garment of life is torn to pieces!
Where the devils too have no authority,
beyond the East and West!

§5. SIN AND LOVE

Sin:

My soul was blazing with the flames of sin
My youth was wandering astray in the desolate valleys of lust
The days of my youth were passed in wild pleasures
The wine of sin splashed in the tavern of my youth
The god of love had no passage into my sanctuary of sin
The houri of chastity was lost in my desert of false fidelity
The pleasure of transgression was carrying me like a helpless straw
The calamitous wave of sin constantly tossed me about
The flowers of my garden, which belonged to my youth,
which perfumed the environment of my childhood, were worn-out
 and ruined
In short, I became in youth a tool for Satan's delight
I became a man, smeared in the filth of sin

Love:

And now as I consume the wine of your perpetual love
I am ashamed of baseless, lust-loving pleasure
My bestial desires have taken flight from my heart,
and in their stead I have embraced a virtuous desire

dalīl-e rāh-e vafā banī haiñ ẓiyā-e ulfat kī pāk kirneñ
phir apne "firdaus-e gum-shudah" kī talāsh meñ rah sipār hūñ maiñ
huʾā hūñ be-dār kāñp-kar ik muhīb ḳhvāboñ ke silsile se
aur ab namūd-e saḥar kī ḳhāt̤ir sitam-kash-e intiz̤ār hūñ maiñ

bahār-e taqdīs-e jāvidāñ kī mujhe phir ik bār ārzū hai
phir ek pākīzah zindagī ke liye bahut be-qarār hūñ maiñ
mujhe muḥabbat ne maʿṣiyat ke jahannamoñ se bachā liyā hai
mujhe javānī kī tīrah-o-tār pastiyoñ se uṭhā liyā hai

§6. MUKĀFĀT

rahī hai ḥaẓrat-e yazdāñ se dostī merī
rahā hai zuhd se yārānah ustuvār mirā
guzar gaʾī hai taqaddus meñ zindagī merī
dil ahriman se rahā hai satezah-kār mirā
kisī pah rūḥ numāyāñ nah ho sakī merī
rahā hai apnī umangoñ pah iḳhtiyār mirā

dabāʾe rakkhā hai sīne meñ apnī āhoñ ko
vahīñ diyā hai shab-o-roz pech-o-tāb unheñ
zabān-e shauq banāyā nahīñ nigāhoñ ko
kiyā nahīñ kabhī vaḥshat meñ be-naqāb unheñ
ḳhayāl hī meñ kiyā parvarish gunāhoñ ko
kabhī kiyā nah javānī se bahrah-yāb unheñ

yih mil rahī hai mire ẓabt̤ kī sazā mujh ko
kih ek zahr se lab-rez hai shabāb mirā
ażīyatoñ se bharī hai har ek be-dārī
mahīb-o-rūḥ-sitāñ hai har ek ḳhvāb mirā
ulajh rahī haiñ navāʾeñ mire sarodoñ kī
fashār-e ẓabt̤ se be-tāb hai rubāb mirā
magar yih ẓabt̤ mire qahqahoñ kā dushman thā
payām-e marg-e javānī thā ijtināb mirā

lo ā gaʾī haiñ vuh ban-kar muhīb taṣvīreñ
vuh ārzūʾeñ kih jin kā kiyā thā ḳhūñ maiñ ne
lo ā gaʾe haiñ vuhī pai-ravān-e ahrīman
kiyā thā jin ko siyāsat se sar-nigūñ maiñ ne
kabhī nah jān pah dekhā thā yih ʿażāb-e alīm
kabhī nahīñ ai mire baḳht-e vāzh-gūñ maiñ ne

The pure rays of love's light have become my guide to faithfulness
I am committed anew to the search for my "Lost Paradise"
Trembling from horrible dreams, I have awoken,
and now as the dawn has appeared I will endure the tyranny of
waiting
Once more I long for the eternal spring of sanctity
Once again I am very anxious for a pure life
Love has saved me from the hells of sin
It has lifted me out from the dark depravities of youth

§6. RETRIBUTION

My friendship with the Lord God has endured
My rapport with abstinence has remained strong
My life has passed in holiness
My heart remains locked in battle with the Devil
No one could see into my soul
My control over my desires has remained

I have suppressed my sighs and kept them in my chest
where I twisted and twined them night and day
I could not turn my glances into a tongue of yearning
I never unveiled them in moments of madness
Only in thought did I nurture sin
I never let them partake of youth

I am being punished for my restraint
My youth is brimming with poison
My every awakening is full of torment
My every dream is terrible and seizes my soul
The melodies of my songs are being entangled
Under the pressure of my control, my instrument is in agony
But this control was an enemy of my mirth
My abstinence was a message of the death of youth

Look, they have come as terrible images,
those desires that I murdered
Look, those same followers of the Devil have come,
those I made miserable through my chastisement
I never saw this excruciating torment in my soul,
never before, Oh my unfortunate fate!

magar yih jitnī aẕīyat bhī deñ mujhe kam hai
kiyā hai rūḥ ko apnī bahut zabūñ maiñ ne
use nah hone diyā maiñ ne ham-navā-e shabāb
nah us pah chalne diyā shauq kā fusūñ maiñ ne
ai kāsh chhup-ke kahīñ ik gunāh kar letā
ḥalāvatoñ se javānī ko apnī bhar letā
gunāh ek bhī ab tak kiyā nah kyoñ maiñ ne?

§7. ḤUZN-E INSĀN (AFLĀṬŪNĪ ʿISHQ PAR EK ṬANZ)

jism aur rūḥ meñ āhang nahīñ,
laẕẕat-andoz-e dil-āvezī-e mauhūm hai tū
ḳhastah-e kash-ma-kash-e fikr-o-ʿamal!
tujh ko hai ḥasrat-e iẓhār-e shabāb
aur iẓhār se maʿẕūr bhī hai
jism nekī ke ḳhayālāt se mafrūr bhī hai
is qadar sādah-o-maʿṣūm hai tū
phir bhī nekī hī kiye jātī hai
kih dil-o-jism ke āhang se maḥrūm hai tū

jism hai rūḥ kī ʿaẓmat ke liye zīnah-e nūr
mambaʿ-e kaif-o-surūr!
nā-rasā āj bhī hai shauq-e parastār-e jamāl
aur insāñ hai kih hai jādah-kash-e rāh-e ṭavīl
(rūḥ-e yūnāñ pah salām!)
ik zimistāñ kī ḥasīñ rāt kā hangām-e tapāk
us kī laẕẕāt se āgāh hai kaun?
ʿishq hai tere liye naġhmah-e ḳhām
kih dil-o-jism ke āhang se maḥrūm hai tū!

jism aur rūḥ ke āhang se maḥrūm hai tū!
varnah shab-hā-e zimistāñ abhī be-kār nahīñ
aur nah be-sūd haiñ ayyām-e bahār!
āh insāñ kih hai vahmoñ kā paristār abhī
ḥusn be-chāre ko dhokā sā diye jātā hai
ẕauq-e taqdīs pah majbūr kiye jātā hai!
ṭūṭ jāʾeñge kisī roz mazāmīr ke tār
muskarā de kih hai tābindah abhī terā shabāb
hai yihī ḥaẓrat-e yazdāñ ke tamasḳhur kā javāb!

But no matter how much trouble they give me, it is not enough
I have abased my soul so thoroughly
I could not let it sing with youth
or let the spell of desire be cast upon it
Oh, if only I had secretly committed one sin,
If only I had filled my youth with sweetness
Why have I still not committed even one sin?

§7. THE AFFLICTION OF MAN (A SATIRE OF PLATONIC LOVE)

There is no harmony in your body and soul
You take pleasure in illusory delights,
wearied by the struggle of thought and action!
You long to express youth,
and are incapable of expression too
The body has fled from righteous thoughts
You are so simple and innocent,
and yet you continue doing only good
for you are deprived of the concord of heart and body

The body is a ladder of light for the soul's magnitude,
a fountain of intoxication and exhilaration!
Even today the passion of worshippers of beauty remains unfulfilled,
and it is man who is a traveler on a long road
(Peace be unto the Greek soul!)
The tumult of ardor on a beautiful winter's night—
who knows of its pleasure?
Love for you is a crude song,
for you are deprived of the concord of heart and body!

You are deprived of the concord of body and soul!
Otherwise these winter nights would not be worthless,
and the days of spring would not be without benefit!
Ah man, who now is a worshipper of illusions
Beauty tricks the poor fellow,
forces him to have a taste for the sacred!
Someday the strings of the instrument will break
Smile, for your youth right now is glowing
This is the answer to the joke of the Lord God!

§8. ITTIFĀQĀT

āj, is sāʿat-e duzdīdah-o-nā-yāb meñ bhī,
jism hai k͟hvāb se lażżat-kash-e k͟hamyāzah tirā
tere mizhgāñ ke tale nīñd kī shabnam kā nazūl
jis se dhul jāne ko hai ġhāzah tirā
zindagī tere liye ras bhare k͟hvāboñ kā hujūm
zindagī mere liye kāvish-e be-dārī hai;
ittifāqāt ko dekh
is ḥasīñ rāt ko dekh
toṛ de vahm ke jāl
chhoṛ de apne shabistānoñ ko jāne kā k͟hayāl,
k͟hauf-e mauhūm tirī rūḥ pah kyā ṭārī hai!
itnā be-ṣarfah nahīñ terā jamāl
is zimistāñ kī junūñ-k͟hez ḥasīñ rāt ko dekh!
āj, is sāʿat-e duzdīdah-o-nā-yāb meñ bhī
tishnagī rūḥ kī āsūdah nah ho
jab tirā jism javānī meñ hai naisān-e bahār
rang-o-nak'hat kā fashār!

phūl haiñ, ghās hai, ashjār haiñ, dīvāreñ haiñ
aur kuchh sāʾe kih haiñ muk͟htaṣar-o-tīrah-o-tār,
tujh ko kyā is se ġharaż hai kih k͟hudā hai kih nahīñ?
dekh pattoñ meñ laraztī huʾī kirnoñ kā nafūż
sarsarātī huʾī baṛhtī hai ragoñ meñ jaise
avvalīñ bādah gusārī meñ naʾī tund sharāb,
tujh ko kyā is se ġharaż hai kih k͟hudā hai kih nahīñ?

kah-kashāñ apnī tamannāʾoñ kā hai rāh-gużār
kāsh us rāh pah mil-kar kabhī parvāz kareñ
ik naʾī zīst kā dar-bāz kareñ!
āsmāñ dūr hai lekin yih zamīñ hai nazdīk
ā isī k͟hāk ko ham jalvah-gah-e rāz kareñ!
rūḥeñ mil saktī nahīñ haiñ to yih lab hī mil jāʾeñ,
ā isī lażżat-e jāved kā āġhāz kareñ!
ṣubḥ jab bāġh meñ ras lene ko zambūr āʾe
us ke būsoñ se hoñ mad-hosh saman aur gulāb
shab-namī ghās pah do paikar-e yak͟h-bastah mileñ,
aur k͟hudā ho to pashemāñ ho jāʾe!

§8. ACCIDENTS

Today, even in this stolen and rare moment,
as your body stretches, gathering the pleasures of sleep,
and under your eyelashes a cataract of sleep's dew
is about to wash away your makeup,
life for you is a swarm of luscious dreams; and
life for me is the struggle to stay awake!
Look at these accidents
Look at this beautiful night
Tear the nets of illusions
Forget about returning to your bedroom
Why should a phantom fear overcome your soul!
Your beauty is not so worthless
Look at this maddening, beautiful winter night!
Today, even in this stolen and rare moment,
why shouldn't the soul's thirst be quenched,
when your body in its youth is a spring cloud,
a compression of color and fragrance!

There are flowers; there is grass; there are trees; there are walls,
and some shadows which are shortened and dark and obscure
Why do you care whether God exists or not?
Look how trembling rays of light penetrate through the leaves,
just like fresh and strong wine creeps and advances
in the veins after the first swig
Why do you care whether God exists or not?

The Milky Way is the pathway of our desires
If only we could meet on that path and fly away,
open the doors to a new life!
The heavens are far away, but this earth is near
Come, let's make this dust a place for secrets to be revealed!
If souls cannot meet, then let these lips meet
Come, let's experience everlasting pleasure!
In the morning, when the bee comes into the garden for nectar
and from its kisses the jasmine and roses grow intoxicated,
let two frozen bodies be found on the dewy grass,
and if there is a God let him be ashamed!

§9. SHĀʿIR-E DAR-MĀÑDAH

zindagī tere liye bistar-e sanjāb-o-samūr
aur mere liye afrang kī daryūzah-garī
ʿāfiyat-koshī-e ābā ke ṯufail,
maiñ hūñ dar-māñdah-o-be-chārah adīb
ḳhastah-e fikr-e maʿāsh!
pārah-e nān-e javīñ ke liye mŏḥtāj haiñ ham
maiñ, mire dost, mire saiñkṛoñ arbāb-e vaṯan
yaʿnī afrang ke gulzāroñ ke phūl!
tujhe ik shāʿir-e dar-māñdah kī ummīd nah thī
mujh se jis roz sitārah tirā vā-bastah huʾā
tū samajhtī thī kih ik roz mirā żĕhn-e rasā
aur mire ʿilm-o-hunar
baḥr-o-bar se tirī zīnat ko guhar lāʾeñge!
mere raste meñ jo ḥāʾil hoñ mire tīrah naṣīb
kyoñ duʿāʾeñ tirī be-kār nah jāʾeñ
tere rātoñ ke sujūd aur niyāz
(us kā bāʿis mirā ilḥād bhī hai!)

ai mirī shamʿ-e shabistān-e vafā,
bhūl jā mere liye
zindagī ḳhvāb kī āsūdah farāmoshī hai!
tujhe maʿlūm hai mashriq kā ḳhudā koʾī nahīñ
aur agar hai, to sarā-pardah-e nisyān meñ hai
tū "masarrat" hai mirī, tū mirī "be-dārī" hai
mujhe āġhosh meñ le
do "anā" mil-ke jahāñ soz baneñ
aur jis ʿahd kī hai tujh ko duʿāʾoñ meñ talāsh
āp hī āp huvaidā ho jāʾe!

§10. INTIQĀM

us kā chĕhrah, us ke ḳhadd-o-ḳhāl yād āte nahīñ
ik shabistāñ yād hai
ik barahnah jism ātish-dāñ ke pās
farsh par qālīn, qālīnoñ pah sej
dhāt aur patthar ke but
goshah-e dīvār meñ hañste huʾe!
aur ātish-dāñ meñ angāroñ kā shor

§9. WRETCHED POET

Life for you is a bed of fur
And for me, begging from the Europeans
Because of the retreat of my forefathers,
I am a miserable and helpless littérateur
worn out by the worries of my livelihood!
In need of a piece of barley bread
are we—me, my friends, my thousands of fellow countrymen,
that is, the flowers of the Europeans' gardens!
You did not hope for a wretched poet
On the day your star was bound to me,
you thought that one day my clever mind
and my knowledge and skill
would bring pearls to adorn you from the land and sea
When ill-fortunes block my path,
why shouldn't your prayers,
your nightly prostrations and supplications, be useless?
(My disbelief, too, is its reason!)

O my candle of the chamber of faithfulness,
forget it all for my sake
Life is the tranquil forgetfulness of dreams!
You know well there is no god of the East,
and if there is, then he is behind a curtain of forgetfulness.
You are my "joy"; you are my "wakefulness"
Take me in your embrace
so two "I's" may become one and set the world ablaze,
so the era you seek in your prayers
may manifest itself on its own.

§10. REVENGE

I don't remember her face, her features
I remember a bedroom,
a naked body near the fireplace
a carpet on the floor, on the carpet a bed,
metal and stone idols
laughing in the corners of the walls!
And in the fireplace, the clamor of coals

un butoñ kī be-ḥisī par ḳhashmgīñ
ujlī ujlī ūñchī dīvāroñ pah ʿaks
un farangī ḥākimoñ kī yādgār
jin kī talvāroñ ne rakkhā thā yahāñ
sang-e bunyād-e farang!

us kā chĕhrah us ke ḳhadd-o-ḳhāl yād āte nahīñ
ik barahnah jism ab tak yād hai
ajnabī ʿaurat kā jism,
mere "hoñṭoñ" ne liyā thā rāt bhar
jis se arbāb-e vat̤an kī be-basī kā intiqām
vuh barahnah jism ab tak yād hai!

§11. HAMAH ŪST

ḳhayābān-e saʿdī meñ
rūsī kitāboñ kī dukkān par ham khaṛe the
mujhe rūs ke chīdah ṣanʿat-garoñ ke
naʾe kār-nāmoñ kī ik ʿumr se tishnagī thī!
mujhe rūsiyoñ ke "siyāsī hamah ūst" se koʾī raġhbat nahīñ hai
magar żarre żarre meñ
insāñ ke jauhar kī tābindagī dekhne kī tamannā hameshah rahī hai!
aur us shām to marsidah kī ʿarūsī thī,
us shauḳh, dīvānī laṛkī kī ḳhāt̤ir
mujhe ek nāzuk-sī sauġhāt kī justjū thī—

vuh merā nayā dost ḳhālid
żarā dūr, taḳhte ke pīchhe khaṛī
ik tanū-mand lekin fusūñ-kār,
qafqāz kī rahne-vālī ḥasīnah se shīr-o-shakar thā!
yih bhūkā musāfir,
jo daste ke sāth
ek ḳhīme meñ, ik dūr uftādah ṣaḥrā meñ
muddat se ʿuzlat-guzīñ thā,
baṛī iltijāʾoñ se
is ḥūr-e qafqāz se kah rahā thā:
"najāne kahāñ se milā hai
tumhārī zabāñ ko yih shahd
aur lahje ko mastī!
maiñ kaise batāʾūñ

angry at the idols' senselessness
Photographs on the tall, white walls,
the memorial to those Western rulers
whose swords here set
the foundation-stone of Europe!

I do not remember her face, her features
I still remember a naked body,
a foreign woman's body,
Through the night my "lips" took
revenge for the impotence of my countrymen
I still remember that naked body!

§11. PANTHEISM

On Saʿdī Avenue,
at a Russian bookshop, we were standing
For a long time I had been craving
for the new achievements of Russia's outstanding artists!
I have no affection for the Russians' "political pantheism,"
but I have come to desire to see the luster of man's intellect
in each and every particle!
Besides, that evening it was Marsidah's wedding,
I was in search of a nice gift
for that coquettish, crazy girl—

My new friend Khalid
stood nearby under a signboard
and talked up a robust but enchanting
beauty from the Caucasus!
This hungry traveler,
who had been isolated for a long time,
away with his unit
in a tent in a faraway desert.
With great supplication,
he was saying to this houri from the Caucasus,
"Who knows where
your language found this sweetness,
and your way of speaking found its intoxication!
How can I tell you

main̄ kis darjah dil-dādah hūn̄ rūsiyon̄ kā
mujhe ishtirākī tamaddun se kitnī muḥabbat hai,
kaise batāʾūn̄!
yih mumkin hai tum mujh ko rūsī sikā do?
kih rūsī adībon̄ kī sar-chashmah-gāhon̄ ko main̄ dekhnā chāhtā hūn̄!"

vuh parvardah-e ʿashvah-bāzī
kanakhyon̄ se yūn̄ dekhtī thī
kih jaise vuh un sar-nigūn̄ ārzūʾon̄ ko pahchāntī ho,
jo kartī hain̄ aks̈ar yūn̄-hī rū-shināsī
kabhī dostī kī tamannā,
kabhī ʿilm kī pyās ban-kar!
vuh kholhe hilātī thī, han̄stī thī
ik sochī samjhī ḥisābī lagāvaṭ se,
jaise vuh un ḳhufyah sar-chashmah-gāhon̄ ke har rāz ko jāntī ho,
vuh taḳhte ke pīchhe khaṛī, qahqahe mārtī, loṭtī thī!

kahā main̄ ne ḳhālid se:
"bahrūpiʾe!
is vilāyat men̄ ẓarb-e mas̈al hai
"kih onṭon̄ kī saudā-garī kī lagan ho
to ghar un ke qābil banāʾo——,
aur is shahr men̄ yūn̄ to ustāniyān̄ an-ganit hain̄
magar is kī ujrat bhalā tum kahān̄ de sakoge!"
vuh phir muẓt̤arab ho-ke, be-iḳhtiyārī se han̄sne lagī thī!
vuh bolī:
"yih sach hai
kih ujrat to ik shāhī bhar kam nah hogī,
magar faujiyon̄ kā bharosah hī kyā hai,
bhalā tum kahān̄ bāz āʾoge
āḳhir zabān̄ sīkne ke bahāne
ḳhiyānat karoge!"
vuh han̄stī huʾī
ik naʾe mashtarī kī t̤araf multafat ho gaʾī thī!

to ḳhālid ne dekhā
kih rūmān to ḳhāk men̄ mil chukā hai——
use khen̄ch-kar jab main̄ bāzār men̄ lā rahā thā,
lagātār karne lagā vuh maqūlon̄ men̄ bāten̄:
"zabān̄ sīknī ho to ʿaurat se sīkho!
jahān̄-bhar men̄ rūsī adab kā nahīn̄ koʾī s̈ānī!

the extent of my devotion to Russians.
I love socialist civilization so much,
how can I tell you!
Would it be possible for you to teach me Russian?
For I want to glimpse the wellsprings of Russian literature!"

This one raised into coquetry
was looking sly,
as if she recognized those shameful desires
which often show their face this way,
sometimes as the desire for friendship,
sometimes as the thirst for knowledge!
She shook her hips and laughed
with a knowing and calculating coquetry,
as if she knew every secret of that hidden spring
Standing under the sign, she was laughing her head off!

I said to Khalid:
"You fraud!
In this land there is a proverb
'If one loves selling camels
then he should make his house worthy of them,'
and in this city there are countless female tutors,
but how will you pay her fee!"
The lady became agitated, and then without choice began to laugh!
She said:
"This is true
for the fee wouldn't be less than a full Shahi coin,
But what is a soldier's trust,
You are never going to give up
pretending to learn a language,
breaching my trust!"
Laughing,
she turned to a new customer!

Then Khalid saw
that the romance had fallen into dust—
When I grabbed him and brought him to the market,
he talked in proverbs:
    "If you have to learn a language, learn it from a woman!
    There is no equal to Russian literature anywhere in the world!

vuh qafqāz kī ḥūr, mazdūr ʿaurat!
jo dunyā ke mazdūr sab ek ho jāʾeñ
āġhāz ho ik nayā daurah-e shādmānī!"

mire dostoñ meñ bahut ishtirākī haiñ,
jo har muḥabbat meñ māyūs ho-kar,
yūñ-hī ik naʾe daurah-e shādmānī kī ḥasrat meñ
karte haiñ dil-jūʾī ik dūsre kī,
aur ab aisī bātoñ pah maiñ
zer-e lab bhī kabhī muskarātā nahīñ hūñ!

aur us shām jashn-e ʿarūsī meñ
ḥusn-o-maʾe-o-raqṣ-o-naġhmah ke t̤ūfān bahte rahe the,
farangī sharābeñ to ʿanqā thīñ
lekin maʾe-e nāb-e qazvīn-o-ḳhullār-e shīrāz ke daur-e paiham se,

rangīñ labāsoñ se,
ḳhvush-bū kī be-bāk lahroñ se,
be-sāḳhtah qahqahoñ, hamhamoñ se,
mazāmīr ke zer-o-bam se,
vuh hangāmah barpā thā,
maḥsūs hotā thā
t̤ahrān kī āḳhirī shab yihī hai!
achānak kahā marsidah ne:
"tumhārā vuh sāthī kahāñ hai?
abhī ek ṣofe pah dekhā thā maiñ ne
use sar ba-zānū!"

to ham kuchh pareshān se ho gaʾe
aur kamrah bah kamrah use ḍhūñḍne mil-ke nikle!

lo ik goshah-e nīm-raushan meñ
vuh ishtirākī zamīñ par paṛā thā
use ham hilāyā kiye aur jhañjhoṛā kiye
vuh to sākit thā, jāmid thā!
rūsī adīboñ kī sar-chashmah-gāhoñ kī us ko ḳhabar ho gaʾī thī?

§12. TEL KE SAUDĀGAR

buḳhārā samarqand ik ḳhāl-e hindū ke badle!
bajā hai, buḳhārā samarqand bāqī kahāñ haiñ?

That houri of the Caucuses, a working woman!
If all the workers of the world unite
a new age of happiness would begin!"

Among my friends, there are many socialists,
who, becoming despondent in love,
try to console each another
in their desire for a new age of happiness,
and now I don't even secretly smirk
at their words!

That night, at the wedding celebration,
a storm of beauty and wine and dance and song was flowing
European liquor was scarce,
but with the constant rounds of the pure wine of Qazvin and the Khullar wine of Shiraz,
with colorful clothes
with fearless flows of fragrances,
with spontaneous laughter and clamor,
with the bass and trebles of the flutes,
there was such a commotion,
it seemed as if
it was Tehran's last night!
Suddenly Marsidah said:
"Where is that friend of yours?
I just saw him on a sofa,
his head on his knees!"

Then we became a bit worried
And having searched room to room for him together we went outside!
Lo, there in a half-lit corner
the socialist was lying on the ground
We kept shaking him over and over again
He was silent, unmoving!
Had he gotten news of the wellsprings of Russian literature?

§12. OIL MERCHANTS

Bukhara and Samarqand for a Hindu-black mole!
Very well, but what remains of Bukhara and Samarqand?

bukhārā samarqand nīñdoñ meñ mad-hosh,
ik nīl-gūñ khāmushī ke ḥijāboñ meñ mastūr
aur rah-rau'oñ ke li'e un ke dar band,
so'ī hu'ī mah-jabīnoñ kī palkoñ ke mānind,
rūsī "hamah ūst" ke tāziyānoñ se ma'ẕūr
do mah-jabīneñ!

bukhārā samarqand ko bhūl jā'o
ab apne darakhshandah shahroñ kī
ṭahrān-o-mashhad ke saqf-o-dar-o-bām kī fikr kar lo,
tum apne na'e daur-e hosh-o-'amal ke dil-āvez chasmoñ ko
apnī na'ī ārzū'oñ ke un khūb-ṣūrat kināyoñ ko
maḥfūẓ kar lo!

un ūñche darakhshandah shahroñ kī
kotah faṣīloñ ko mazbūṭ kar lo
har ik burj-o-bār-o-par apne nigah-bāñ chaṛhā do,
gharoñ meñ havā ke sivā,
sab ṣadā'oñ kī sham'eñ bujhā do!
kih bāhar faṣīloñ ke nīche
ka'ī din se rah-zan haiñ khīmah-figan,
tel ke būṛhe saudāgaroñ ke labāde pahan-kar,
vuh kal rāt yā āj kī rāt kī tīragī meñ,
chale ā'eñge ban-ke mĕhmāñ
tumhāre gharoñ meñ,
vuh da'vat kī shab jām-o-mīnā luñḍhā'eñge
nācheñge, gā'eñge,
be-sākhtah qahqahoñ hamhamoñ se
vuh garmā'eñge khūn-e maḥfil!

magar pau phuṭegī
to palkoñ se kho doge khvud apne murdoñ kī qabreñ
bisāṭ-e ẓiyāfat kī khākistar-e sokhtah ke kināre
bahā'oge āñsū!

bahā'e haiñ ham ne bhī āñsū!
——go ab khāl-e hindū kī arzish nahīñ hai
'iẕār-e jahāñ par vuh ristā hu'ā gahrā nāsūr
afrang kī āz-e khūñ-khvār se ban chukā hai——
bahā'e haiñ ham ne bhī āñsū,
hamārī nigāhoñ ne dekhe haiñ

Bukhara and Samarqand are intoxicated in their slumber,
covered in blue veils of silence,
their doors closed to travelers
like the eyelids of sleeping moon-faced women,
two moon-faced women
crippled by the whips of Russian "pantheism"!

Forget about Bukhara and Samarqand
Worry now for your shining cities,
the roofs, doors, and terraces of Tehran and Mashhad,
the pleasant fountains of your new age of sense and action,
these beautiful metaphors of your new hopes,
protect them!

Strengthen the low walls
of these tall, shining cities
Post your sentries on every tower and gate
Extinguish the lanterns of all sounds
except for the wind in your homes!
For outside, beneath the walls
some days ago robbers, dressed up as old oil-merchants,
pitched their tents
In the darkness, tonight or tomorrow
they will come as guests
into your homes
They will spill their drinks at the night's banquet
They will dance, they will sing
With unfeigned laughter and merriment,
they will warm the blood of the gathering!

But when dawn breaks,
you will dig the graves of your dead with your own eyelashes
At the ashes of the banquet's spread,
you will shed tears!

We too have shed tears!
—though now the Hindu mole has no value
that deep, oozing boil on the cheek of the world
that arose from the West's bloodthirsty desire—
We too have shed tears
Our eyes have seen

saiyāl sāyoñ ke mānind ghulte hu'e shahr
girte hu'e bām-o-dar
aur mīnār-o-gumbad,
magar vaqt meḥrāb hai
aur dushman ab us kī ḳhamīdah kamar se guẓartā hu'ā
us ke nichle ufaq par laṛhaktā chalā jā rahā hai!
hamāre barahnah-o-kāhīdah jismoñ ne
vuh qaid-o-band aur vuh tāziyāne sahe haiñ
kih un se hamārā sitam-gar
ḳhvud apne alā'o meñ jalne lagā hai!

mire hāth meñ hāth de do!
mire hāth meñ hāth de do!
kih dekhī haiñ maiñ ne
himālah-o-alvand kī choṭiyoñ par anā kī shu'ā'eñ,
uñhīñ se vuh ḳhvurshīd phūṭegā āḳhir
buḳhārā samarqand bhī sāl-hā-sāl se
jis kī ḥasrat ke daryūzah-gar haiñ!

§13. MANN-O-SALVÂ

"ḳhudā-e bar-tar,
yih dāriyūsh-e buzurg kī sar-zamīñ,
yih naushīrvān-e 'ādil kī dād-gāheñ,
taṣavvuf-o-ḥikmat-o-adab ke nigār-ḳhāne,
yih kyoñ siyah-post dushmanoñ ke vujūd se
āj phir ubalte hu'e se nāsūr ban rahe haiñ?"

"ham is ke mujrim nahīñ haiñ, jān-e 'ajam nahīñ haiñ
vuh pahlā angrez
jis ne hindūstāñ ke sāḥil pah
lā-ke rakkhī thī jins-e saudāgarī
yih us kā gunāh hai
jo tire vaṭan kī
zamīn-e gul-posh ko
ham apne siyāh qadmoñ se rauñdte haiñ!

yih shahr apnā vaṭan nahīñ hai,
magar farangī kī rah-zanī ne
usī se nā-chār ham ko vā-bastah kar diyā hai,
ham us kī tahẕīb kī bulandī kī chhipkalī ban-ke rah ga'e haiñ!

cities dissolving like flowing shadows,
falling roofs and doors
and minarets and domes
But time is an arch
and the enemy, now passing over its zenith,
is rolling down its lower horizon!
Our naked and emaciated bodies
have endured those prisons, chains, and whips
that through them our tyrant
has started to burn in his own fire!

Put your hand in mine!
Put your hand in mine!
For I have seen
rays of the light of "I am" on the peaks of Alwand and the Himalayas
from there, that sun will finally rise
for which
Bukhara and Samarqand have longingly begged for years!

§13. MANNA AND QUAILS

"God on high,
this land of Darius the Great,
these courts of Naushirvan the Just,
these galleries of Sufism, wisdom, and literature,
why today, in the presence of dark-skinned enemies,
are they again becoming a festering sore?"

We are not guilty of this crime, beloved Persia, we are not
That first Englishman
who brought his wares
to the shore of India
It is his fault
that we are trampling
the rose-covered soil
of your homeland with our dark feet!

This city is not our home,
but the highway-robbery of the European
has bound us to it perforce
We have become the house-lizards in the heights of his civilization!

vuh rāh-zan jo yih sochtā hai:
"kih eshiyā hai koʾī ʿaqīm-o-amīr bīvah
jo apnī daulat kī be-panāhī se mubtalā ik fashār meñ hai,
aur us kā āġhosh-e ārzū-mand vā mire intiz̤ār meñ hai,
aur eshiyāʾī,
qadīm ḳhvājah-sarāʾoñ kī ik nazhād-e kāhil,
ajal kī rāhoñ pah tez-gāmī se jā rahe haiñ"——

magar yih hindī
gurisnah-o-pā-barahnah hindī
jo sālik-e rāh haiñ
magar rāh-o-rasm-e manzil se be-ḳhabar haiñ
gharoñ ko vīrān kar-ke,
lākhoñ ṣuʿūbatoñ sah-ke
aur apnā lahū bahā-kar
agar kabhī sochte haiñ kuchh to yihī,
—kih shāyad uñhī ke bāzū
najāt dilvā sakeñge mashriq ko
ġhair ke be-panāh biphre huʾe sitam se—
yih sochte haiñ:
—yih ḥādis̤ah hī kih jis ne pheñkā hai
lā-ke un ko tire vat̤an meñ
vuh āñch ban jāʾe,
jis se phuñk jāʾe,
vuh jarās̤īm kā akhāṛā,
jahāñ se har bār jang kī bū-e tund uṭhtī hai
aur dunyā meñ phailtī hai!—

maiñ jāntā hūñ
mire bahut se rafīq
apnī udās, be-kār zindagī ke
dirāz-o-tārīk fāṣiloñ meñ
kabhī kabhī bheṛiyoñ ke mānind
ā nikalte haiñ, rah-guzāroñ pah
justajū meñ kisī ke do "sāq-e ṣandalīñ" kī!
kabhī darīchoñ kī oṭ meñ
nā-tavāñ patangoñ kī phaṛphaṛāhaṭ pah
hosh se be-niyāz ho-kar vuh ṭūṭte haiñ;
vuh dast-e sāʾil
jo sāmne un ke phailtā hai
is ārzū meñ

That highway-robber thinks:
"Asia is a barren and rich widow
being pressured for her unprotected wealth
Her arms open in longing await me
And the Asians,
a languid race of ancient eunuchs,
travel with haste on the roads of death"——

But these Indians,
these hungry and barefoot Indians,
who are travelers on the Path
but unaware of the ways and customs of the destination
Destroying homes,
enduring thousands of hardships,
and shedding their own blood,
they think, if they think at all,
—perhaps these arms
will bring liberation to the East
from the inescapable and uncontrolled cruelty of the outsider—
They think
—this event which took them
and flung them into your homeland,
it could become a flame
that could flare up
the germ-ridden arena
from which the stench of war rises every time
and spreads throughout the world!—

I know that
many of my companions,
in the long and dark distances
of their sad and worthless lives
sometimes emerge on the roads
like wolves
in search of two "sandalwood flanks"!
Sometimes seeing the fluttering of helpless moths
in the window screens
they lose their senses and break down;
the beggar's hand
that opens in front of them
longing that

kih un kī baḳhshish se
pārah-e nān, mann-o-salvâ kā rūp bhar le,
vuhī kabhī apnī nāzukī se
vuh rah sujhātā hai
jis kī manzil pah shauq kī tishnagī nahīñ hai!

tū in manāẓir ko dekhtī hai!
tū sochtī hai:
——yih sang-dil, apnī buz-dilī se
farangiyoñ kī muḥabbat-e nā-ravā kī zanjīr meñ bañdhe haiñ
uñhī ke dam se yih shahr ubaltā huʾā sā nāsūr ban rahā hai——!

muḥabbat-e nā-ravā nahīñ hai
bas ek zanjīr,
ek hī āhanī kamand-e ʿaẓīm
phailī huʾī hai,
mashriq ke ik kināre se dūsre tak,
mire vaṭan se tire vaṭan tak,
bas ek hī ʿankabūt kā jāl hai kih jis meñ
ham eshiyāʾī asīr ho-kar taṛap rahe haiñ!
muġhūl kī ṣubḥ-e ḳhūñ-fishāñ se
farang kī shām-e jāñ-sitāñ tak!
taṛap rahe haiñ
bas ek hī dard-e lā-davā meñ,
aur apne ālām-e jāñ-guzā ke
is ishtirāk-e girāñ-bahā ne bhī
ham ko ik dūsre se ab tak
qarīb hone nahīñ diyā hai!

§14. TAMĀSHĀ-GAH-E LĀLAH-ZĀR

tamāshā-gah-e lālah-zār,
    "tiyātar" pah merī nigāheñ jamī thīñ
    mire kān "mūzīk" ke zer-o-bam par lage the,
    magar merā dil phir bhī kartā rahā thā
    ʿarab aur ʿajam ke ġhamoñ kā shumār
        tamāshā-gah-e lālah-zār!

tamāshā-gah-e lālah-zār,
    ab īrāñ kahāñ hai?
    yih ʿishqī kā shahkār—"Īrān kī rustaḳhez!"

their gift
of a chunk of bread would transform into manna and quails,
and through its tenderness
would someday show the way
to a place without the thirst of longing!

You see these spectacles!
You think:
—These cold-hearted people, through their own cowardice,
are bound in a chain of indecent love for the Europeans;
because of them, this city is becoming a festering sore . . . !

This is not indecent love
but just a chain,
one great iron noose
which spreads
from one end of the East to the other,
from my homeland to yours
There is just one spider's web in which
we Asians are bound and writhing!
From the blood-scattering morning of the Mongols
to the fatal evening of the Europeans!
We are writhing
in one single pain without cure,
and even this prized partnership
of shared, soul-destroying afflictions
has not yet let us
come close to one another!

§14. THE TULIP FIELD THEATER

The Tulip Field Theater
    my eyes were fixed on the "théâtre"
    my ears were set on the treble and bass of "musique"
    but my heart kept on
    counting the pains of Arabia and Persia
        the theater of the tulip field!

The Tulip Field Theater,
    where is Iran now?
    this masterpiece of 'Ishqi—"Iran's Resurrection!"

ab īrāñ hai ik nauḥah-gar pīr-zāl
hai muddat se afsurdah jis kā jamāl,
madā'in kī vīrāniyoñ par 'ajam ashk-rez,
vuh naushīrvāñ aur zardusht aur dāriyūsh,
vuh farhād-o-shīrīñ, vuh kai-ḳhusrav-o-kai-qubād
"ham ik dāstāñ haiñ vuh kirdār the dāstāñ ke!
ham ik kārvāñ haiñ vuh sālār the kārvāñ ke!"
tah-e ḳhāk jin ke mazār
tamāshā-gah-e lālah-zār!

tamāshā-gah-e lālah-zār,
magar nauḥah-ḳhvānī kī yih sar-girānī kahāñ tak?
kih manzil hai dushvār ġham se ġham-e jāvidāñ tak!
vuh sab the kushādah-dil-o-hosh-mand-o-parastār-e rabb-e karīm
vuh sab ḳhair ke rāh-dāñ, rah-shinās
hameñ āj mŏḥsin-kush-o-nā-sipās!
vuh shāhanshahān-e 'aẓīm
vuh pindār-e raftah kā jāh-o-jalāl-e qadīm
hamārī hazīmat ke sab be-bahā tār-o-pū the,
fanā un kī taqdīr, ham un kī taqdīr ke nauḥah-gar haiñ
usī kī tamannā meñ phir sog-vār
tamāshā-gah-e lālah-zār!

tamāshā-gah-e lālah-zār,
'arūs-e javāñ-sāl-e fardā, ḥijāboñ meñ mastūr
gurisnah-nigah, zūd-kāroñ se ranjūr
magar ab hamāre na'e ḳhvāb kābūs-e māẓī nahīñ haiñ,
hamāre na'e ḳhvāb haiñ, ādam-e nau ke ḳhvāb
jahān-e tag-o-dau ke ḳhvāb!
jahān-e tag-o-dau, madā'in nahīñ,
kāḳh-e faġhfūr-o-kusrâ nahīñ
yih us ādam-e nau kā māvâ nahīñ
na'ī bastiyāñ aur na'e shahryār
tamāshā-gah-e lālah-zār!

§15. NAMRŪD KĪ ḲHUDĀ'Ī

yih qudsiyoñ kī zamīñ
jahāñ falsafī ne dekhā thā, apne ḳhvāb-e saḥar-gahī meñ,

Now Iran is an old woman in mourning
whose beauty faded years ago
Persia weeps on the ruins of Ctesiphon,
that Naushirvan and Zarathustra and Darius,
that Farhad and Shirin, that Kai Khusrau and Kai Qubad
"We are a legend; they were a legend's characters!
We are a caravan; they were a caravan's chiefs!"
whose tombs are beneath the dust
the theater of the tulip field!

The Tulip Field Theater,
how long will the melancholy of singing laments last?
for the journey from grief to eternal grief is arduous!
They were all openhearted, wise worshipers of a kind god
They all knew the road of virtue
Today we are ungrateful and unthankful!
Those great emperors,
the ancient rank and grandeur of that past pride,
they were the priceless warp and weft of our defeat
Annihilation was their fate; we are the mourners of their fate,
afflicted with that same desire
the theater of the tulip field!

The Tulip Field Theater,
the young bride of tomorrow, concealed in veils
upset with hungry-eyed and hasty men,
but now our dreams are not the nightmare of the past,
our new dreams are dreams of a new Adam,
dreams of a world of striving!
A world of striving, not Ctesiphon,
not the palaces of Faghfur and Khusrau
These are not the abode of that new Adam
new habitations and new kings
the theater of the tulip field!

§15. THE LORDSHIP OF NIMROD

This land of the holy,
where in his early morning sleep the philosopher saw

havā-e tāzah-o-kisht-e shādāb-o-chashmah-e jāñ-firoz kī ārzū kā partav!
yihīñ musāfir pahuñch ke ab sochne lagā hai:
"vuh ḳhvāb kābūs to nahīñ thā?
—vuh ḳhvāb kābūs to nahīñ thā?"

ai falsafah-go,
kahāñ vuh royā-e āsmānī?
kahāñ yih namrūd kī ḳhudāʾī!
tū jāl buntā rahā hai, jin ke shikastah tāroñ se apne mauhūm falsafe ke
ham us yaqīñ se, ham us ʿamal se, ham us muḥabbat se,
āj māyūs ho chuke haiñ!

koʾī yih kis se kahe kih āḳhir
gavāh kis ʿadl-e be-bahā ke the ʿahd-e tātār ke ḳharābe?
ʿajam, vuh marz-e t̤ilism-o-rang-o-ḳhayāl-o-naġhmah
ʿarab, vuh iqlīm-e shīr-o-shahd-o-sharāb-o-ḳhurmā
faqat̤ navā-sanj the dar-o-bām ke ziyāñ ke
jo un pah guzrī thī
us se bad-tar dinoñ ke ham ṣaid-e nā-tavāñ haiñ!

koʾī yih kis se kahe:
dar-o-bām,
āhan-o-chob-o-sang-o-sīmāñ ke
ḥusn-e paivand kā fusūñ the
bikhar gayā vuh fusūñ to kyā ġham?
aur aise paivand se umīd-e vafā kise thī?

shikast-e mīnā-o-jām bar-ḥaq,
shikast-e rang-e ʿiżār-e maḥbūb bhī gavārā
magar—yahāñ to khañḍar diloñ ke,
(—yih nauʿ-e insāñ kī
kah-kashāñ se buland-o-bar-tar t̤alab ke ujṛe huʾe madāʾin—)
shikast-e āhang-e ḥarf-o-maʿnī ke nauḥah-gar haiñ!

maiñ āne-vāle dinoñ kī dahshat se kāñptā hūñ
mirī nigāheñ yih dekhtī haiñ
kih ḥarf-o-maʿnī ke rabt̤ kā
ḳhvāb-e lażżat-āgīñ bikhar chukā hai,
kih rāste nīm-hoshmandoñ se,
nīñd meñ rāh-po gadāʾoñ se
"ṣūfiyoñ" se bhare paṛe haiñ

a ray of longing for a fresh wind, a lush field, a soul-quenching stream!
Arriving here a traveler has begun to wonder:
"Was that dream a nightmare?
—Was that dream a nightmare?"

O philosopher,
where is that heavenly vision?
And in its place this lordship of Nimrod!
With broken strings you've woven the nets of your illusory philosophy
Today, we have lost hope
in that certainty, in that action, in that love!

To whom should we say this: that in the end
the ruins of the age of the Tartars were witness to priceless justice?
Persia, the land of magic and color and thought and song
Arabia, the clime of milk and honey and drink and dates
only sang of the destruction of homes,
those days that passed on them—
we are the helpless prey of worse days!

To whom should we say this:
that houses,
of iron, wood, stone, and silver
had the magical beauty of connection
If their spell was broken then what grief?
And who hoped for fidelity in such a connection?

That the cup and goblet will break is inevitable,
that the color of the beloved's cheek will fade is also acceptable
but here, the hearts' ruins
(—these ruined cities of mankind's search,
taller and greater than the galaxy—)
lament the broken harmony of word and meaning!

I tremble with fear for the days to come
My eyes see
that the pleasant dream
of the connection of word and meaning has shattered
for the roads are filled with halfwits
with sleepwalking beggars
with "Sufis"

ḥayāt ḳhālī hai ārzū se
hamārī tahżīb, kuhnah bīmār jāñ ba-lab hai!

§16. VUH ḤARF-E TANHĀ (JISE TAMANNĀ-E VAṢL-E MAʿNĀ)

hamāre aʿẓā jo āsmāñ kī t̤araf duʿā ke liye uṭhe haiñ,
(tum āsmāñ kī t̤araf nah dekho!)
maqām-e nāzuk pah ẓarb-e kārī se jāñ bachāne kā hai vasīlah
kih apnī maḥrūmiyoñ se chhupne kā ek ḥīlah?
buzurg-o-bar-tar ḳhudā kabhī to (bihisht bar-ḥaq,)
hameñ ḳhudā se najāt degā
kih ham haiñ is sar-zamīñ pah jaise vuh ḥarf-e tanhā,
(magar vuh aisā jahāñ nah hogā) ḳhamosh-o-goyā,
jo ārzū-e viṣāl-e maʿnī meñ jī rahā ho
jo ḥarf-o-maʿnī kī yak-dilī ko taras gayā ho!

hameñ maʿarrī ke ḳhvāb de do
(kih sab ko baḳhsheñ ba-qadr-e żauq-e nigah tabassum)
hameñ maʿarrī kī rūḥ kā iẓt̤irāb de do
(jahāñ gunāhoñ ke ḥauṣle se mile taqaddus ke dukh kā marʾham)
kih us kī be-nūr-o-tār āñkheñ
dirūn-e ādam kī tīrah rātoñ
ko chhedtī thīñ
usī jahāñ meñ firāq-e jāñ-kāh-e ḥarf-o-maʿnī
ko dekhtī thīñ
bihisht us ke liye vuh maʿṣūm sādah lauḥoñ kī ʿāfiyat thā
jahāñ vuh nange badan pah jābir ke tāziyānoñ se bach-ke
rāh-e farār pāʾeñ
vuh kafsh-e pā thā, kih jis se ġhurbat kī reg-e hazyāñ

se roz-e furṣat qarār pāʾeñ
kih ṣulb-e ādam kī, rĕḥm-e ḥavvā kī ʿuzlatoñ meñ
nihāyat-e intiẓār pāʾeñ!

(bihisht ṣifr-e ʿaẓīm, lekin hameñ vuh gum-gashtah handase haiñ
baġhair jin ke koʾī masāvāt kyā banegī
viṣāl-e maʿnī se ḥarf kī bāt kyā banegī?)
ham is zamīñ par azal se pīrānah sar haiñ, mānā
magar abhī tak haiñ dil tavānā

Life is void of striving
Our civilization is ancient, sick, on its last breath!

§16. THAT LONELY WORD (WHICH LONGS TO UNITE WITH MEANING)

Our arms are lifted to the sky in prayer—
(Don't look at the sky!)
Is this a means to escape a fatal blow to a tender spot
or a deception to hide from us our deprivations?
Great and high God (Paradise is a certainty) will sometime
deliver us from god
for we on this earth are like that lonely word,
(but it won't be such a world) silent as well as articulate,
which lives in longing for union with meaning,
which has craved the concord of word and meaning!

Give us the dreams of Maʿarrī
(give each a smile according to his taste)
Give us the agitation of Maʿarrī's soul
(where through courageous sins we find the salve for sacred pain)
for his lightless and dark eyes
    pierced the dark nights
        of man's inner being
In that world they saw
            the heart-breaking separation of word and meaning
Paradise for him was the retreat of the innocent and simple
in which, saved from tyrant's whips on naked bodies,
                they would find a road to flee away
it was the sandals by which respite from the roasting sand of
  estrangement
            could be had for a day
there in the seclusion of the loins of Adam and the womb of Eve
                they would reach the end of waiting!

(Paradise is a great zero, but we are those lost numbers
without which no equation can be made
without union with meaning what will a word become?)
True, we on this earth have been old and aged from the beginning,
but even now our heart is strong

aur apnī zhūlīdah kāriyoṅ ke ṭufail dānā
hameṅ ma'arrī ke ḳhvāb de do
(bihisht meṅ bhī nashāṭ, yak-rang ho to, ġham hai
ho ek sā jām-e shahd sab ke liye to sam hai)
kih ham abhī tak haiṅ is jahāṅ meṅ vuh ḥarf-e tanhā
(bihisht rakh lo, hameṅ ḳhvud apnā javāb de do!)
jise tamannā-e vaṣl-e ma'nā . . .

§17. ZINDAGĪ SE ḌARTE HO?

——zindagī se ḍarte ho?
zindagī to tum bhī ho, zindagī to ham bhī haiṅ!
ādmī se ḍarte ho?
ādmī to tum bhī ho, ādmī to ham bhī haiṅ!
ādmī zabāṅ bhī hai, ādmī bayāṅ bhī hai,
is se tum nahīṅ ḍarte!
ḥarf aur ma'nī ke ristah-hā-e āhan se, ādmī hai vā-bastah
ādmī ke dāman se zindagī hai vā-bastah
is se tum nahīṅ ḍarte!
"an-kahī" se ḍarte ho
jo abhī nahīṅ ā'ī, us ghaṛī se ḍarte ho
us ghaṛī kī āmad kī āgahī se ḍarte ho!

——pahle bhī to guzre haiṅ,
daur nā-rasā'ī ke, "be-riyā" ḳhudā'ī ke
phir bhī yih samajhte ho, hech ārzū-mandī
yih shab-e zabāṅ-bandī, hai rah-e ḳhudāvandī!
tum magar yih kyā jāno,
lab agar nahīṅ hilte, hāth jāg uṭhte haiṅ
hāth jāg uṭhte haiṅ, rāh kā nishāṅ ban-kar
nūr kī zabāṅ ban-kar
hāth bol uṭhte haiṅ, ṣubḥ kī aẕāṅ ban-kar
roshnī se ḍarte ho?
roshnī to tum bhī ho, roshnī to ham bhī haiṅ,
roshnī se ḍarte ho!

——shahr kī faṣīloṅ par
dev kā jo sāyah thā pāk ho gayā āḳhir
rāt kā labādah bhī
chāk ho gayā āḳhir, ḳhāk ho gayā āḳhir

and is wise, through our twisted works
Give us the dreams of Maʿarrī
(If in paradise the pleasure is just uniform, then that is suffering
If there is the same cup of honey for everyone then it is poison)
For even now in this world we are that lonely word
(Keep your paradise, give us our answer!)
which longs for union with meaning . . .

§17. ARE YOU AFRAID OF LIFE?

—Are you afraid of life?
You too are life, we too are life!
Are you afraid of man?
You too are man, we too are man!
Man is language, man is expression,
You are not afraid of this!
Man is bound to the iron bond of word and meaning
Life is bound to the garment of man
You are not afraid of this!
Are you afraid of the "unsaid"?
Are you afraid of the moment that has not arrived
Are you even afraid of knowing when that moment has come!

—Periods of failure, of "guileless" domination
have passed before
Yet still you believe, desire is nothing,
and this night of bound tongues is the road to power!
But what do you know about it
If lips do not move, hands rise up
Hands rise up and become a sign of the path
become a tongue of light
Hands cry out, becoming the morning call to prayer
Are you afraid of light?
You too are light, we too are light
Are you even afraid of light!

—From the ramparts of the city
the demon's shadow has finally been removed
The cloak of night
has finally been torn, has finally turned to dust

izhdihām-e insāñ se fard kī navā ā'ī
żāt kī ṣadā ā'ī
rāh-e shauq meñ jaise rāh-rau kā ḳhūñ lapke
ik nayā junūñ lapke!
ādmī chalak uṭṭhe
ādmī hañse dekho, shahr phir base dekho
tum abhī se ḍarte ho?
hāñ, abhī to tum bhī ho, hāñ, abhī to ham bhī haiñ,
tum abhī se ḍarte ho!

§18. DIL, MIRE ṢAḤRĀ-NAVARD-E PĪR DIL

naġhmah dar jāñ, raqṣ bar pā, ḳhandah bar lab
dil, tamannā'oñ ke be-pāyāñ alā'o ke qarīb!

dil, mire ṣaḥrā-navard-e pīr dil
reg ke dil-shād shahrī, reg tū
aur reg hī terī ṭalab
reg kī nak'hat tirī paikar meñ, terī jāñ meñ hai!

reg ṣubḥ-e 'īd ke mānind zar-tāb-o-jalīl,
reg ṣadyoñ kā jamāl,
jashn-e ādam par bichhaṛ-kar milne-vāloñ kā viṣāl,
shauq ke lamḥāt ke mānind āzād-o-'aẓīm!

reg naġhmah-zan
kih żarre reg-zāroñ kī vuh pā-zeb-e qadīm
jis pah paṛ saktā nahīñ dast-e la'īm,
reg-e ṣaḥrā zar-garī kī reg kī lahroñ se dūr
chashmah-e makr-o-riyā shahroñ se dūr!

reg shab be-dār hai, suntī hai har jābir kī chāp
reg shab be-dār hai, nigrāñ hai mānind-e naqīb
dekhtī hai sāyah-e āmir kī chāp
reg har 'ayyār, ġhārat-gar kī maut
reg istibdād ke ṭuġhyāñ ke shor-o-shar kī maut
reg jab uṭhtī hai, uṛ jātī hai har fātiḥ kī nīñd
reg ke nezoñ se zaḳhmī, sab shahanshāhoñ ke ḳhvāb!

(reg, ai ṣaḥrā kī reg
mujh ko apnī jāgte żarroñ ke ḳhvāboñ kī
na'ī ta'bīr de!)

From the throng of mankind the voice of the individual has come
The sound of the self has come
as if the blood of the traveler on the road of desire quickens,
kindling a new madness!
An overflow of men
Look at men laughing, look at the city inhabited once more
Are you afraid of now?
Yes, you too are now, we too are now
Are you even afraid of now!

§18. HEART, MY OLD DESERT-WANDERING HEART

A song in its soul, a dance in its feet, a smile on its lips
my heart, near the endless bonfire of desires!

Heart, my old desert-wandering heart
sand's joyous citizen, sand you are,
      and sand alone is that which you seek
The fragrance of sand is in your body, in your soul!

Sand, golden and glorious like the morning of a festival
Sand, the beauty of centuries
the union of those separated at the birth of Adam,
like moments of passion, free and great!

Sand strikes a tune
as its grains are those ancient anklets
that the hand of the vile cannot grasp
Sand of the desert is far away from the sand-waves of the goldsmith,
far away from the fountain of deceit and dissimulation, from cities!

Sand keeps awake at night; it hears the footsteps of every tyrant
Sand keeps awake at night; it keeps watch like a herald
It sees the footsteps of the dictator's shadow
Sand, the death of every agent, of every plunderer
Sand, the death of the tumult of despotism's transgression
When sand arises, the sleep of every conqueror flees
The dreams of all emperors are wounded by the spears of sand!

(Sand, O desert sand,
grant me a new interpretation
            of the dreams of your grains!)

reg ke żarro, ubhartī ṣubḥ tum,
ā'o ṣaḥrā kī ḥadoñ tak ā gayā roz-e ṭarab
dil, mire ṣaḥrā-navard-e pīr dil,
ā chūm reg!
hai ḳhayāloñ ke parī-zādoñ se bhī ma'ṣūm reg!

reg raqṣāñ, māh-o-sāl-e nūr tak raqṣāñ rahe
us kā abresham malā'im, narm-ḳhū, ḳhandāñ rahe!

dil, mire ṣaḥrā-navard-e pīr dil
yih tamannā'oñ kā be-pāyāñ alā'o
rāh-gum-kardoñ kī mash'al, us ke lab par "ā'o! ā'o!"

tere māẓī ke ḳhazif rezoñ se jāgī hai yih āg
āg kī qirmiz zabāñ par imbisāṭ-e nau ke rāg
dil, mire ṣaḥrā-navard-e pīr dil,
sar-garānī kī shab-e raftah se jāg!
kuchh sharar āġhosh-e ṣarṣar meñ haiñ gum,
aur kuchh zīnah bah zīnah shǒ'loñ ke mīnār par chaṛhte hu'e
aur kuchh tah meñ alā'o kī abhī,
muẓṭarib, lekin mużabżab ṭifl-e kam-sin kī ṭaraḥ!
āg zīnah, āg rangoñ kā ḳhazīnah
āg un lażżāt kā sar-chashmah hai
jis se letā hai ġhazā 'ushshāq ke dil kā tapāk!
chob-e ḳhushk angor, us kī mai hai āg
sarsarātī hai ragoñ meñ 'īd ke din kī ṭaraḥ!

āg kāhin, yād se utrī hu'ī ṣadyoñ kī yih afsānah-ḳhvāñ
āne-vāle qarn-hā kī dāstāneñ lab pah haiñ
dil, mirā ṣaḥrā-navard-e pīr dil sun-kar javāñ!

āg āzādī kā, dil-shādī kā nām
āg paidā'ish kā, afzā'ish kā nām
āg ke phūloñ meñ nasrīñ, yāsmin, sumbul, shaqīq-o-nastaran

āg ārā'ish kā, zebā'ish kā nām
āg vuh taqdīs, dhul jāte haiñ jis se sab gunāh
āg insānoñ kī pahlī sāñs ke mānind ik aisā karam
'umr kā ik ṭūl bhī jis kā nahīñ kāfī javāb!

yih tamannā'oñ kā be-pāyāñ alā'o gar nah ho
is laq-o-daq meñ nikal ā'eñ kahīñ se bheṛiye
is alā'o ko sadā roshan rakho!

Grains of sand, you are the rising dawn
Come, the day of joy has reached the desert's edge
Heart, my old desert-wandering heart,
Come and kiss the sand!
Sand is even more innocent than the fairies of imagination!

May sand keep dancing, for months and years of light may it dance
May its raw silk remain soft, soft-natured, and laughing!

Heart, my old desert-wandering heart
this endless bonfire of desires
this torch for those who have lost their way, on its lips, "Come! Come!"
this fire is awakened by the broken fragments of your past
On the crimson tongue of fire is a song of new joy
Heart, my old desert-wandering heart,
wake up from the dizziness of last night!
Some sparks are lost in the embrace of the wind
Some are advancing rung by rung up the minaret of flames
Some, right now, are in the depths of the bonfire
agitated, but hesitating like a young child!
Fire, a ladder; fire, a treasure-trove of colors
Fire, a fountain of desires
that feed the ardor of lovers' hearts!
A vine of withered grapes, its wine is fire
creeping in its veins like the day of festival!

Fire is a soothsayer, the storyteller of centuries fallen from memory
On its lips are tales of centuries to come
Hearing it, my heart, my old desert-wandering heart, is made young!

Fire is the name of freedom, of delight
Fire is the name of birth, of growth
Among its flowers are the dog rose, jasmine, hyacinth, the poppy, and the white rose
Fire is the name of adornment, of beauty
Fire is that purity by which all sins are washed away
Fire, like the first breath of man, is a gift
for which the expanse of one life is not enough of an answer!

If there were not this endless bonfire of desires,
wolves, from somewhere, would enter this desert
Keep this fire burning always!

(reg-e ṣaḥrā ko bashārat ho kih zindah hai alāʾo,
bheṛiyoñ kī chāp tak ātī nahīñ!)

āg se ṣaḥrā kā rishtah hai qadīm
āg se ṣaḥrā ke ṭeṛhe, reñgne-vāle,
girah-ālūd, zhūlīdah daraḳht
jāgte haiñ naġhmah dar jāñ, raqṣ bar-pā, ḳhandah bar-lab
aur manā lete haiñ tanhāʾī meñ jashn-e māhtāb
un kī shāḳheñ ġhair marʾī ṭabl kī āvāz par detī haiñ tāl
beḳh-o-bun se āne lagtī hai ḳhudāvandī jalājil kī ṣadā!

āg se ṣaḥrā kā rishtah hai qadīm
rah-rauʾoñ, ṣaḥrā-navardoñ ke liʾe hai rah-numā
kārvānoñ kā sahārā bhī hai āg
aur ṣaḥrāʾoñ kī tanhāʾī ko ham kartī hai āg!

āg ke chāroñ ṭaraf pashmīnah-o-dastār meñ lipṭe huʾe
afsānah-go
jaise gird-e chasm mizhgāñ kā hujūm;
un ke ḥairat-nāk, dil-kash tajriboñ se
jab damak uṭhtī hai ret,
żarrah żarrah bajne lagtā hai misāl-e sāz-e jāñ
gosh bar āvāz rahte haiñ daraḳht
aur hañs dete haiñ apnī ʿārifānah be-niyāzī se kabhī!

yih tamannāʾoñ kā be-pāyāñ alāʾo gar nah ho
reg apnī ḳhalvat-e be-nūr-o-ḳhvud-bīñ meñ rahe
apnī yaktāʾī kī taḥsīñ meñ rahe
is alāʾo ko sadā roshan rakho!

yih tamannāʾoñ kā be-pāyāñ alāʾo gar nah ho
eshiyā, afrīqah pahnāʾī kā nām
(be-kār pahnāʾī kā nām)
yūrop aur amrīkah dārāʾī kā nām
(takrār-e dārāʾī kā nām!)

merā dil, ṣaḥrā navard-e pīr dil
jāg uṭhā hai, mashriq-o-maġhrib kī aisī yak-dilī
ke kārvānoñ kā nayā royā liʾe:
yak-dilī aisī kih hogī fahm-e insāñ se varāʾ
yak-dilī aisī kih ham sab kah uṭheñ
"is qadar ʿujlat nah kar
izhdihām-e gul nah ban!"
kah uṭheñ ham:

(Glad tidings to the desert sand, for the bonfire is alive,
the footfall of the wolves does not come near!)

The desert's bond with fire is ancient
Through fire, the desert's crooked, crawling,
knotted, twisted trees
awaken, a song in their soul, a dance in their feet, a smile on their lips
and, in solitude, celebrate the festival of moonlight
Their branches keep time to the beat of an unseen drum
From their roots and stems comes the sound of divine bells!

The desert's bond with fire is ancient
For travelers, for desert-wanderers it is a guide
Fire is an aid to the caravans, as well,
and lessens the solitude of the desert!

All around the fire, wrapped in wool and turbans
storytellers
like a crowd of lashes around an eye
When, from their astonishing, heart-gripping experiences,
sand glistens,
every grain of sand resounds like the instrument of the soul
The ears of the trees remain fixed on this voice,
and laugh sometimes too at their own mystic indifference!

If there were not this endless bonfire of desires,
sand would remain in its lightless, self-absorbed solitude,
acclaiming its own uniqueness
Keep this fire burning forever!

If there were not this endless bonfire of desires,
Asia and Africa would be the name for an empty space
(the name for useless space)
Europe and America the name for dominance
(the name for reiteration of dominance!)

My heart, my old desert-wandering heart
has awakened, with a new dream of caravans
of a solidarity of the East and West
Such a solidarity that will be beyond the understanding of man
Such a solidarity that we'd all say:
"Do not make such haste
Do not become a throng of roses!"
We'd say:

"tū ġham-e kul to nah thī
ab lażżat-e kul bhī nah ban
roz-e āsāʾish kī be-dardī nah ban
yak-dilī ban, aisā sunnāṭā nah ban,
jis meñ tābistāñ kī do-pahroñ kī
be-ḥāsil kasālat ke sivā kuchh bhī nah ho!"

is "jafā-gar" yak-dilī ke kārvāñ yūñ āʾeñge
dast-e jādū-gar se jaise phūṭ nikle hoñ ṭilism,
ʿishq-e ḥāsil-ḳhez se, yā zor-e paidāʾī se jaise nā-gahāñ
khul gaʾe hoñ mashriq-o-maġhrib ke jism,
——jism, ṣadyoñ ke ʿaqīm!

kārvāñ farḳhundah pai, aur un kā bār
kīsah kīsah taḳht-e jam-o-tāj-e kai
kūzah kūzah fard kī saṭvat kī mai
jāmah jāmah roz-o-shab mĕḥnat kā ḳhai
naġhmah naġhmah ḥurriyat kī garm lai!

sāliko, fīroz-baḳhto, āne-vāle qāfilo
shahr se lauṭoge tum to pāʾoge
ret kī sar-ḥad pah jo rūḥ-e abad ḳhvābīdah thī
jāg uṭhī hai "shikvah-hā-e nai" se vuh
ret kī tah meñ jo sharmīlī saḥar roʾīdah thī
jāg uṭhī hai ḥurriyat kī lai se vuh!

itnī doshīzah thī, itnī mard nā-dīdah thī ṣubḥ
pūchh sakte the nah us kī ʿumr ham!
dard se hañstī nah thī,
żarroñ kī raʿnāʾī pah bhī hañstī nah thī,
ek maḥjūbānah be-ḳhabrī meñ hañs detī thī ṣubḥ!
ab manātī hai vuh ṣaḥrā kā jalāl
jaise ʿazz-o-jal ke pāʾoñ kī yihī mĕḥrāb ho!
zer-e mĕḥrāb ā gaʾī ho us ko be-dārī kī rāt
ḳhvud janāb-e ʿazz-o-jal se jaise ummīd-e zifāf

(sāre nā-kardah gunāh us ke maʿāf!)

ṣubḥ-e ṣaḥrā, shād-bād!
ai ʿarūs-e ʿazz-o-jal, farḳhundah rū, tābindah ḳhū
tū ik aise ḥujrah-e shab se nikal-kar āʾī hai
dast-e qātil ne bahāyā thā jahāñ har sej par
saiñkṛoñ tāroñ kā ruḳhshandah lahū, phūloñ ke pās!

"You were not the pain of all
Now don't became the pleasure of all as well
Do not become the indolence of the day of rest
Become solidarity, do not become a stillness
in which there is nothing but
the fruitless laziness of summer afternoons!"

The caravans of this "oppressive" solidarity will come
like a spell from the hand of a sorcerer,
as if from fruitful love or from the force of creation, suddenly
the bodies of the East and West opened,
—bodies, barren for centuries!

Caravans with happy feet, and their load
in bag after bag, the throne of Jamshed and the crown of Kai
in jug after jug, the wine of the majesty of the individual
in robe after robe, the "bravo!" of hard work done day and night
in song after song, the warm melody of freedom!

Pilgrims, victors, caravans to come
When you return from the city, you will find that,
on the border of sand, the soul of eternity, which was sleeping,
has awakened from the "lament of the reed"
That bashful morning planted in the depths of sand
has awakened by the songs of freedom!

The morning was so virgin, had never been touched by men
We couldn't even ask her age!
She did not laugh from pain,
she didn't even laugh at the colorfulness of the grains of sand,
She used to laugh in a shy, careless manner!
Now she celebrates the glory of the desert
as if it were the very arch of the feet of the Glorious and Majestic!
She spent the night awake under the arch
as if in hope of consummating a marriage with the Glorious and
Majestic himself
(who forgives all her uncommitted sins!)

Morning of the desert, rejoice!
O bride of the Glorious and Majestic, happy, bright-faced
you have come leaving a night chamber
where the executioner let flow the shining blood
of thousands of stars near every flower on the bed!

ṣubḥ-e ṣaḥrā, sar mire zānū pah rakh-kar dāstāñ

un tamannā ke shahīdoñ kī nah kah
un kī nīmah-ras umangoñ, ārzūʾoñ kī nah kah
jin se milne kā koʾī imkāñ nahīñ
shahd terā jin ko nosh-e jāñ nahīñ!
āj bhī kuchh dūr, is ṣaḥrā ke pār
dev kī dīvār ke nīche nasīm
roz-o-shab chaltī hai mubʿham ḳhauf se sahmī huʾī
jis t̤araḥ shahroñ kī rāhoñ par yatīm
naġhmah bar-lab tā kih un kī jāñ kā sunnāṭā ho dūr!

āj bhī is reg ke żarroñ meñ haiñ
aise żarre, āp hī apne ġhanīm
āj bhī is āg ke shoʿloñ meñ haiñ
vuh sharar jo is kī tah meñ par-barīdah rah gaʾe
miśl-e ḥarf-e nā-shunīdah rah gaʾe!
ṣubḥ-e ṣaḥrā, ai ʿarūs-e ʿazz-o-jal
ā kih un kī dāstāñ duhrāʾeñ ham
un kī ʿizzat, un kī ʿaz̤mat gāʾeñ ham

ṣubḥ, ret aur āg, ham sab kā jalāl!
yak-dilī ke kārvāñ un kā jamāl
āʾo!
is tahlīl ke ḥalqe meñ ham mil jāʾeñ
āʾo!
shād-bād apnī tamannāʾoñ kā be-pāyāñ alāʾo!

§19. EK AUR SHAHR

ḳhvud-fahmī kā armāñ hai tārīkī meñ rū-posh,
tārīkī ḳhvud be-chasm-o-gosh!
ik be-pāyāñ ʿujlat rāhoñ kī alvand!

sīnoñ meñ dil yūñ jaise chasm-e āz-e ṣayyād
tāzah ḳhūñ ke pyāse afrangī mardān-e rād
ḳhvud dev-e āhan ke mānind

daryā ke do sāḥil haiñ aur donoñ hī nā-paid
shar hai dast-e siyah aur ḳhair kā ḥāmil rū-e safed!
ik bār-e mizhgāñ, ik lab-ḳhand!

Morning of the desert, do not put your head on my knee and tell the
    story
of those martyrs of desire
Do not tell of their half-risen hopes, their longings
with whom there is no hope of meeting,
to whom your honey was not sweet!
Today still a little farther, across this desert
below the wall of the demon, the breeze
day and night moves trembling from some unknown fear
like orphans on the city streets
who have a song on their lips to keep away the silence in their souls!

Today, still, among the grains of sand there are
grains that are their own enemy
Today still in these flames there are
sparks that remain with clipped wings,
    remain like an unheard word!
Morning of the desert, O bride of the Glorious and Majestic
Come, let's retell their tale
let's sing of their virtue, of their greatness!

Morning, sand and fire, the majesty of us all!
The caravan of solidarity, their beauty
        Come!
Let's meet in this circle of praise
        Come!
Joy to the endless bonfire of our desires!

§19. ANOTHER CITY

The desire for self-understanding hides its face in darkness,
    darkness itself without eyes and ears!
[From] a boundless haste, the roads [become] a high mountain
    [Mt. Alvand]!

The hearts in their chests like the covetous eye of a hunter
thirsty for fresh blood, valiant Western heroes
    just like [their] demons of iron

The river has two shores, and both are unattainable
Evil is a black hand, and the bearer of goodness a white face!
    one weighing down the eyes, one with a smile on its lips!

sab paimāne be-ṣarfah jab sīm-o-zar mīzān
jab żauq-e ʿamal kā sar-chashmah be-maʿnī hiżyān

jab dahshat har lamḥah jāñ-kand!

yih sab ufqī insāñ haiñ, yih in ke samāvī shahr
kyā phir in kī kamīñ meñ vaqt ke t̤ūfāñ kī ik lahr?
kyā sab vīrānī ke dil-band?

§20. REG-E DĪROZ

ham muḥabbat ke ḳharāboñ ke makīñ
vaqt ke t̤ūl-e alam-nāk ke parvardah haiñ
ek tārīk azal, nūr-e abad se ḳhālī!

ham jo ṣadyoñ se chale haiñ to samajhte haiñ kih sāḥil pāyā
apnī tahżīb kī pā-kobī kā ḥāṣil pāyā!

ham muḥabbat ke nihāñ-ḳhānoñ meñ basne-vāle
apnī pā-mālī ke afsānoñ pah hañsne-vāle
ham samajhte haiñ nishān-e sar-e manzil pāyā!

ham muḥabbat ke ḳharāboñ ke makīñ
kunj-e māẓī meñ haiñ bārāñ-zadah t̤āʾir kī t̤araḥ āsūdah,
aur kabhī fitnah-e nā-gāh se ḍar-kar chauñkeñ
to raheñ sadd-e nigah nīñd ke bhārī parde
ham muḥabbat ke ḳharāboñ ke makīñ!
aise tārīk ḳharābe kih jahāñ
dūr se tez palaṭ jāʾeñ ẓiyā ke āhū
ek, bas ek, ṣadā gauñjtī ho
shab-e ālām kī "yā hū! yā hū!"

ham muḥabbat ke ḳharāboñ ke makīñ
reg-e dīroz meñ ḳhvāboñ ke shajar būte rahe
sāyah nā-paid thā, sāye kī tamannā ke tale sote rahe!

§21. ZAMĀNAH ḲHUDĀ HAI

"zamānah ḳhudā hai, ise tum burā mat kaho"
magar tum nahīñ dekhte——zamānah faqat̤ resmān-e ḳhayāl

All measures are useless when silver and gold are the scale
when the fountain of the appreciation of action is meaningless nonsense
when at every moment terror threatens the soul!

These are all horizontal men; these, their high-rising cities
Does a wave of the storm of time lie to ambush them?
Are all the beloved children of destruction?

§20. THE SANDS OF YESTERDAY

We are the residents of the ruins of love
raised by the grievous expanse of Time
a dark Beginning, void of the light of the End!

We, who for centuries have traveled, believe we have reached a shore
obtained the reward of our dance of civilization!

We reside in the hidden chambers of love
We scoff at tales of being trampled under foot
We believe we have found a sign of the destination!

We are the residents of the ruins of love
content like a rain-soaked bird in a corner of the past,
and if ever a sudden tumult should frighten us and we awake
then the heavy curtain of sleep would remain a barrier to our vision
We are the residents of the ruins of love!
Ruins so dark that
deer of light would retreat from afar
One, just one voice would echo
the "O my God! O my God!" of the night of suffering

We are the residents of the ruins of love
We planted trees of dreams in the sands of the past
The shade was non-existent; we slept under the desire for shade!

§21. TIME IS GOD

"Time is God, you should not speak badly of it"
But you do not see—time is only a rope of thought

sabuk-māyah, nāzuk, t̤avīl
judāʾī kī arzāñ sabīl!

vuh ṣubḥeñ jo lākhoñ baras pesh-tar thīñ,
vuh shāmeñ jo lākhoñ baras baʿd hoñgī,
uñheñ tum nahīñ dekhte, dekh sakte nahīñ
kih maujūd haiñ, ab bhī, maujūd haiñ vuh kahīñ,
magar yih nigāhoñ ke āge jo rassī tanī hai
ise dekh sakte ho, aur dekhte ho
kih yih vuh ʿadam hai
jise hast hone meñ muddat lagegī
sitāroñ ke lamḥe, sitāroñ ke sāl!

mire ṣaḥn meñ ek kam-sin banafshe kā paudā hai
t̤ayyārah koʾī kabhī us ke sar par se guẓre
to vuh muskarātā hai aur lahlahātā hai
goyā vuh t̤ayyārah, us kī muḥabbat meñ
ʿahd-e vafā ke kisī jabr-e t̤āqat-rubā hī se guẓrā!

vuh ḳhūsh ĕʿtimādī se kahtā hai:
"lo dekho, kaise isī ek rassī ke donoñ kināroñ
se ham tum bañdhe haiñ!
yih rassī nah ho to kahāñ ham meñ tum meñ
ho paidā yih rāh-e viṣāl?"
magar hijr ke un vasīloñ ko vuh dekh saktā nahīñ
jo sarāsar azal se abad tak tane haiñ!

jahāñ yih zamānah——hanūz-e zamānah
faqat̤ ik girah hai!

§22. AFSĀNAH-E SHAHR

shahr ke shahr kā afsānah, vuh ḳhvush-fahm, magar sādah musāfir
kih jiñheñ ʿishq kī lalkār ke rah-zan ne kahā: "āʾo!
dikhlāʾeñ tumheñ ek dar-e bastah ke asrār kā ḳhvāb—"
shahr ke shahr kā afsānah, vuh dil jin ke bayābāñ meñ
kisī qat̤rah-e gum-gashtah ke nā-gāh larazne kī ṣadā ne yih kahā:
"āʾo dikhlāʾeñ tumheñ ṣubḥ ke honṭoñ pah tabassum kā sarāb!"

shahr ke shahr kā afsānah, vuhī ārzū-e ḳhastah ke lañgṛāte huʾe pair
kih haiñ āj bhī afsāne kī duzdīdah-o-zhūlīdah lakīroñ pah ravāñ

of little value, thin, long
the cheap road of separation!

Those mornings that were millions of years before
those evenings that will be millions of years from now
you do not see them, cannot see them
though they are present, even now, they are present somewhere,
but this rope that is stretched before the eyes
you can see this, and do see this
for this is that non-existence
which in becoming being will take a long while
moments of stars, years of stars!

In my courtyard is a young violet plant
Whenever an airplane passes over its head
it smiles and waves
as if that airplane, in its love
passed by just from the enervating compulsion of its pledge of faithfulness!
It says with full confidence:
"Look how to both ends of this very rope
you and I are bound!
If there was not this rope, then where in us, in you,
would the path to our union by found?"
But it cannot see those causes of separation
that are stretched from end to end, from the beginning to the end of time
where this time—the now of time—
is only a knot!

§22. LEGEND OF THE CITY

The city and its legend, those beguiled but simple travelers
to whom the thief of love's defiant cry said: "Come!
I shall show you in a dream what lies behind the closed door—"
The city and its legend, those hearts in whose desert
the voice of the unexpected trembling of an errant drop said:
"Come, I shall show you the mirage of a smile on the morning's lips!"

The city and its legend, those limping feet of worn-out longing
that still move on the stolen and twisted lines of legend

un asīroñ kī t̤arah jin ke rag-o-reshah kī zanjīr kī jhankār

bhī tham jāʾe to kah uṭṭheñ: "kahāñ?
ab kahāñ jāʾeñge ham?
jāʾeñ ab tāzah-o-nā-dīdah nigāhoñ ke zimistāñ meñ kahāñ?"
un asīroñ kī t̤arah jin ke liye vaqt kī be-ṣarfah salāḳheñ
nah kabhī sard nah garm, aur nah kabhī saḳht nah narm
nah rihāʾī kī paẕīrā, nah asīrī hī kī sharm!

shahr ke shahr kā afsānah, vuh rūḥeñ jo sar-e pul ke sivā
aur kahīñ vaṣl kī joyā hī nahīñ
pul se jinheñ pār utarne kī tamannā hī nahīñ
is kā yārā hī nahīñ!

§23. YIH ḲHALĀ PUR NAH HUʾĀ

żěhn ḳhālī hai
ḳhalā nūr se, yā naġhme se
yā nak'hat-e gum-rāh se bhī
pur nah huʾā
żěhn ḳhālī hī rahā
yih ḳhalā ḥarf-e tasallī se,
tabassum se,
kisī āh se bhī pur nah huʾā
ik nafī larzish-e paiham meñ sahī
jahd-e be-kār ke mātam meñ sahī
ham jo nā-ras bhī haiñ, ġham dīdah bhī haiñ
is ḳhalā ko
(isī děhlīz pah soʾe huʾe
sar-mast gadā ke mānind)
kisī mīnār kī taṣvīr se,
yā rang kī jhankār se
yā ḳhvāboñ kī ḳhvush-būʾoñ se
pur kyoñ nah kareñ?
kih ajal ham se bahut dūr
bahut dūr rahe?
nahīñ, ham jānte haiñ
ham jo nā-ras bhī haiñ, ġham-dīdah bhī haiñ
jānte haiñ kih ḳhalā hai vuh jise maut nahīñ

like those prisoners who, even if the clinking of the chain of their nerves and fibers
stopped, would cry out: "Where?
    Now where should we go?
Where should we go now in the winter of fresh and unseen sights?"
Like those prisoners for whom the valueless bars of time
are never cold or warm, and never hard or soft
They neither welcome their release, nor feel shame at their imprisonment!

The city and its legend, those souls that
seek no other union except the one on the bridge,
    who do not even long to cross the bridge
    nor have the strength for it!

§23. THIS VOID WAS NOT FILLED

The mind is empty,
    an emptiness unfilled
        by light or by song
            or even by lost perfume
The mind is empty still
    an emptiness unfilled
        by a comforting word, by a smile
            or even by a sigh
A nothingness in constant tremor, yes
    in mourning of useless exertion, yes
We who are unfulfilled, who have known sorrow
Why should we not fill
this emptiness
    (like a drunken beggar
        asleep on this doorstep)
with the picture of a minaret
    or with the buzzing of color
        or with the fragrance of dreams?
So that death would remain far away,
    far away from us?
No, we know,
    we who are unfulfilled, who have known sorrow
we know the emptiness is the absence of death

kis liye nūr se, yā naġhme se
yā ḥarf-e tasallī se ise "jism" banā'eñ
aur phir maut kī vā-raftah paẕīrā'ī kareñ?
na'e hañgāmoñ kī tajlīl kā dar bāz kareñ
ṣubḥ-e takmīl kā āġhāz kareñ?

§24. ṬALAB KE TALE

gul-o-yāsmin kal se nā-āshnā,
kal se be-ĕʿtinā
gul-o-yāsmin apne jismoñ kī hai'at meñ fard
magar——kal se nā-āshnā, kal se be-ĕʿtinā
kisī marg-e mabram kā dard
un ke dil meñ nahīñ!

faqaṭ apnī tārīḳh kī be-sar-o-pā ṭalab ke tale
ham dabe haiñ!
ham apne vujūdoñ kī pinhāñ taheñ
kholte tak nahīñ
ārzū bolte tak nahīñ!
yih tārīḳh merī nahīñ aur terī nahīñ
yih tārīḳh hai izdiḥām-e ravāñ
usī izdiḥām-e ravāñ kī yih tārīḳh hai,
yih vuh chīḳh hai
jis kī takrār apne man-o-tū meñ hai
vuh takrār jo apnī tahẕīb kī hū meñ hai!

tujhe is pah ḥairat nahīñ
ham is izdiḥām-e ravāñ ke nishān-e qadam par chale jā rahe haiñ
baṛhe jā rahe haiñ
kih ham ẓulmat-e shab meñ tanhā
paṛe rah nah jā'eñ——
baṛhe jā rahe haiñ,
nah jīne kī ḳhāṭir
nah is se fizūñ zindah rahne kī ḳhāṭir
baṛhe jā rahe haiñ, kisī ʿaib se
rahzan-e marg se bach nikalne kī ḳhāṭir,
judā'ī kī ḳhāṭir!
kisī fard ke ḳhauf se baṛh rahe haiñ
jo bāṭin ke ṭūṭe darīchoñ ke pīchhe
sharārat se hañstā chalā jā rahā hai—

Why should we make it "body" with light or song
    or with a comforting word
and then accept death without a second thought?
Why should we open the door to new celebrations
    and begin the dawn of fulfillment?

§24. IN SEARCH

The rose and jasmine are not aware of tomorrow,
        not concerned with tomorrow
The rose and jasmine are unequaled in their bodily form
but—not aware of tomorrow, not concerned with tomorrow
The pain of some inevitable death
    is not in their hearts!

In the absurd search for our history
we are overcome!
We do not reveal
the hidden depths of our beings
We do not express our desires!
This history is not mine and is not yours
This history is a flowing crowd
It is the history of this flowing crowd
that is the cry
    repeated in our "You" and "I"
repeated in the being of our civilization!

Are you not surprised that
we are moving in the footsteps of this flowing crowd
We are advancing
so that we do not stay
    lying alone in the darkness of night—
We are advancing,
not to live,
    not to remain more alive
We are advancing to escape from some defect,
    from the clutches of the highwayman of death,
for the sake of separation!
We are advancing because we fear some individual
who behind the broken windows of the inner world
laughs mischievously—

§25. GUMĀÑ KĀ MUMKIN—JO TŪ HAI MAIÑ HŪÑ!

karīm sūraj,
jo ṭhanḍe patthar ko apnī golāʾī
de rahā hai
jo apnī hamvārī de rahā hai——
(vuh ṭhanḍā patthar jo mere mānind
bhūre sabzoñ meñ
daur-e reg-o-havā kī yādoñ meñ lauṭtā hai)
jo bahte pānī ko apnī daryā-dilī kī
sarshārī de rahā hai
——vuhī mujhe jāntā nahīñ hai
magar mujhī ko yih vahm shāyad
kih āp apnā s̱ubūt apnā javāb hūñ maiñ!
mujhe vuh pahchāntā nahīñ hai
kih merī dhīmī ṣadā
zamāne kī jhīl ke dūsre kināre
se ā rahī hai

yih jhīl vuh hai kih jis ke ūpar
hazāroñ insāñ
ufaq ke mutvāzī chal rahe haiñ
ufaq ke mutvāzī chalne-vāloñ ko pār lātī hai
vaqt lahreñ——
jiñheñ tamannā, magar, samāvī ḳhirām kī ho
uñhī ko pātāl zamzamoñ kī ṣadā sunātī haiñ
vaqt lahreñ
uñhīñ ḍubotī haiñ vaqt lahreñ!
tamām mallāḥ is ṣadā se sadā hirāsāñ, sadā gurīzāñ
kih jhīl meñ ik ʿumūd kā chor chhup-ke baiṭhā hai
us ke gesū ufaq kī chhat se laṭak rahe haiñ——
pukārtā hai: "ab āʾo, āʾo!
azal se maiñ muntaẓar tumhārā——
maiñ gumbadoñ ke tamām rāzoñ ko jāntā hūñ
daraḳht, mīnār, burj, zīne mire hī sāthī
mire hī mutvāzī chal rahe haiñ
maiñ har havāʾī jahāz kā āḳhirī basīrā
samandaroñ par jahāz-rānoñ kā maiñ kinārā
ab āʾo, āʾo!
tumhāre jaise kaʾī fasānoñ ko maiñ ne un ke

§25. THE POSSIBILITY OF SUPPOSITION: THAT YOU ARE, I AM

The munificent sun
giving its roundness
giving its smoothness
to the cold stone—
(the cold stone that like me
rolls in brown meadows
in memories of the age of sand and wind)
giving its generous profusion
to flowing water
—It does not know me
yet perhaps I alone imagine
that I am my own proof, my own answer!
It does not recognize me
for my faint voice
is coming from
the other side of the lake of time

This is the lake on which
thousands of men
are moving parallel to the horizon
Those moving parallel to the horizon are carried across by
time-waves—
Yet to those who long for a celestial journey
to them the voices of the underworld murmur:
time-waves
time-waves drown them!
Mariners are always frightened, they always flee this voice
for a thief of verticality sits hidden in the lake
his curls dangle from the roof of the horizon—
He calls: "Come, come now!
I have waited for you from the Beginning—
I know all the secrets of the domes
trees, minarets, towers, ladders are my companions alone
move parallel to me alone
I am the final resting place of all airplanes
on the seas I am the shore of every mariner
Come, come now!
I have placed several tales like you

abad ke āġhosh meñ utārā—”
tamām mallāḥ is kī āvāz se gurīzāñ
ufaq kī shah-rāh-e mubtażil par tamām sahme huʾe ḳhirāmāñ——
magar samāvī ḳhirām-vāle
jo past-o-bālā ke āstāñ par jame huʾe haiñ
ʿumūd ke is ṭanāb hī se utar rahe haiñ
isī ko thāme huʾe bulandī pah chaṛh rahe haiñ!

isī ṭaraḥ maiñ bhī sāth in ke utar gayā hūñ
aur aise sāḥil par ā lagā hūñ
jahāñ ḳhudā ke nishān-e pā ne panāh lī hai
jahāñ ḳhudā kī ẓaʿīf āñkheñ
abhī salāmat bachī huʾī haiñ
yihī samāvī ḳhirām merā naṣīb niklā
yihī samāvī ḳhirām jo merī ārzū thā——

magar najāne
vuh rāstah kyoñ chunā thā maiñ ne
kih jis pah ḳhvud se viṣāl tak kā gumāñ nahīñ hai?
vuh rāstah kyoñ chunā thā maiñ ne
jo ruk gayā hai diloñ ke ib'hām ke kināre?
vuhī kinārā kih jis ke āge gumāñ kā mumkin
jo tū hai maiñ hūñ!

magar yih sach hai,
maiñ tujh ko pāne kī (ḳhvud ko pāne kī) ārzū meñ
nikal paṛā thā
us ek mumkin kī justajū meñ
jo tū hai maiñ hūñ
maiñ aise chĕhre ko dhūñḍtā thā
jo tū hai maiñ hūñ
maiñ aisī taṣvīr ke taʿāqub meñ ghūmtā thā
jo tū hai maiñ hūñ!

maiñ is taʿāqub meñ
kitne āġhāz gin chukā hūñ
(maiñ us se ḍartā hūñ jo yih kahtā
hai mujh ko ab koʾī ḍar nahīñ hai)
maiñ is taʿāqub meñ kitnī galyoñ se
kitne chaukoñ se,
kitne gūñge mujassimoñ se, guzar gayā hūñ

into the embrace of their End—"
Sailors flee from his voice
on the common highway of the horizon all travelers tremble—
But the celestial travelers,
gathered at the threshold of high and low,
are descending with the tent-rope of this verticality alone
grasping this alone they are advancing on the heights!

I have descended along with them
and arrived on a shore
where the footprint of God has found refuge
where the weak eyes of God
have now escaped to safety
this celestial journey became my fate
this celestial journey I had longed for—

But who knows
why did I choose that road
on which there is not the supposition of union with myself?
Why did I choose that road
that has stopped at the edge of the heart's uncertainty?
The very edge ahead of which is the possibility of supposition
that you are, I am!

But this much is true,
I emerged
in hope of finding you (of finding myself)
in search of that one possibility
that you are, I am
I searched for a face
that you are, I am
I wandered in pursuit of a picture
that you are, I am!

In this pursuit
I have counted so many beginnings
(I am afraid of the one who says
he now has no fear)
In this pursuit, I have passed so many alleyways
so many thoroughfares
so many mute statues

maiñ is taʿāqub meñ kitne bāġhoñ se,
kitnī añdhī sharāb rātoñ se
kitnī bāhoñ se,
kitnī chāhat ke kitne biphre samandaroñ se
guzar gayā hūñ
maiñ kitnī hosh-o-ʿamal kī shamʿoñ se,
kitne īmāñ ke gumbadoñ se
guzar gayā hūñ
maiñ is taʿāqub meñ kitne āġhāz kitne anjām gin chukā hūñ——
ab is taʿāqub meñ koʾī dar hai
nah koʾī ātā huʾā zamānah
har ek manzil jo rah gaʾī hai
faqaṭ guzartā huʾā fasānah
tamām raste, tamām pūchhe savāl, be-vazn ho chuke haiñ
javāb, tārīḳh rūp dhāre
bas apnī takrār kar rahe haiñ——
"javāb ham haiñ——javāb ham haiñ——
hameñ yaqīñ hai javāb ham haiñ——"
yaqīñ ko kaise yaqīñ se duhrā rahe haiñ kaise!
magar vuh sab āp apnī ẓid haiñ
tamām, jaise gumāñ kā mumkin
jo tū hai maiñ hūñ!

tamām kunde (tū jāntī hai)
jo saṭḥ-e daryā pah sāth daryā ke tairte haiñ
yih jānte haiñ yih ḥādis̤ah hai,
kih jis se in ko,
(kisī ko) koʾī mafar nahīñ hai!
tamām kunde jo saṭḥ-e daryā pah tairte haiñ,
nahang bannā—yih un kī taqdīr meñ nahīñ hai
(nahang kī ibtidā meñ hai ik nahang shāmil
nahang kā dil nahang kā dil!)
nah un kī taqdīr meñ hai phir se daraḳht bannā
(daraḳht kī ibtidā meñ hai ik daraḳht shāmil
daraḳht kā dil daraḳht kā dil!)
tamām kundoñ ke sāmne band vāpasī kī
tamām rāheñ
vuh saṭḥ-e daryā pah jabr-e daryā se tairte haiñ
ab in kā anjām ghāṭ haiñ jo
sadā se āġhosh vā kiye haiñ
ab in kā anjām vuh safīne

In this pursuit I have passed so many gardens
so many wine-blind nights
so many arms
so many raging oceans of so many desires
I have passed
so many candles of awareness and action,
so many domes of faith
I have passed
In this pursuit I have counted so many beginnings, so many ends—
now in this pursuit there is neither a door
nor a coming age
every destination left behind
is only a passing story
All roads, all known questions have become meaningless
Answers, assuming the form of history,
only repeat themselves—
"We are the answers—we are the answers—
we are certain that we are the answers—"
how they repeat certainty with such certainty!
But they themselves are their own negation
all, like the possibility of supposition
that you are, I am!

All the logs (you know)
that flow with the river on the surface of the river
they know this is an event from which
for them (for anyone)
there is no escape!
For all the logs that flow on the surface of the river
to become crocodiles—this is not their fate
(the beginning of a crocodile contains a crocodile
the heart of a crocodile is the heart of a crocodile!)
to become trees again is not their fate
(the beginning of a tree contains a tree
the heart of a tree is the heart of a tree!)
Before the logs all roads of return
are closed
They flow with the force of the river on the surface of the river
Now their end is the ghats
that have always opened their embrace
Now their end is those ships

abhī nahīñ jo safīnah-gar ke qiyās meñ bhī
ab in kā anjām
aise aurāq jin pah ḥarf-e siyah chhapegā
ab in kā anjām vuh kitābeñ——
kih jin ke qārī nahīñ, nah hoñge
ab in kā anjām aise ṣūrat-garoñ ke parde
abhī nahīñ jin ke koʾī chĕhre
kih un pah āñsū ke rang utreñ,
aur un meñ āyindah
un ke royā ke naqsh bhar de!

ġharīb kundoñ ke sāmne band vāpasī kī
tamām rāheñ
baqā-e mauhūm ke jo raste khule haiñ ab tak
hai un ke āge gumāñ kā mumkin——
gumāñ kā mumkin, jo tū hai maiñ hūñ!
jo tū hai, maiñ hūñ!

§26. ḤASAN KŪZAH-GAR

jahāñ-zād, nīche galī meñ tire dar ke āge
yih maiñ soḳhtah-sar ḥasan kūzah-gar hūñ!
tujhe ṣubḥ bāzār meñ būṛhe ʿaṭṭār yūsif
kī dukkān par maiñ ne dekhā
to terī nigāhoñ meñ vuh tāb-nākī
thī maiñ jis kī ḥasrat meñ nau sāl dīvānah phirtā rahā hūñ
jahāñ-zād, nau sāl dīvānah phirtā rahā hūñ!
yih vuh daur thā jis meñ maiñ ne
kabhī apne ranjūr kūzoñ kī jānib
palaṭ-kar nah dekhā——
vuh kūze mire dast-e chābuk ke putle
gil-o-rang-o-rauġhan kī maḳhlūq-e be-jāñ
vuh sar-goshiyoñ meñ yih kahte:
"ḥasan kūzah-gar ab kahāñ hai?
vuh ham se, ḳhvud apne ʿamal se,
ḳhudāvand ban-kar ḳhudāʾoñ ke mānind hai rū-e gardāñ!"
jahāñ-zād nau sāl kā daur yūñ mujh pah guzrā
kih jaise kisī shahr-e madfūn par vaqt guzre;
taġhāroñ meñ miṭṭī

that are not yet even conceived of by shipbuilders
Now their end is
those pages on which black words will be printed
Now their end is those books—
that have no readers, nor ever will
Now their end is those painters' canvases
that now have no faces
that the colors of tears would fall on them,
and the future fill them
with the form of their dream!

Before the poor logs all roads of return
are closed
Those roads of imagined eternity are still open now
ahead of them is the possibility of supposition—
the possibility of supposition that you are, I am!
that you are, I am!

§26. HASAN THE POTTER

Jahanzad, in the alley below in front of your door
It is I, love-struck Hasan the Potter
In the bazaar this morning, in the old apothecary Yusuf's shop
I saw you
in your glances was the brilliance
in whose pursuit I have wandered madly for nine years
Jahanzad, I have wandered madly for nine years!
During that time
I never turned and looked
at my grieving pots—
Those pots, effigies of my deft hands,
lifeless creations of clay and color and varnish,
in whispers they used to say:
"Where is Hasan the Potter now?
Through us, through his own work,
he became a god, and like the gods he turns away his face!"
Jahanzad, those nine years passed over me
they way time passes over a buried city;
The buckets of clay

kabhī jis kī ḳhvush-bū se vā-raftah hotā thā meñ
sang-bastah paṛī thī
ṣurāḥī-o-mīnā-o-jām-o-sabū aur fānūs-o-guldāñ
mirī hech-māyah maʿīshat ke, iz̤hār-e fan ke sahāre
shikastah paṛe the
maiñ ḳhvud, maiñ ḥasan kūzah-gar pā bah gil, ḳhāk bar sar, barahnah,
sar-e "chāk" zhūlīdah mū, sar ba-zānū,
kisī ġham-zadah devatā kī t̤araḥ vāhimah ke
gil-o-lā se ḳhvāboñ ke saiyāl kūze banātā rahā thā—
jahāñ-zād, nau sāl pahle
tū nā-dāñ thī lekin tujhe yih ḳhabar thī
kih maiñ ne, ḥasan kūzah-gar ne
tirī qāf kī sī ufaq-tāb āñkhoñ
meñ dekhī hai vuh tāb-nākī kih jis se mire jism-o-jāñ, abr-o-mahtāb kā
rah-guzar ban gaʾe the
jahāñ-zād baġhdād kī ḳhvāb gūñ rāt,
vuh rod-e dajlah kā sāḥil,
vuh kashtī, vuh mallāḥ kī band āñkheñ,
kisī ḳhastah-jāñ, ranjbar, kūzah-gar ke liʾe
ek hī rāt vuh kah-rubā thī
kih jis se abhī tak hai paivast us kā vujūd——
us kī jāñ, us kā paikar
magar ek hī rāt kā żauq daryā kī vuh lahr niklā
ḥasan kūzah-gar jis meñ ḍūbā to ubhrā nahīñ hai!

jahāñ-zād, us daur meñ roz, har roz
vuh soḳhtah-baḳht ā-kar
mujhe dekhtī chāk par pā bah-gil, sar ba-zānū,
to shānoñ se mujh ko hilātī——
(vuhī chāk jo sāl-hā-sāl jīne kā tanhā sahārā rahā thā!)
vuh shānoñ se mujh ko hilātī:
"ḥasan kūzah-gar hosh meñ ā
ḥasan apne vīrān ghar par naz̤ar kar
yih bachchoñ ke tannūr kyoñkar bhareñge?
ḥasan, ai muḥabbat ke māre
muḥabbat amīroñ kī bāzī,
ḥasan, apne dīvār-o-dar par naz̤ar kar"
mire kān meñ yih navā-e ḥazīñ yūñ thī jaise
kisī ḍūbte shaḳhṣ ko zer-e girdāb koʾī pukāre!

I used to lose myself in their fragrance
they have hardened into stone
Flasks, goblets, cups, and pitchers; lanterns and flowerpots—
my only means of subsistence, of expressing my art—
broken
I, Hasan the Potter, my feet stuck in mud, dust in my hair

naked at the "wheel" with disheveled hair, my head on my knees,
like some grief-stricken god of hallucination
I used to shape the flow of dreams into pots with clay and water—
Jahanzad, nine years ago
You were naive but you knew
that I, Hasan the Potter,
saw in your eyes, like Mt. Qaf, illuminating the horizon
the brilliance by which my body and soul had become a pathway

of clouds and moonlight
Jahanzad, that dream-colored night in Baghdad,
the shore of the Tigris,
the boat, the closed eyes of the boatman,
for some worn-out, afflicted potter
that one night was the amber
in which his being is still caught—
his soul, his body
That one night's delight caused the river to surge
and Hasan the Potter drowned, and he has never surfaced!

Jahanzad, at that time, every day, every single day
the ill-fortuned one came and
saw me at the wheel, my feet stuck in mud, my head on my knees,
She shook me by the shoulders—
(that wheel that for years and years was my only means of living!)
She shook me by the shoulders:
"Hasan the Potter! Come to your senses
Hasan, look at your ruined house
how will the children's bellies be filled?
Hasan, O victim of love,
love is the game of the rich,
Hasan, look at your house and home"
In my ears her troubled voice was like
crying to someone trapped in a whirlpool!

vuh ashkoñ ke ambār phūloñ ke ambār the hāñ
magar maiñ ḥasan kūzah-gar shahr-e auhām ke un
k̤harāboñ kā majżūb thā jin
meñ koʾī ṣadā koʾī jumbish
kisī murġh-e parrāñ kā sāyah
kisī zindagī kā nishāñ tak nahīñ thā!

jahāñ-zād, meñ āj terī galī meñ
yahāñ rāt kī sard-gūñ tīragī meñ
tire dar ke āge khaṛā hūñ
sar-o-mū pareshāñ
darīche se vuh qāf kī sī ṭilismī nigāheñ
mujhe āj phir jhāñktī haiñ
zamānah, jahāñ-zād vuh chāk hai jis pah mīnā-o-jām-o-sabū
aur fānūs-o-guldāñ
ke mānind bante bigaṛte haiñ insāñ
maiñ insāñ hūñ lekin
yih nau sāl jo ġham ke qālib meñ guzre!
ḥasan kūzah-gar āj ik todah-e k̤hāk hai jis
meñ nam kā aṡar tak nahīñ hai
jahāñ-zād bāzār meñ ṣubḥ ʿaṭṭār yūsif
kī dukkān par terī āñkheñ
phir ik bār kuchh kah gaʾī haiñ
in āñkhoñ kī tābindah shok̤hī
se uṭṭhī hai phir todah-e k̤hāk meñ nam kī halkī sī larzish
yihī shāyad is k̤hāk ko gil banā de!

tamannā kī vusʿat kī kis ko k̤habar hai, jahāñ-zād lekin
tū chāhe to ban jāʾūñ meñ phir
vuhī kūzah-gar jis ke kūze
the har kāk̤h-o-kū aur har shahr-o-qaryah kī nāzish
the jin se amīr-o-gadā ke musākin darak̤hshāñ
tamannā kī vusʿat kī kis ko k̤habar hai
jahāñ-zād lekin
tū chāhe to maiñ phir palaṭ jāʾūñ un apne mahjūr kūzoñ kī jānib
gil-o-lā ke sūkhe taġhāroñ kī jānib
maʿīshat ke, iẓhār-e fan ke sahāroñ kī jānib
kih maiñ us gil-o-lā se, us rang-o-rauġhan
se phir vuh sharāre nikālūñ kih jin se
diloñ ke k̤harābe hoñ roshan!

That heap of tears was, in truth, a heap of flowers
and I, Hasan the Potter, was the ecstatic hermit of the ruins
of a city of illusions in which there was not
any sound, any movement
the shadow of any bird in flight
any sign of life!

Jahanzad, today in your alleyway
here in the cold darkness of the night
I stand in front of your door
my head and hair disheveled
From the window, those Qaf-like enchanting eyes
peer at me again
Time, Jahanzad, is the wheel on which, like goblets, cups, pitchers,
lanterns, and flowerpots,
men are being formed and disfigured
I am a man, but
one who passed nine years in the mold of grief!
Hasan the Potter is today a heap of dust in which
there is not even a trace of moisture
Jahanzad, in the bazaar this morning
in the perfumer Yusuf's shop, your eyes
once again have said something
From the brilliant playfulness of those eyes
the gentle movement of moisture has risen again in this heap of dust
Perhaps this will turn dust into clay again!

Who knows the extent of longing, Jahanzad, but
if you desire, then I will become again
that potter whose pots
were the delight of every balcony and lane, every city and village
by which the homes of every rich man and beggar were lit
Who knows the extent of longing,
Jahanzad, but
if you desire, then I will again turn toward my deserted pots
toward those dried-up buckets of clay and water
toward my means of subsistence, of expressing my art
So that, with that clay and water, with that color and varnish
I would again bring forth those sparks by which
the hearts' ruins would be illuminated!

§27. ḤASAN KŪZAH-GAR (2)

ai jahāñ-zād,
nashāṭ us shab-e be-rāh ravī kī
maiñ kahāñ tak bhūlūñ?
zor-e mai thā, kih mire hāth kī larzish thī
kih us rāt koʾī jām girā ṭūṭ gayā——
tujhe ḥairat nah huʾī!
kih tire ghar ke darīchoñ ke kaʾī shīshoñ par
us se pahle kī bhī darzeñ thīñ bahut——
tujhe ḥairat nah huʾī!

ai jahāñ-zād,
maiñ kūzoñ kī ṭaraf, apne taġhāroñ kī ṭaraf
ab jo baġhdād se lauṭā hūñ,
to maiñ sochtā hūñ——
sochtā hūñ: tū mire sāmne āʾīnah rahī
sar-e bāzār, darīche meñ, sar-e bistar-e sanjāb kabhī
tū mire sāmne āʾīnah rahī,
jis meñ kuchh bhī naẓar āyā nah mujhe
apnī hī ṣūrat ke sivā
apnī tanhāʾī-e jāñ-kāh kī dahshat ke sivā!
likh rahā hūñ tujhe ḳhaṭ
aur vuh āʾīnah mire hāth meñ hai
is meñ kuchh bhī naẓar ātā nahīñ
ab ek hī ṣūrat ke sivā!
likh rahā hūñ tujhe ḳhaṭ
aur mujhe likhnā bhī kahāñ ātā hai?
lūḥ-e āʾīnah pah ashkoñ kī phuvāroñ hī se
ḳhaṭ kyoñ nah likhūñ?

ai jahāñ-zād,
nashāṭ us shab-e be-rāh ravī kī
mujhe phir lāʾegī?
vaqt kyā chīz hai tū jāntī hai?
vaqt ik aisā patangā hai
jo dīvāroñ pah, āʾīnoñ pah,
paimānoñ pah, shīshoñ pah,
mire jām-o-sabū, mere taġhāroñ pah
sadā reñgtā hai
reñgte vaqt ke mānind kabhī

§27. HASAN THE POTTER (2)

O Jahanzad,
    the pleasure of that night of errant wandering
        how could I forget?
Was it the strength of the wine, or the trembling of my hand
    that on that night a cup fell and shattered—
You were not surprised!
For on many of your windowpanes
there are cracks from before—
You were not surprised!

O Jahanzad,
    now that I have returned from Baghdad
to my pots, to my buckets,
    I think—
I think: "You have been a mirror in front of me
in the bazaar, at the window, by the bed of fur sometimes
you have been a mirror in front of me,
in which nothing appeared to me
    except my own face
except the terror of my own soul-exhausting solitude!
I am writing you a letter
    and that mirror is in my hand
nothing appears in it
    now except a single face!
I am writing you a letter
    and what do I know of writing?
Why should I not write a letter
        on the mirror tablet with the drizzle of tears?

O Jahanzad,
    the pleasure of that night of errant wandering
        will it bring me back again?
What sort of thing is time, do you know?
Time is a sort of moth
which on the walls, on the mirrors,
    on the bowls, on the glasses,
        on my cup and pitcher, in my buckets filled with clay
            is always crawling
Like crawling time

lauṭ-ke āʾegā ḥasan kūzah-gar-e soḳhtah-jāñ bhī shāyad!

ab jo lauṭā hūñ, jahāñ-zād,
to maiñ sochtā hūñ:
shāyad is jhoñpṛe kī chhat pah yih makṛī mirī maḥrūmī kī——
jise tantī chalī jātī hai, vuh jālā to nahīñ hūñ maiñ bhī?
yih siyah jhoñpṛā maiñ jis meñ paṛā sochtā hūñ
mere aflās ke rauñde huʾe ajdād kī
bas ek nishānī hai yihī
un ke fan, un kī maʿīshat kī kahānī hai yihī
maiñ jo lauṭā hūñ to vuh soḳhtah-baḳht
ā-ke mujhe dekhtī hai
der tak dekhtī rah jātī hai
mere is jhoñpṛe meñ kuchh bhī nahīñ——
khel ik sādah muḥabbat kā
shab-o-roz ke is baṛhte huʾe khokhale-pan meñ jo kabhī khelte haiñ
kabhī ro lete haiñ mil-kar, kabhī gā lete haiñ
aur mil-kar kabhī hañs lete haiñ
dil ke jīne ke bahāne ke sivā aur nahīñ——
ḥarf sarḥad haiñ, jahāñ-zād, maʿānī sarḥad
ʿishq sarḥad hai, javānī sarḥad
ashk sarḥad haiñ, tabassum kī ravānī sarḥad
dil ke jīne ke bahāne ke sivā aur nahīñ——
(dard-e majrūmī kī,
tanhāʾī kī sarḥad bhī kahīñ hai kih nahīñ?)

mere is jhoñpṛe meñ
kitnī hī ḳhvush-būʾeñ haiñ
jo mire gird sadā reñgtī haiñ
usī ik rāt kī ḳhvush-bū kī ṭaraḥ reñgtī haiñ——
dar-o-dīvār se lapṭī huʾī is gird kī ḳhvush-bū bhī hai
mere aflās kī, tanhāʾī kī,
yādoñ kī, tamannāʾoñ kī ḳhvush-būʾeñ bhī,
phir bhī is jhoñpṛe meñ kuchh bhī nahīñ——
yih mirā jhoñpṛā tārīk hai, gandah hai, purā gandah hai
hāñ, kabhī dūr daraḳhtoñ se parindoñ kī ṣadā ātī hai
kabhī anjīroñ ke, zaitūnoñ ke bāġhoñ kī mahak ātī hai
to meñ jī uṭhtā hūñ
to maiñ kahtā hūñ kih lo āj nahā-kar niklā!
varnah is ghar meñ koʾī sej nahīñ, ʿiṭr nahīñ hai,

Hasan the Potter will perhaps return, burnt up by love!

Now that I have returned, Jahanzad,
I think:
perhaps the spider on the ceiling of this hut is my deprivation—
what it keeps on spinning, am I not like that web?
This dark hut in which I am lying and thinking
this is the one memorial
of my forefathers laid waste by destitution
the story of their art, of their way of life is just this
When I have returned, that ill-fated one
comes and looks at me
for a long time she keeps on looking at me
in this hut of mine there is nothing—
A game of simple love
night and day in this growing hollowness we
play
we meet and cry, we sing
and we laugh
there is nothing more than this pretense to stay alive—
words are a border, Jahanzad, meaning a border
love is a border, youth a border
tears are a border, the effortless smile a border
there is nothing more than this pretense to stay alive—
(Is there a limit to the pain of deprivation,
of solitude somewhere or not?)

In this hut of mine
how many sweet smells there are
that always crawl around me
they crawl like the sweet smells of that one night—
there is another sweet smell of this dust coiling around this house
The sweet smells of my poverty, my solitude
my memories, my desires
yet still in this hut there is nothing at all—
This hut of mine is dark, it is filthy, completely a shambles
Yes, from faraway trees the sounds of birds come
And sometimes the fragrances of gardens of figs, of olives come
then I liven up
then I say, look, today wash yourself and leave!
Although in this house there is no bed, there is no perfume,

koʾī pankhā bhī nahīñ,
tujhe jis ʿishq kī ḳhū hai
mujhe us ʿishq kā yārā bhī nahīñ!

tū hañsegī, ai jahāñ-zād, ʿajab bāt
kih jażbāt kā ḥātim bhī maiñ
aur ashyā ke parastār bhī maiñ
aur s̱arvat jo nahīñ us kā t̤alab-gār bhī maiñ!
tū jo hañstī rahī us rāt tażabżub pah mire
merī do-rangī pah phir se hañs de!
ʿishq se kis ne magar pāyā hai kuchh apne sivā?
ai jahāñ-zād,
hai har ʿishq savāl aisā kih ʿāshiq ke sivā
us kā nahīñ koʾī javāb
yihī kāfī hai kih bāt̤in kī ṣadā gūñj uṭhe!

ai jahāñ-zād
mire goshah-e bāt̤in kī ṣadā hī thī
mire fan kī ṭhiṭhartī huʾī ṣadyoñ
ke kināre gūñjī
terī āñkhoñ ke samandar kā kinārā hī thā
ṣadyoñ kā kinārā niklā
yih samandar jo mirī żāt kā āʾīnah hai
yih samandar jo mire kūzoñ ke bigṛe huʾe
bante huʾe sīmāʾoñ kā āʾīnah hai
yih samandar jo har ik fan kā
har ik fan ke parastār kā
āʾīnah hai

§28. ḤASAN KŪZAH GAR (3)

jahān-zād,
vuh ḥalab kī kārvāñ-sarā kā ḥauẓ, rāt vuh sukūt
jis meñ ek dūsare se ham-kinār tairte rahe
muḥīt̤ jis t̤araḥ ho dāʾire ke gird ḥalqah-zan
tamām rāt tairte rahe the ham
ham ek dūsare ke jism-o-jāñ se lag-ke
tairte rahe the ek shād-kām ḳhauf se
kih jaise pānī āñsūʾoñ meñ tairtā rahe
ham ek dūsare se mut̤maʾin zavāl-e ʿumr ke ḳhilāf

there is not even a fan,
the kind of love you are used to
    I do not have the courage for that love!

You will laugh, O Jahanzad, it's a strange thing
that I am generous with emotions
and a worshipper of things, too
I seek wealth that I do not have!
When you laughed that night at my indecision
laugh at my two-facedness again!
But who ever got anything from love except himself?
O Jahanzad,
Every love is a question for which except for the lover
    there is no other answer
this is enough for the voice of the inner being to resound!

O Jahanzad
    this sound from the corners of my inner being
        on the shore of the icy centuries of my art
            echoed
This was the shore of the ocean of your eyes
        The edge of centuries emerged
This ocean which is the mirror of my self
this ocean which is the mirror of the disfigured
        forming faces of the mirror
This is the ocean of which every single art
    ever single worshiper of art
        is a mirror

§28. HASAN THE POTTER (3)

Jahanzad,
    the pool at the caravansary in Aleppo, the silence of the night
in which we swam embracing
the way a circumference surrounds a circle
all night we kept on swimming
joining with each other's body and soul
        we swam on with joyous fear
the way water would swim in tears
Secure in each other against the decline of age

tairte rahe
tū kah uṭhī: "ḥasan yahāñ bhī kheñch lā'ī
jāñ kī tishnagī tujhe!"
(lo apnī jāñ kī tishnagī ko yād kar rahā thā maiñ
kih merā ḥalq āñsū'oñ kī be-bahā saḳhāvatoñ
se shād-kām ho gayā!)
magar yih vahm dil meñ tairne lagā kih ho nah ho
mirā badan kahīñ ḥalab ke ḥauẓ hī meñ rah gayā—
nahīñ, mujhe dū'ī kā vāhimah nahīñ
kih ab bhī rabṭ-e jism-o-jāñ kā ětibār hai mujhe
yihī vuh ětibār thā
kih jis ne mujh ko āp meñ samo diyā——
maiñ sab se pahle "āp" hūñ
agar hamīñ hoñ——tū ho aur maiñ hūñ——phir bhī maiñ
har ek shai se pahle āp hūñ!
agar maiñ zindah hūñ to kaise "āp" se daġhā karūñ?
kih terī jaisī 'aurateñ, jahān-zād,
aisī uljhaneñ haiñ
jin ko āj tak ko'ī nahīñ "sulajh" sakā
jo maiñ kahūñ kih maiñ "sulajh" sakā to sarbasar
fareb apne āp se!
kih 'auratoñ kī sāḳht hai vuh ṭanz apne āp par
javāb jis kā ham nahīñ——

(labīb kaun hai? tamām rāt jis kā żikr
tere lab pah thā——
vuh kaun tere gesū'oñ ko kheñchtā rahā
laboñ ko nauchtā rahā
jo maiñ kabhī nah kar sakā
nahīñ yih sach hai——maiñ hūñ yā labīb ho
raqīb ho to kis liye tirī ḳhvud-āgahī kī be-riyā nishāṭ-e nāb kā
jo ṣad navā-o-yak navā ḳhirām-e ṣubḥ kī ṭaraḥ
labīb har navā-e sāz-gār kī nafī sahī!)
magar hamārā rābṭah viṣāl-e āb-o-gil nahīñ, nah thā kabhī
vujūd-e ādmī se āb-o-gil sadā birūñ rahe
nah har viṣāl-e āb-o-gil se ko'ī jām yā sabū hī ban sakā

jo in kā ek vāhimah hī ban sake to ban sake!

jahān-zād,
ek tū aur ek vuh aur ek maiñ

we swam on
You spoke: "Hasan, here too the thirst of your soul
has drawn you!"
(As I remembered the thirst of my soul
my throat, through the invaluable bounty of tears,
became joyous!)
But this fear began to swim in my heart:
had my body remained somewhere in that pool in Aleppo?—
No, I have no conception of duality
for even now I have faith in the connection of body and soul
This was that very faith
that mixed me in myself—
Before everything else I am "myself"
If we ourselves are—if you are and I am—still
before every thing I am myself!
If I am alive then how can I deceive "myself"?
For women like you, Jahanzad,
are such riddles
that even today no one can "unravel"
If I said that I was able to "unravel" you that would be
to deceive myself!
For women's form is a laughing at itself
to which we have no answer—

(Who was Labib? whose name was on
your lips all night—
Who was he who grabbed your locks
and tore at your lips
which I could never do
No this is true—Whether Labib or I
why should we compete for your self-aware and sincere pure pleasure
whether as a hundred voices or one voice, like a morning stroll
Labib is the negation of every singer's voice, certainly!)
But our bond is not the union of water and clay, nor was it ever
the being of man always remained outside of water and clay
not from every union of water and clay could even a cup or pitcher be made
If anything, it could only be an illusion!

Jahanzad,
You, he, and I

yih tīn zāviye kisī muṣallaṡ-e qadīm ke
hameshah ghūmte rahe
kih jaise merā chāk ghūmtā rahā
magar nah apne āp kā koʾī surāġh pā sake——
muṡallaṡ-e qadīm ko maiñ toṛ dūñ, jo tū kahe, magar nahīñ
jo siḥr mujh pah chāk kā vuhī hai is muṡallaṡ-e qadīm kā
nigāheñ mere chāk kī jo mujh ko dekhtī haiñ
ghūmte huʾe
sabū-o-jām par tirā badan, tirā hī rang, terī nāzukī
baras paṛī
vuh kīmiyā-garī tire jamāl kī baras paṛī
maiñ sail-e nūr-e andarūñ se dhul gayā!
mire dirūñ kī ḳhalq yūñ galī galī nikal paṛī
kih jaise ṣubḥ kī ażāñ sunāʾī dī!
tamām kūze bante bante "tū" hī ban-ke rah gaʾe
nashāt̤ is viṣāl-e rah-guzar kī nā-gahāñ mujhe nigal gaʾī——
yihī payālah-o-ṣarāḥī-o-sabū kā marḥalah hai vuh
kih jab ḳhamīr-e āb-o-gil se vuh judā huʾe
to un ko simt-e rāh-e nau kā kāmrāniyāñ mileñ——
(maiñ ik ġharīb kūzah-gar
yih intihā-e maʿrifat
yih har payālah-o-ṣarāḥī-o-sabū kī intihā-e maʿrifat
mujhe ho is kī kyā ḳhabar?)

jahān-zād,
intiz̤ār āj bhī mujhe hai kyoñ vuhī magar
jo nau-baras ke daur-e nā-sazā meñ thā?
ab intiz̤ār āñsūʾoñ ke dajlah kā
nah gum-rahī kī rāt kā
(shab-e gunah kī lażżatoñ kā itnā żikr kar chukā
vuh ḳhvud gunāh ban gaʾīñ!)
ḥalab kī kārvāñ-sarā ke ḥauẓ kā, nah maut kā
nah apnī is shikast-ḳhvurdah żāt kā
ik intiz̤ār-e be-zamāñ kā tār hai bañdhā huʾā!
kabhī jo chand ṡāniye zamān-e be-zamāñ meñ ā-ke ruk gaʾe
to vaqt kā yih bār mere sar se bhī utar gayā
tamām raftah-o-gużashtah ṣūratoñ, tamām ḥādiṡoñ
ke sust qāfile
mire dirūñ meñ jāg uṭhe
mire dirūñ meñ ik jahān-e bāz-yāftah kī rel-pel jāg uṭhī
bihisht jaise jāg uṭhe ḳhudā ke lā-shuʿūr meñ!

These three angles of an ancient triangle
always keep going around
as my potter's wheel keeps going around
but could not find any trace of itself—
I would break this ancient triangle, if you asked, but no
the wheel's spell on me is the same as that of the ancient triangle
As the eyes of my wheel look at me
turning
your body, your color, your slenderness
rained down upon the pitcher and the cup
That alchemy of your beauty rained down
I was washed in the flood of an inner light!
My inner creation came out into alley upon alley
as if the morning's call to prayer sounded!
All the pots being made became "you"
The pleasure of that meeting on the road suddenly devoured me—
This was that stage of the cup and flask and pitcher
that when separated from the constitution of water and clay
found success in the direction of a new road—
(I am a poor potter
what would I know of the limit of mystic knowledge
this mystic limit of every cup and goblet and pitcher
what would I know of this?)

Jahanzad,
why do I wait today
just as I did for those foolish nine years?
Now I wait, not for a Tigris of tears
nor for a night of waywardness
(I have recounted so much the pleasures of the night of sin
that they have themselves become sinful!)
not for the pool at a caravansary in Aleppo, nor for death
nor for this destroyed self of mine
A thread of timeless waiting spins out!
Sometimes, when a few moments came and stopped in timeless time
then this burden of time was lifted from my head
All coming and past circumstances, all moments'
lazy caravans
awoke inside me
inside me, the throng of a restored world awoke
like paradise would wake in the unconscious of God!

maiñ jāg uṭhā ġhanūdagī kī ret par paṛā huʾā
ġhanūdagī kī ret par paṛe huʾe vuh kūze jo
—mire vujūd se birūñ—
tamām rezah rezah ho-ke rah gaʾe the
mere apne āp se firāq meñ,
vuh phir se ek kul bane (kisī navā-e sāz-gār kī t̤araḥ)
vuh phir se ek raqṣ-e be-zamāñ bane
vuh royat-e azal bane!

§29. ḤASAN KŪZAH-GAR (4)

jahāñ-zād, kaise hazāroñ baras baʿd
ik shahr-e madfūn kī har galī meñ
mire jām-o-mīnā-o-guldāñ ke reze mile haiñ
kih jaise vuh is shahr-e barbād kā ḥāfiz̤ah hoñ!
(ḥasan nām kā ik javāñ kūzah-gar——ik naʾe shahr meñ——
apne kūze banātā huʾā, ʿishq kartā huʾā
apne māẓī ke tāroñ meñ ham se piroyā gayā hai
hamīñ meñ (kih jaise hamīñ hoñ) samoyā gayā hai
kih ham tum vuh bārish ke qat̤re the jo rāt-bhar se,
(hazāroñ baras reñgtī rāt-bhar)
ik darīche ke shīshoñ pah girte huʾe sāñp lahreñ
banāte rahe haiñ,
aur ab is jagah vaqt kī ṣubḥ hone se pahle
yih ham aur yih nau-javāñ kūzah-gar
ek royā meñ phir se piroʾe gaʾe haiñ!)

jahāñ-zād——
yih kaisā kuhnah parastoñ kā amboh
kūzoñ kī lāshoñ meñ utrā hai
dekho!
yih vuh log haiñ jin kī āñkheñ
kabhī jām-o-mīnā kī lim tak nah pahuñcheñ
yihī āj is rang-o-rauġhan kī maḳhlūq-e be-jāñ
ko phir se ulaṭne palaṭne lage haiñ
yih in ke tale ġham kī chingāriyāñ pā sakeñge
jo tārīḳh ko khā gaʾī thīñ?
vuh t̤ūfān, vuh āñdhiyāñ pā sakeñge
jo har chīḳh ko khā gaʾī thīñ?

I awoke, lying on the sand of drowsiness
Lying on the sand of drowsiness those pots which
            —outside of my being—
had entirely shattered into pieces
                in separation from myself
they again became whole (like a pleasing tune)
they became again a timeless dance
they became an aspect of the Beginning!

§29. HASAN THE POTTER (4)

Jahanzad, how after thousands of years
in every alleyway of a buried city
the shards of my cups and goblets and flowerpots have been found
as if they are the memory of this ruined city
(Hasan is the name of a young potter—in a new city—
making his pots, loving
strung together with us in the strings of his past
mixed in us (as though he were us)
for you and I are those drops of rain which all night
(crawling all night for thousands of years)
have made snake lines
                on the window-panes,
and now at this place, before time's morning
we and this young potter
    once again have been strung together in a vision!)

Jahanzad—
    What a crowd of past-worshipers
        has descended on the corpses of the pots
            look!
Those people whose eyes
    never reached into the depths of a cup or goblet
today they have again begun to turn over
    lifeless creations of this color and glaze
Will they be able to find under them the sparks of suffering
    that had devoured history?
Will they find the typhoons, the dust storms
    that devoured every scream?

iñheñ kyā k̲habar kis dhanak se mire rang āʾe—
(mire aur is nau-javāñ kūzah-gar ke?)
iñheñ kyā k̲habar kaun-sī titliyoñ ke paroñ se?
iñheñ kyā k̲habar kaun se ḥusn se?
kaun sī żāt se, kis k̲hadd-o-k̲hāl se
maiñ ne kūzoñ ke chĕhre utāre?
yih sab log apne asīroñ meñ haiñ
zamānah, jahāñ-zād, afsūñ-zadah burj hai
aur yih log us ke asīroñ meñ haiñ—
javāñ kūzah-gar hañs rahā hai!
yih maʿṣūm vaḥshī kih apne hī qāmat se zhūlīdah dāman

haiñ joyā kisī ʿaẓmat-e nā-rasā ke—
iñheñ kyā k̲habar kaisā āsīb-e mubram mire ġhār sīne pah thā
jis ne mujh se (aur is kūzah-gar se) kahā:
"ai ḥasan kūzah-gar, jāg
dard-e risālat kā roz-e bashārat tire jām-o-mīnā

kī tishnah-labī tak pahuñchne lagā hai!"
yihī vuh nidā, jis ke pīchhe ḥasan nām kā
yih javāñ kūzah-gar bhī
piyā pai ravāñ hai zamāñ se zamāñ tak
k̲hizāñ se k̲hizāñ tak!

jahāñ-zād maiñ ne—ḥasan kūzah-gar ne—
bayābāñ bayābāñ yih dard-e risālat sahā hai
hazāroñ baras baʿd yih log
rezoñ ke chunte huʾe
jān sakte haiñ kaise
kih mere gil-o-k̲hāk ke rang-o-rauġhan
tire nāzuk aʿẓā ke rangoñ se mil-kar
abad kī ṣadā ban gaʾe the?
maiñ apne masāmoñ se, har por se,
terī bāñhoñ kī pahnāʾiyāñ
jażb kartā rahā thā
kih har āne-vāle kī āñkhoñ ke maʿbad pah jā-kar
chiṛhāʾūñ—
yih rezoñ kī tahżīb pā leñ to pā leñ
ḥasan kūzah-gar ko kahāñ lā sakeñge?
yih us ke pasīne ke qaṭre kahāñ gin sakeñge?
yih fan kī tajallī kā sāyah kahāñ pā sakeñge?

What do they know of the rainbow from which my colors came—
(mine and this young potter's?)
What do they know from which of the butterflies' wings?
What do they know from which beauty?
From what self, from what features
did I take the faces of the pots?
All these people are their own prisoners
Time, Jahanzad, is an enchanted tower,
and these people are among its prisoners—
The young potter is laughing!
These innocent savages whose clothes are disheveled by their very own stature
they are in search of some unattainable grandeur—
What do they know of the evil spirit that lay in the cave of my breast
which said to me (and to this potter):
"O Hasan the Potter, wake up
the day of the enunciation of the pain of prophecy has begun to reach
the thirstiness of your cup and goblet!"
This is the very voice behind which a young potter
also named Hasan
is moving unceasingly from age to age
from autumn to autumn!

Jahanzad, I—Hasan the Potter—
have endured this pain of revelation in desert after desert
A thousand years from now these people
sifting through the shards
how can they know how
the color and glaze of my clay and dust
upon meeting the colors of delicate parts of your body
had become the voice of the End?
How in my pores, in every inch
I drew in
the expanse of your arms
that I should go and offer [them] at the temple of every coming person's eyes
If they find the civilization of the shards, so be it
How will they find Hasan the Potter?
How will they count the drops of his sweat?
How will they obtain the shadow of the manifestation of art?

jo baṛhtā gayā hai zamāñ se zamāñ tak
ḳhizāñ se ḳhizāñ tak
jo har naujavāñ kūzah-gar kī naʾī żāt meñ
aur baṛhtā chalā jā rahā hai!
vuh fan kī tajallī kā sāyah kih jis kī badaulat
hamah ʿishq haiñ ham
hamah kūzah-gar ham
hamah-tan ḳhabar ham, hamah be-ḳhabar ham
ḳhudā kī ṭaraḥ apne fan ke ḳhudā sar-ba-sar ham!
(ārzūʾeñ kabhī pā-yāb to sar-yāb kabhī,
tairne lagte haiñ be-hoshī kī āñkhoñ meñ kaʾī chĕhre
jo dekhe bhī nah hoñ
kabhī dekhe hoñ kisī ne to surāġh un kā
kahāñ se pāʾe?
kis se īfā huʾe añdoh ke ādāb kabhī
ārzūʾeñ kabhī pā-yāb to sar-yāb kabhī!)

yih kūzoñ ke lāshe, jo in ke liye haiñ
kisī dāstān-e fanā ke vaġhairah vaġhairah——
hamārī ażāñ haiñ, hamārī ṭalab kā nishāñ haiñ
yih apne sukūt-e ajal meñ bhī yih kah rahe haiñ:
"vuh āñkheñ hamīñ haiñ jo andar khulī haiñ
tumheñ dekhtī haiñ, har ik dard ko bhāñptī haiñ
har ik ḥusn ke rāz ko jāntī haiñ
kih ham ek sunsān ḥujre kī us rāt kī ārzū haiñ
jahāñ ek chĕhre, daraḳhtoñ kī shāḳhoñ ke mānind
ik aur chĕhrah pah jhuk-kar, har insāñ ke sīne meñ
ik barg-e gul rakh gayā thā
usī shab kā duzdīdah bosah hamīñ haiñ!"

§30. MERE BHĪ HAIÑ KUCHH ḲHVĀB

ai ʿishq-e azal-gīr-o-abad-tāb, mere bhī haiñ kuchh ḳhvāb

mere bhī haiñ kuchh ḳhvāb!
is daur se, is daur ke sūkhe huʾe daryāʾoñ se,
phaile huʾe ṣaḥrāʾoñ se, aur shahroñ ke vīrānoñ se
vīrānah-garoñ se maiñ ḥazīñ aur udās!
ai ʿishq-e azal-gīr-o-abad-tāb
mere bhī haiñ kuchh ḳhvāb!

which has advanced from age to age
from autumn to autumn
which in the new self of every young potter
advances further!
That shadow of the manifestation of art through whose bounty
we are all love
we are all potters
we are all aware, entirely unaware
like God we are wholly the gods of our art!
(The longings are sometimes shallow and sometimes deep,
then some faces begin to swim in unconscious eyes
that would not even be seen
even if they were seen, then how would someone
find their sign?
how would they fulfill the etiquette of grief
The longings are sometimes shallow then sometimes deep!)

These corpses of pots, which for them are
the et cetera, et cetera of some tale of annihilation,
our calls to prayer, our signs of searching
Even in their silence of death they say:
"We are those eyes that are open inside
We are watching you, we comprehend every pain
we know the secret of every beauty
for we are the longing of that night in a desolate chamber
where one face, like the branches of trees
bending upon another face, in the chest of every man
had placed a flower petal
We are the stolen kiss of that night!"

§30. I TOO HAVE SOME DREAMS

O love, embracing the Beginning and illuminating the End, I too
have some dreams
I too have some dreams!
This age, the dried-out rivers of this age,
the outspread deserts, the ruins of cities,
their destroyers leave me sad and forlorn!
O love, embracing the Beginning and illuminating the End,
I too have some dreams!

ai ʿishq-e azal-gīr-o-abad-tāb, mere bhī haiñ kuchh ḳhvāb

mere bhī haiñ kuchh ḳhvāb
vuh ḳhvāb kih asrār nahīñ jin ke hameñ āj bhī maʿlūm
vuh ḳhvāb jo āsūdagī-e martabah-o-jāh se,
ālūdagī-e gird-e sar-e rāh se maʿṣūm!
jo zīst kī be-hūdah kashākash se bhī hote nahīñ maʿdūm
ḳhvud zīst kā mafhūm!

ai ʿishq-e azal-gīr-o-abad-tāb,
ai kāhin-e dānish-var-o-ʿālī-guhar-o-pīr
tū ne hī batāʾī hameñ har ḳhvāb kī taʿbīr
tū ne hī sujhāʾī ġham-e dil-gīr kī tasḳhīr
ṭūṭī tire hāthoñ hī se har ḳhauf kī zanjīr
ai ʿishq-e azal-gīr-o-abad-tāb, mere bhī haiñ kuchh ḳhvāb

mere bhī haiñ kuchh ḳhvāb!

ai ʿishq-e azal-gīr-o-abad-tāb,
kuchh ḳhvāb kih madfūn haiñ ijdād ke ḳhvud-sāḳhtah asmār ke nīche
ujṛe huʾe maẕhab ke banā-reḳhtah auhām kī dīvār ke nīche
shīrāz ke majẕūb-e tunak-jām ke afkār ke nīche
tahẕīb-e nigūñ-sār ke ālām ke ambār ke nīche!

kuchh ḳhvāb haiñ āzād magar baṛhte huʾe nūr se marʿūb
nai ḥauṣlah-e ḳhvub hai, nai himmat-e nā-ḳhvub
go ẕāt se baṛh-kar nahīñ kuchh bhī uñheñ maḥbūb
haiñ āp hī us ẕāt ke jā-rūb
——ẕāt se maḥjūb

kuchh ḳhvāb haiñ jo girdish-e ālāt se joyandah-e tamkīn

hai jin ke liye bandagī-e qāẓī-e ḥājāt se is dahr kī tazʾīn

kuchh jis ke liye ġham kī masāvāt se insān kī taʾmīn

kuchh ḳhvāb kih jin kā havas-e jaur hai āʾīn
dunyā hai nah dīn!

kuchh ḳhvāb haiñ parvardah-e anvār, magar un kī saḥar gum
jis āg se uṭhtā hai muḥabbat kā ḳhamīr, us ke sharar gum
hai kul kī ḳhabar un ko magar juz kī ḳhabar gum

O love, embracing the Beginning and illuminating the End, I too
    have some dreams
        I too have some dreams
Those dreams whose mysteries are not known to us even today
Those dreams which are free from the comfort of station and rank,
from the pollution of the dust of the road!
Which are not annihilated even by the foolish struggle of life,
        which are themselves the meaning of life!

O love embracing the Beginning and illuminating the End,
O wise, noble, and old soothsayer
You alone told us the interpretation of every dream
You alone showed us how to overcome the suffering of melancholy
By your hands alone, every chain of fear broke
O love embracing the Beginning and illuminating the End, I too
    have some dreams
        I too have some dreams!

O love embracing the Beginning and illuminating the End,
Some dreams are buried under the made-up tales of our ancestors
under the wall of illusions raised by a ruined religion
under the thoughts of the easily intoxicated fakir of Shiraz
under the heap of sorrows of a shamed civilization!

Some dreams are free but frightened by the advancing light
they have neither the courage for good nor the strength for non-good
Though they have no beloved greater than the self
they themselves are the broom of that self
        —concealed from the self

There are some dreams that seek grandeur in the turning of
    machines
for which servitude to the Judge of the Necessities is the adornment
    of this age
There are some for whom the equality of suffering is the ornament of
    man
some dreams whose lust for tyranny is the rule
        neither the world nor religion!

Some dreams are raised by lights, but their dawn is lost
the fire from which the leaven of love rises, its sparks are lost
they know of the whole but have lost trace of the part

yih ḳhvāb haiñ vuh jin ke liye martabah-e dīdah-e tar hech
dil hech hai, sar itne barābar haiñ kih sar hech
—— ʿarẓ-e hunar hech!

ai ʿishq-e azal-gīr-o-abad-tāb
yih ḳhvāb mire ḳhvāb nahīñ haiñ kih mire ḳhvāb haiñ kuchh aur
kuchh aur mire ḳhvāb haiñ, kuchh aur mirā daur
ḳhvāboñ ke naʾe daur meñ nai mor-o-malaḳh nai asad-o-ṡaur

nai lażżat-e taslīm kisī meñ nah kisī ko havas-e jaur
——sab ke naʾe t̤aur!

ai ʿishq-e azal-gīr-o-abad-tāb,
mere bhī haiñ kuchh ḳhvāb!
har ḳhvāb kī saugand!
har chand kih vuh ḳhvāb haiñ sar-bastah-o-rū-band
sīne meñ chhupāʾe huʾe goyāʾī-e doshīzah-e lab-ḳhand
har ḳhvāb meñ ajsām se afkār kā, mafhūm se guftār kā paivand

ʿushshāq ke lab-hā-e azal-tishnah kī paivastagī-e shauq ke mānind

(ai lamḥah-e ḳhvursand!)

ai ʿishq-e azal-gīr-o-abad-tāb, mere bhī haiñ kuchh ḳhvāb

vuh ḳhvāb haiñ āzādī-e kāmil ke naʾe ḳhvāb
har saʿī-e jigar-doz ke ḥāsil ke naʾe ḳhvāb
ādam kī vilādat ke naʾe jashn pah lahrāte jalājil ke naʾe ḳhvāb

is ḳhāk kī sat̤vat kī manāzil ke naʾe ḳhvāb
yā sīnah-e gītī meñ naʾe dil ke naʾe ḳhvāb
ai ʿishq-e azal-gīr-o-abad-tāb
mere bhī haiñ kuchh ḳhvāb
mere bhī haiñ kuchh ḳhvāb!

These are dreams for which the rank of a weeping eye is nothing
the heart is nothing, heads are so equal that heads are nothing
—the breadth of art nothing!

O love, embracing the Beginning and illuminating the End
These dreams are not my dreams for my dreams are something more
Something more are my dreams, something more is my age
In the new age of dreams there are neither ants and locusts nor the Lion and the Bull
In no one is there the pleasure of submission or the lust for tyranny
—a new way for all!

O love, embracing the Beginning and illuminating the End,
I too have some dreams!
The oath of every dream!
Although the heads and faces of those dreams are covered
Hidden in [their] breast, the eloquence of a smiling virgin
In every dream the grafting of thoughts with bodies, of speech with meaning
like the connection with desire of the lips of lovers thirsting for eternity
(O happy moment!)

O love, embracing the Beginning and illuminating the End, I too have some dreams
These dreams are new dreams of complete freedom
new dreams of the rewards of every heart-piercing effort
new dreams of the waving bells on the new celebration of Man's birth
new dreams of destinations of majesty for this dust
or new dreams of a new heart in the chest of the world
O love, embracing the Beginning and illuminating the End,
I too have some dreams
I too have some dreams!

NOTES

INTRODUCTION

1. Urdu is usually written in the calligraphic right-to-left *nastạ̈līq* script shared with Persian and derived from Arabic, whereas Hindi is preferentially written in the left-to-right *devanāgarī* script, also commonly used now for Sanskrit, as well as other languages, such as Nepali. Hindi and Urdu can be represented in either script, and are frequently written (though not usually published) in various forms of the Roman alphabet, especially on the Internet, mobile devices, and product labels.

2. Urdu meter is quantitative and based on particular patterns of syllables of certain lengths (not stress, as in English and German). Hindi meter is also based on syllable length, but focuses on the number of syllables of particular lengths in a particular line with less attention to fitting them into a particular pattern.

3. The ghazal consists of two-line couplets, where the second is usually an answer to the first. They are generally not connected in a linear narrative but rather a thematic one, in which they address the suffering and experiences of a lover pining for an unnamed beloved, who could be human or divine.

4. Iftikhar Dadi's study of "South Asian Muslim Modernism" similarly points to the complexity of that genealogy in the visual arts. He describes the variegated "tradition" of the Pakistani artists he describes as involving a "genealogy [that] includes fragments from Persianate humanism, Hindu and Buddhist mythology, the orientalist construction of the discipline of Islamic art, colonial governmentality, nineteenth-century theological and modernist reform, modern pan-Islamism, twentieth-century metropolitan and transnational artistic modernism, and mid-twentieth-century nationalism and developmentalism, and contemporary debates on race, gender, and globalization." Iftikhar Dadi, *Modernism and the Art of Muslim South Asia* (Chapel Hill, NC: University of North Carolina Press, 2010), 2.

5. For a discussion of Sufism in Urdu and Persian poetry, see the work of Annemarie Schimmel, especially *As Through a Veil: Mystical Poetry in Islam* (New York: Columbia University Press, 1982). For a discussion of the problematic equation

of "Sufism" with mysticism and a view of Sufis as social actors, see Nile Green, *Sufism: A Global History* (Malden, MA: Wiley-Blackwell, 2012).

6. Two recent compilations that showcase the current state of research are Peter Brooker, Andrzej Gasiorek, Deborah Longworth, and Andrew Thacker, eds., *The Oxford Handbook of Modernisms* (New York, Oxford University Press, 2010); and Mark Wollaeger with Matt Eatough, eds., *The Oxford Handbook of Global Modernisms* (New York: Oxford University Press, 2012). Both also have fine introductions. For a 2009 evaluation of the state of modernist studies, see Douglas Mao and Rebecca L. Walkowitz, "The Changing Profession: The New Modernist Studies," *PMLA* 123, no.3 (2008): 737–48.

7. I take this apt term from the Brooker et al., "Introduction," in *The Oxford Handbook of Modernisms*. They clarify, "This doesn't mean that the aesthetic, which was championed in different ways by various modernists, as well as by such influential critics as Clement Greenberg and Theodor Adorno, has been bracketed off or jettisoned [in modernist studies since the late 1980s], but rather that it is no longer assumed to be the principal issue at stake in discussions of modernism and its legacies" (2). For an excellent discussion of New Modernist studies in relation to previous literary criticism, see Douglas Mao and Rebecca L. Walkowitz, "Introduction: Modernisms Bad and New," in *Bad Modernisms*, ed. Douglas Mao and Rebecca L. Walkowitz (Durham, NC: Duke University Press, 2006), 1–18.

8. As the enthusiasm for modernism spills over into South Asian literary studies, other work will hopefully expand both the study of its aesthetic and of its social and cultural history. We can hope that more studies of the little avant-garde magazine, so central to modernism in Hindi, Urdu, Bengali, and elsewhere, will become a site for more extensive research, as well as of cultural heritage preservation. For an example addressing Hindi, see Alok Rai, "Reading Pratik through Agyeya: Reading Agyeya through Pratik," in *Hindi Modernism*, ed. Vasudha Dalmia (Delhi: Manohar, 2012), 17–29. There is strong work on the emergence of print culture in the colonial period that will hopefully get extended forward through the twentieth century (e.g., Ulrike Stark, *An Empire of Books: The Naval Kishore Press and the Diffusion of the Printed Word in South Asia* [New Delhi: Permanent Black, 2007]).

9. N. M. Rāshid, "Tamhīd," in *Īrān meñ ajnabī aur dūsarī naẓmeñ* (Lahore: Goshah-e adab, 1957), 25.

10. N. M. Rāshid, *Māvarā* (Lahore: Maktabah-e urdū, [1941]), 23.

11. N. M. Rāshid, "Tamhīd," in *Īrān meñ ajnabī*, 25. This is a frequent trope also taken up later by traditionalists. See the description of Salīm Aḥmad's reading of Ġhālib versus Mīr as a modern versus a traditional poet in A. Sean Pue, "In the Mirror of Ghalib: Postcolonial Reflections on Indo-Muslim Selfhood," *The Indian Economic and Social History Review* 48, no. 4 (2011): 571–92.

12. N. M. Rāshid, "Tamhīd," 31.

13. N. M. Rāshid, *Lā=Insān* (Lahore: al-Miṡāl, 1969), 21.

14. N. M. Rāshid, *Māvarā*, 29.

15. N. M. Rāshid, *Lā=Insān*, 34.

16. See Laura Anne Doyle and Laura A. Wikiel, eds., *Geomodernisms: Race, Modernism, Modernity* (Bloomington, IN: Indiana University Press, 2005). Two other similar terms contend with "geomodernism" in contemporary modernist studies, and these are "planetary" and "global" modernism. Following the lead of Gayatri Spivak, a number of scholars have turned away from the rational ordering of the "global" to consider the "planetary." Gayatri Spivak, *Death of A Discipline* (New York: Columbia University Press, 2003). Others contend that the "planetary" "conjures the distraction of the interplanetary, whereas 'global' suggests horizons that shift with the curve of the earth and the position of the observer." Mark Wollaeger, "Introduction," in *Oxford Handbook of Global Modernisms*, 5. While none of these terms are particularly satisfying, they all point toward a similar formulation.

17. Laura Anne Doyle, "Modernist Studies and Inter-Imperiality in the Longue Durée," in *The Oxford Handbook of Global Modernisms*, ed. Mark Wollaeger with Matt Eatough (New York: Oxford University Press, 2012), 684–85; Edward Said, *Culture and Imperialism* (New York: Vintage Books, 1994), 186–90.

18. Laura Anne Doyle and Laura A. Wikiel, "Introduction: The Global Horizons of Modernism," in *Geomodernisms*, 3.

19. Muġhannī Tabassum, "N. M. Rāshid: muḳhtaṣar ḥālāt-e zindagī," in *N. M. Rāshid: fikr-o-fan*, ed. Kuñvar Muḥammad Aḳhlāq Ḳhāñ Shahryār and Muġhannī Tabassum (Hyderabad, India: Maktabah-e shĕʻr-o-ḥikmat, 1971), 10.

20. These writings have been collected in N. M. Rāshid, *Rāshid: Rāvī meñ*, edited by Saʻādat Saʻīd and Muḥammad Rafīq (Lahore: Department of Urdu, Government College University, 2010). See also Salīm Aḳhtar, "N. M.Rāshid kā matrūk kalām," in *Maqālāt-e ḥalqah-e arbāb-e żauq*, ed. Suhail Aḥmad (Lahore: Polimar Publications, 1990), 190–217.

21. N. M. Rashed's daughter Nasreen Rashed recently edited and had published a number of their early letters. See N. M. Rāshid, *N. M. Rāshid ke ḳhuṭūṭ, apnī ahiliyah ke nām,* ed. Nasrīn Rāshid (Islamabad: A. R. Printers, 2010).

22. A brainchild of Muḥammad ʻInāyatu'l-lâh Ḳhān Mashriqī, the Ḳhāksār movement was founded in 1931–1932. Characterized by a commitment to military-style discipline and organization, the movement was organized into detachments, forming a "shadow government" of the local colonial state. Rashed held the rank of *sālār* (commander) of Multan in the movement and commanded a *dāshtah* (detachment) of twenty-five soldiers. With its emphasis on uniforms, marching, and militarization, the Ḳhāksār movement had fascistic aspirations, but they did so while carrying shovels not weapons. Rumors of a meeting between Mashriqi and Hitler, which probably never actually took place, were capitalized on by his followers. Though nominally an apolitical and noncommunal service organization, the Ḳhāksār movement used Islamic symbols and attracted Muslims almost exclusively. As a Muslim movement with political aspirations, it was an alternative to the Muslim League based almost entirely in Punjab. Mashriqi used Islamic titles to characterize his position—calling himself an *amīr*, and his followers *raʻiyyat*

(subjects). Yet he criticized religious authorities, like *maulvīs* and *mullās*, whom he blamed for excessive sectarianism, ritualism, and illiteracy, and also Sufis and their leaders *(pīr)*, whom he saw as pacifistic and held responsible for the decline of Muslim political power. Although a relatively minor organization, largely ignored by nationalist historians, the Ḳhāksārs were still subject to intense surveillance by the colonial state. See Iftikhar H. Malik, "Regionalism or Personality Cult? Allama Mashriqi and the Tehreek-i-Khaksar in pre-1947 Punjab," in *Region and Partition: Bengal, Punjab and the Partition of the Subcontinent*, ed. Ian Talbot and Gurharpal Singh (Karachi: Oxford University Press, 1999), 42–94; and Muhammad Aslam Malik, *Allama Inayatullah Mashraqi: A Political Biography* (Karachi: Oxford University Press, 2000).

23. In a late interview, Rashed explains his participation as the result of a "psychological crisis." N. M. Rāshid, "N. M. Rāshid se ek muṣāhibah," interview by Nasrīn Anjum Bhaṭṭī, in *Rāshid ba-qalam-e ḳhwud,* ed. Sa'ādat Sa'īd and Nasrīn Anjum Bhaṭṭī (Lahore: Department of Urdu, Government College, 2010), 55–56.

24. N. M. Rāshid, "Ḥālāt-o-kavā'if," in *N. M. Rāshid: ek muṭāla'ah*, ed. Jamīl Jālibī (Karachi: Maktabah-e uslūb, 1986). 9.

25. N. M. Rāshid, *Īrān meñ ajnabī aur dūsarī naẓmeñ* (Lahore: Goshah-e adab, 1957).

26. H. R. Luthra, *Indian Broadcasting* (New Delhi: Publications Division, Ministry of Information and Broadcasting, Government of India, 1986), 171–72.

27. N. M. Rāshid, "Ḥālāt-o-kavā'if," 10.

28. Tehsin Firaqi recently gathered and published these interviews. See Taḥsīn Firāqī, ed., *Ḥasan Kūzahgar* (Lahore: Department of Urdu, Oriental College), 2010.

29. N. M. Rāshid, *Jadīd fārsī shā'irī: taqrīr az N. M. Rāshid* (Lahore: al-Mis̤āl, 1969); N. M. Rāshid, *Jadid fārsī shā'irī* (Lahore: Majlis-e taraqqī-e adab, 1987).

30. N. M. Rāshid, *Lā = Insān.*

31. N. M. Rāshid, "N. M. Rāshid se ek muṣāḥibah," interviewed by Sa'ādat Sa'īd, 1969, in *Maqālāt-e N. M. Rāshid*, ed. Shīmā Majīd (Islamabad: Alhamra Publishing, 2002), 385.

32. Āftāb Aḥmad, "Rāshid kī yād meñ," *Nayā Daur* 71–72 (1978?): 272.

33. Ě'jāz Ḥusain Baṭālvī, "Āḳhirī majmū'ah, āḳhirī mulāqāt," forward to *Gumāñ kā mumkin*, by N. M. Rāshid (Lahore: Nayā Idārah, 1976), *be.*

34. Ě'jāz Ḥusain Baṭālvī, "Āḳhirī majmū'ah, āḳhirī mulāqāt," *dāl.*

35. Sāqī Fārūqī's account gives the date as October 11. "Ḥasan Kūzahgar," *Nayā daur* 71–72 (1978?): 17. This piece has been translated into English by Rafey Habib and Faruq Hasan as "Hasan the Potter," *Annual of Urdu Studies* 5 (1985): 3–17.

36. Sāqī Fārūqī, "Ḥasan kūzahgar," 17–18; Shahryār Rāshid, "Mere vālid," translated by Intiẓār Ḥusain, in Āftāb Aḥmad, *N. M. Rāshid: shā'ir-o-shaḳhṣ* (Lahore: Māvarā Publishers, 1989), 21.

37. Yāsmīn Rāshid Ḥasan, "Vaẓāḥat," *Bunyād* 1 (2010): 294–98.

38. "N. M. Rāshid kī āḳhirī vaṣiyyat: lāsh ko jalā diyā jā'e aur merī namāz nah paṛhī jā'e," *Chaṭān* 28, no. 43 (27 October 1975), 5.

39. Mīrājī, "Raqṣ," in *N. M. Rāshid: fikr-o-fan*, 235.

40. Faiẓ Aḥmad Faiẓ, "Nūn Mīm Rāshid," *Kitāb* 10, no. 3 (December 1975), 21–22. This article is a transcript of a commemorative address given by Faiz at the Pakistan National Center, Lahore.

41. Recent English-language treatments of the Progressive Writers Association include Talat Ahmed, *Literature and Politics in the Age of Nationalism: The Progressive Writers' Movement in South Asia, 1932–56* (London: Taylor and Francis, 2008) and Priyamvada Gopal, *Literary Radicalism in India: Gender, Nation and the Transition to Independence* (New York: Routledge, 2005). See also Kamran Asdar Ali's forthcoming book, "Surkh Salam (Red Greetings): Communists in a Muslim Land," as well as earlier work by Carlo Coppola, especially "Urdu Poetry 1935–1970: The Progressive Episode" (PhD dissertation, University of Chicago, 1975).

42. For a thorough discussion of these processes, as well as an insightful reading of the very influential Urdu modernist poet Mīrājī, see Geeta Patel, *Lyrical Movements, Historical Hauntings: On Gender, Colonialism, and Desire in Mīrājī's Urdu Poetry* (Stanford: Stanford University Press, 2002).

43. Āftāb Aḥmad, "N. M. Rāshid," *Adab-e laṭīf* 17–18, no. 6–7 (August-September 1943): 5–13. Its argument is similar to one made by Faiz in 1939, reprinted as Faiẓ Aḥmad Faiẓ, "N. M. Rāshid: ibtidāʾī daur-e shāʿirī," in *N. M. Rāshid: ek muṭālaʿah*, ed. Jamīl Jālibī (Karachi: Maktabah-e uslūb, 1986), 80–84.

44. Āftāb Aḥmad, *N. M. Rāshid: shāʿir-o-shakhṣ*, 89, 92.

45. N. M. Rāshid, "Muṣāhibah," in *Lā=Insān*, 2.

46. See C. M. Naim, "The Consequences of the Indo-Pakistan War for Urdu Language and Literature: A Parting of the Ways?" *The Journal of Asian Studies* 28, no. 2 (1969): 269–83.

47. ʿĀlam Ḳhūndmīrī, "N. M. Rāshid, insān aur ḳhudā," in *N. M. Rāshid: fikr-o-fan*, 52.

48. Vazīr Āġhā, "N. M. Rāshid," in *N. M. Rāshid: ek mutālaʿah*, 184.

49. Muġhannī Tabassum, "Mujhe vidāʿ kar," in *N. M. Rāshid: fikr-o-fan*, 265.

50. Fatḥ Muḥammad Malik, *N. M. Rāshid: siyāsat aur shāʿirī*, 135–44.

51. Fatḥ Muḥammad Malik, *N. M. Rāshid: siyāsat aur shāʿirī*, 10–11, 52.

52. Fatḥ Muḥammad Malik, *N. M. Rāshid: siyāsat aur shāʿirī*, 134.

53. Muhammad Iqbal, "Presidential Address Delivered at the Annual Session of the All-India Muslim League, 29th December, 1930," in *Speeches, Writings, and Statements of Iqbal*, edited by Latif Ahmed Sherwani (Lahore: Iqbal Academy, 1977), 3.

CHAPTER ONE

1. While Rashed is celebrated for his decisive break with classical forms, poets had experimented with blank verse over the previous decades. See Ḥanīf Kaifī, *Urdū meñ naẓm-e muʿarrā aur āzād naẓm: ibtidā se 1947 tak* (New Delhi: Uttar Pradesh Urdu Academy, 1982).

2. Aamir R. Mufti, *Enlightenment in the Colony: The Jewish Question and the Crisis of Postcolonial Culture* (Princeton: Princeton University Press, 2007), 141.

3. Farina Mir, *The Social Space of Language: Vernacular Culture in British Colonial Punjab* (Berkeley: University of California Press, 2010).

4. Farina Mir, "Imperial Policy, Provincial Practices: Colonial Language Policy in Nineteenth-century India," *Indian Economic and Social History Review* 43, no. 4 (December 2006): 395–427.

5. Vasudha Dalmia, *The Nationalization of Hindu Traditions: Bhāratendu Hariśchandra and Nineteenth-century Banaras* (Delhi: Oxford University Press, 1997).

6. Dalmia, *The Nationalization of Hindu Traditions*, 217.

7. Dalmia, *The Nationalization of Hindu Traditions*, 291.

8. Using a familiar vocabulary of literary growth and maturation, Lucy Rosenstein explains, "Being a language in its infancy, Khari Boli Hindi did not have the melodiousness, elegance of diction and prosody, and wealth of cultural associations of Braj, a language refined by several hundred years of tradition. Thus the idea of using Khari Boli for verse was anathema to poetry connoisseurs at the end of the 19th and beginning of the 20th century." *New Poetry in Hindi (Nayi Kavita): An Anthology* (New Delhi: Permanent Black, 2002), 2.

9. Allison Busch, *Poetry of Kings: The Classical Hindi Literature of Mughal India* (New York: Oxford University Press, 2011).

10. Frances W. Pritchett, *Nets of Awareness: Urdu Poetry and Its Critics* (Berkeley: University of California, 1994).

11. Muḥammad Ḥusain Āzād, *Ab-e hayat: Shaping the Canon of Urdu Poetry*, trans. and ed. Frances Pritchett with Shamsur Rahman Faruqi (New Delhi: Oxford University Press, 2001), 91–92.

12. A similar movement in English education is described in Gauri Viswanathan, *Masks of Conquest: Literary Study and British Rule in India* (New York: Columbia University Press, 1989), 134.

13. Ḥālī explained, "Love is not restricted to lust, desire, love-games, or the seeking of gratification. It can be affection and attachment of basically any sort: of a man for God, of children for their parents, of parents for their children, of siblings for each other, of a husband for his wife, of a wife for her husband, of a servant for his master, of a subject for a king, of a friend for a friend, of a man for an animal, of people for their place, for their homeland, and for their nation/community (*qaum*). When there is so much space and universality in love, when in our expressions of love there is such baseness, and when the way the beloved is talked about is so shameful, why is it necessary that love should be restricted to just sexual desire and animal lust? Why should one reveal such a hidden secret and make apparent one's meanness and weakness?" Alṭāf Ḥusain Ḥālī, *Muqaddamah-e shĕʿr-o-shāʿirī* (Lucknow: Uttar Pradesh Urdu Academy, 2002 [1893]), 120–21.

14. "There is no better way to spread natural poetry then to express in the ghazal every type of elegant and pure thought. It should become a tool to express all human emotions. Additionally, it should be put forward dressed in such clothing that at first sight it does not appear strange or unfamiliar." Ḥālī, *Muqaddamah-e shĕʿr-o-shāʿirī*, 151–52.

15. Karine Schomer, *Mahadevi Varma and the Chhayavad Age of Modern Hindi Poetry* (Berkeley: University of California Press, 1983), 13.

16. Lucy Rosenstein, *New Poetry in Hindi*, 5.

17. Dipesh Chakrabarty, *Provincializing Europe: Postcolonial Thought and Historical Difference* (Princeton: Princeton University Press, 2000), 168, 170.

18. Aamir R. Mufti, *Enlightenment in the Colony.*

19. N. M. Rāshid, "Dībāchah," in *Māvarā* (Lahore: Maktabah-e urdū, [1941]), 28.

20. Geeta Patel, *Lyrical Movements, Historical Hauntings: On Gender, Colonialism, and Desire in Miraji's Urdu Poetry* (Stanford: Stanford University Press, 2002).

21. N. M. Rāshid, "Dībāchah," in *Māvarā*, 28.

22. N. M. Rāshid, "Dībāchah," in *Māvarā*, 29.

23. In his *Muqaddamah-e shĕʿr-o-shāʿirī*, Ḥālī states that neither meter *(vazan)* nor rhyme *(qāfiyah)* is a constitutive element of poetry, however much they enhance the listener's pleasure. He argues for a distinction between *shĕʿr* and *naẓm* that is the same as the distinction between "poetry" and "verse" in English, whereby verse requires meter and poetry does not. While he agrees that rhyme increases the pleasantness of poetic language, he qualifies this admission: rhyme, especially when paired with refrain *(radīf)* as developed and practiced by Persian poets, can greatly hinder poets in "fulfilling their duty." Because of rhyme, Ḥālī states, a poet cannot simply form a thought and then put it into words. Instead, he must first choose a rhyme and then, if he is able, conform his thought to match the rhyme; otherwise, he must abandon the thought completely. "Thus," Ḥālī writes, "in reality, a poet cannot put an idea into verse by himself; rather, he puts into verse the idea that the rhyme allows" (32).

24. N. M. Rāshid, "Āzād shāʿirī," in *Maqālāt-e N. M. Rāshid*, ed. Shīmā Majīd (Islamabad: Alhamra, 2002), 10. Originally published in *Ilhām* (May 1941).

25. N. M. Rāshid, "Dībāchah," in *Māvarā*, 26–27.

26. Ḥālī, *Muqaddamah-e shĕʿr-o-shāʿirī*, 91–92.

27. Sayyid Akḥtar Aḥmad Akḥtar, "Urdū kī rūmānī shāʿirī aur Akḥtar Shairānī" in Akḥtar Shairānī, *Ṣubḥ-e bahār* (Dehli: Maktabah-e anokhā jāsūs, 1971), 22–28; S. Akḥtar Jaʿfrī, "Dībāchah" in *Akhtar Shairānī aur us kī shāʿirī*, ed. S. Akḥtar Jaʿfrī (Lahore: Āʾinah-e adab, 1964), 20–26.

28. "ai ʿishq kahīñ le chal, is bāp kī bastī se / nafratgah-e ʿālam se, laʿnatgah-e hastī se / in nafs-parastoñ se, is nafs-parastī se / dūr—aur kahīñ le chal! / ai ʿishq kahīñ le chal! // . . . . qudrat ho ḥimāyat par hamdard ho qismat bhī / salmâ bhī ho pahlū meñ salmâ kī muḥabbat bhī / har shai se farāġhāt ho aur terī ʿināyat bhī / ṭifl-e ḥasīñ le chal! / ai ʿishq kahīñ le chal! // ik aisī bihisht āʾeñ vādī meñ pahuñch jāʾeñ / jis meñ kabhī dunyā ke ġham dil ko nah taṛpāʾeñ / aur jis kī bahāroñ meñ jīne ke maze āʾeñ / le chal to vahīñ le chal! / ai ʿishq, kahīñ le chal!" Akḥtar Shairānī, "Ai ʿishq kahīñ le chal," in *Kulliyāt-e Akḥtar Shairānī*, ed. Gopāl Mittal (Delhi: Modern Publishing House, 1997), 32–37.

29. My analysis here draws on Salīm Aḥmad's influential essay "Naʾī naẓm aur pūrā ādmī" (New Verse and the Complete Man) in which he calls Akḥtar Shairānī

not a "complete man" but a poet of only the "upper-half," on the grounds that his poetry, with its persistent praise of "innocence" *(ma'ṣūmiyat)*, is really in tune with the forces of "morality" *(akhlāqiyāt)*. See Salīm Aḥmad, "Na'ī naẕm aur pūrā ādmī," in *Na'ī naẕm aur pūrā ādmī* (Karachi: Adabī Academy, 1962), 19–20.

30. Akhtar Shairānī, "Gujrāt kī rāt," *Kulliyāt-e Akhtar Shairānī*, 179.

31. N. M. Rāshid, "Chand lamḥe Akhtar Shairānī ke sāth," in *Maqālāt-e N. M. Rāshid*, ed. Shīmā Majīd, 351. Originally published in *Akhtaristān*.

32. According to Āġhā 'Abdu'l-ḥamīd, Rashed wrote this poem in the first week of August 1934 when they were both in Multan. Āġhā 'Abdu'l-ḥamīd, "Rāshid: chand khaṭ, chand yādeñ," in *N. M. Rāshid: ek muṭāla'ah*, ed. Jamīl Jālibī (Karachi: Maktabah-e uslūb, 1986), 41–42.

33. N. M. Rāshid, "Āzād shā'irī," in *Maqālāt-e N. M. Rāshid*, ed. Shīmā Majīd. For a similar exegesis, written the day after the poem, see also N. M. Rāshid to Āġhā 'Abdu'l-ḥamīd, Delhi, 1 April 1940, in *N. M. Rāshid: ek muṭāla'ah*, ed. Jamīl Jālibī, 240.

34. Rashed quotes from the piece in the article "Ġhālīb hamāre zamāne meñ," in *N. M. Rāshid: fikr-o-fan*, ed. Kuñvar Muḥammad Akhlāq Khāñ Shahryār and Muġhannī Tabassum (Hyderabad, India: Maktabah-e shĕ'r-o-ḥikmat, 1971), 331–43.

35. Sigmund Freud, "Formulations on the Two Principles of Mental Functioning," in *The Standard Edition of the Complete Psychological Works of Sigmund Freud* (London: Hogarth Press, 1958), 12:218, 224.

36. Sigmund Freud, *Civilization and Its Discontents*, trans. and ed. James Strachey (New York: W. W. Norton and Company, 1961), 33–34.

37. For Fanon, this desire springs from an internalized sense of inferiority and an urge to be acknowledged as white, and he writes, "when my restless hands caress those white breasts, they grasp white civilization and dignity and make them mine." Frantz Fanon, *Black Skins, White Masks*, trans. Charles Lam Markmann (New York: Grove Press, 1967), 63.

38. Alfred Adler (1870–1937) was an early advocate of Freud's theories who later broke with him. He opposed Freud's theory of sexuality by emphasizing "organ inferiority" as the dominant cause of neuroses. Adler's "Individual Psychology" rests on an analogy between psychic life and organic life: as though recovering from the loss of a limb, the patient both consciously and unconsciously seeks to (over)compensate for an unfilled goal, formed during childhood, through the maladjustments of the interrelated "superiority" and "inferiority" complexes. The goal of Adlerian therapy is to discover the mistakes an individual made during his or her formative years and to correct them through treatment. See Alfred Adler, *The Science of Living* (New York: Garden City, 1929).

39. Frantz Fanon, *Black Skins, White Masks*, 81.

40. Frantz Fanon, *Black Skins, White Masks*, 213.

41. Frantz Fanon, *Black Skins, White Masks*, 216.

42. N. M. Rāshid, "Āzād shā'irī," 11.

43. A key work here is Partha Chatterjee, *The Nation and Its Fragments: Colonial and Postcolonial Histories* (Princeton: Princeton University Press, 1993).

44. Ahmed Ali, "The Progressive Writers' Movement and Creative Writers in Urdu," in *Marxist Influences and South Asian Literature*, ed. Carlo Coppola (East Lansing: Asian Studies Center, Michigan State University, 1974), 1:34–44.

45. ʿAzīz Aḥmad, *Taraqqī pasand adab* (New Delhi: Chaman Book Depot, [1945]), 96.

46. Ḥayātu'l-lâh Anṣārī, *N. M. Rāshid par* (New Delhi: Insha Press, 1945).

47. In a comprehensive study of psychological criticism in Urdu, Salīm Aḳhtar notes that Anṣārī is perhaps the first Urdu critic to use Adler. He also comments, "because the sexual elements of Rashed's poetry are the special target of [Anṣārī's] critique, he makes no mention of Freudianism." Salīm Aḳhtar, *Nafsiyātī tanqīd* (Lahore: Majlis-e taraqqī-e adab, 1986), 223.

48. The exact phrase he uses is "*īżā-dihī kī ʿillat*," literally, the "sickness of pain-giving." He cites Adler's chapter on "Love and Marriage" in *The Science of Living*, quoting the passage: "If few persons are properly prepared nowadays for family life it is that they have never learned to see with the eyes, hear with the ears, and feel with the heart of another." Adler argues that the right preparation for love and marriage is to be properly adjusted socially through the development of "social feeling." The development of "social feeling" is obstructed by an inferiority complex, which is often compensated for in the desire to be a "conqueror" in a relationship. Anṣārī explains: "Such a curtain falls upon the thoughts of a man who is a victim of sadism that he cannot form any picture of the pleasure that a woman experiences through her movements and pauses [in love-making], and his gaze remains transfixed on his own movements and pauses." Turning to Rashed's poem "Revenge," Anṣārī notes that the "hero" of Rashed's poem is a victim of this sickness. He continues, "To feel emotions of enmity during love-making with a European woman is somewhat natural, but . . . a man gives pleasure to a woman no matter what country she is from. To not experience this pleasure and to remain fixated on an assumed enmity is nothing other than a psychological illness." Ḥayātu'l-lâh Anṣārī, *N. M. Rāshid par*, 10–11.

49. Ḥayātu'l-lâh Anṣārī, *N. M. Rāshid par*, 99.

50. Ḥayātu'l-lâh Anṣārī, *N. M. Rāshid par*, 99–100.

51. Ḥayātu'l-lâh Anṣārī, *N. M. Rāshid par*, 80.

52. Writing in 1951, progressive poet and critic ʿAli Sardār Jaʿfrī, for example, dismissed the writers of the Ḥalqah-e Arbāb-e Żauq (Circle of People of Taste), a literary organization most strongly associated with the poet Mīrājī, as "lovers of form, ambiguity, and sex" who, "influenced by Europe's degraded literature, focused on the subconscious and unconscious instead of consciousness and, abandoning meaning and matter, focused on form and style." He sees in them an excessive internality as well as formalism. He goes on to note that the lyrical "I" of their poetry "did not bear any type of social responsibility, and it inevitably resulted in ambiguity, pessimism, and escapism." Unable to form a "relationship with the common people," in part because these poets based in the Punjab were writing in Urdu, they "quickly became the victims of European degradation," and their poetry remained the "ugly filth of landlords and the bourgeoisie." ʿAlī Sardār Jaʿfrī, *Taraqqī pasand adab* (Aligarh: Anjuman-e Taraqqī-e Urdū, 1951), 190–91.

53. Anṣārī writes, "the latter half of *Māvarā* is full of emotions of lust *(shahvat)*, but unfortunately these emotions are not free from psychological complexes. In it, there is a lack of attention, sadism, masochism, the pain of conscience, emotional suffocation, and a lack of creative emotion." Drawing on Adler's depiction of Don Juan, he declares that "these poems in reality depict conquests, not the natural expression of the natural faculty." Ḥayātu'l-lâh Anṣārī, *N. M. Rāshid par*, 43–45, 58.

CHAPTER TWO

1. Mug̈hannī Tabassum, "N. M. Rāshid: mukḥtaṣar ḥālāt-e zindagī," in *N. M. Rāshid: fikr-o-fan*, ed. Kuñvar Muḥammad Akḥlāq Ḳhāñ Shahryār and Mug̈hannī Tabassum (Hyderabad, India: Maktabah-e shĕ'r-o-ḥikmat, 1971), 9.

2. 'Alī Sardār Ja'frī, *Eshiyā jāg uṭhā* (Delhi: Maktabah-e shāhrāh, 1952), 13, 9–10.

3. Gayatri Chakravorty Spivak, *Other Asias* (Malden, MA: Blackwell Publishing, 2008), 240, 1.

4. Gayatri Chakravorty Spivak, "Scattered Speculations on the Subaltern and the Popular," *Postcolonial Studies* 8, no. 4 (2005): 476.

5. In contrast to the preoccupation of Western literature with individual experience, "third-world texts," Jameson notoriously asserted, "necessarily project a political dimension in the form of national allegory." For those who "have suffered the experience of colonialism and imperialism," he writes, "the telling of the individual story and the individual experience cannot but ultimately involve the whole laborious telling of the experience of the collectivity itself." Frederic Jameson, "Third-World Literature in the Era of Multinational Capital," *Social Text* 15 (Fall 1986): 65, 69, 67, 85–86. It is important to note in this context that the most prominent response to Jameson's piece came from an Urdu literary critic, Aijaz Ahmad, who disputes Jameson's premise of a "third-world text," noting that in Jameson's essay "difference between the first world and the third is absolutised as an Otherness," while the "so-called third world is submerged within a singular identity of 'experience.'" The catchall category of nationalism ignores the fact that there are "hundreds of nationalisms in Asia and Africa"; "some are progressive, others are not." To Ahmad, the Urdu literary culture that emerged in the 1930s through the efforts of the Progressive Writers Association provides an example of a "socialist and/or communist culture" that is "neither nationalist nor postmodern" (8) in Jameson's terms. In short, Ahmad argues that Jameson's formulation elides the distinction between conservative and progressive politics in the so-called third world. Aijaz Ahmad, "Jameson's Rhetoric of Otherness and the 'National Allegory,'" *Social Text* 17 (Fall 1987): 10, 8.

6. See Aamir R. Mufti, *Enlightenment in the Colony: The Jewish Question and the Crisis of Postcolonial Culture* (Princeton, NJ: Princeton University Press, 2007), 180–85.

7. Aijaz Ahmad, "In the Mirror of Urdu: Recompositions of Nation and Community, 1947–1965" in *Lineages of the Present* (New Delhi: Tulika, 1996), 192.

8. Aḥmad Shāh Paṭras Buk̲hārī, "Tamhīd" in N. M. Rāshid, *Irān meñ ajnabī aur dūsarī nazmeñ* (Lahore: Goshah-e adab, 1957), 7–20; Tabassum Kāshmīrī, *Lā = Rāshid* (Lahore: Nigārishāt, 1994), 9–24; N. M. Rashed, "Interview with N. M. Rashed," *Mahfil* 7, no. 1–2 (1971), 4–5.

9. Aamir R. Mufti, "Aura of Authenticity," *Social Text* 18, no. 3 (2000): 87–103; Aamir R. Mufti, *Enlightenment in the Colony*, 14–21.

10. Aamir R. Mufti, "Aura of Authenticity," 87–88.

11. Aijaz Ahmad, "In the Mirror of Urdu," *Lineages of the Present,* 192.

12. See Shamsur Rahman Faruqi, *Early Urdu Literary Culture and History* (New Delhi: Oxford University Press, 2001).

13. By "comportment" I mean the concept of *adab*, and by "respectable," *sharīf.* For *adab*, see Barbara Daly Metcalf, *Moral Conduct and Authority: The Place of Adab in South Asian Islam* (Berkeley: University of California Press, 1984). For *sharīf,* see David Lelyveld, *Aligarh's First Generation: Muslim Solidarity in British India* (New Delhi: Oxford University Press, 1996 [1978]), 35–101.

14. Muġhannī Tabassum, "N. M. Rāshid: muk̲htaṣar ḥālāt-e zindagī," 10–11.

15. On the ghazal, see Frances W. Pritchett, *Nets of Awareness: Urdu Poetry and Its Critics* (Berkeley: University of California Press, 1994).

16. The foreword is dated 25 October 1955. At the time, Bokhari, Pakistan's first representative at the United Nations, was Under-Secretary of Information at the United Nations, where Rashed was an information officer. Bokhari had been Rashed's professor of English at Government College. He had also been Rashed's superior as the director of All India Radio, where Rashed worked before taking an army commission. For Bokhari, see the excellent website, www.patrasbokhari.com (accessed 2012).

17. Aḥmad Shāh Paṭras Buk̲hārī, "Tamhīd," 15.

18. Ẓiyā Jālandharī, "Īrān meñ ajnabī," in *N. M. Rāshid: fikr-o-fan*, edited by Kuñvar Muḥammad Ak̲hlāq K̲hāñ Shahryār and Muġhannī Tabassum (Hyderabad, India: Maktabah-e shĕʿr-o-ḥikmat, 1971), 149.

19. Sigmund Freud, "The Uncanny," in *Standard Edition of the Complete Psychological Works of Sigmund Freud* (London: Hogarth Press, 1955), 17:236.

20. Aḥmad Shāh Paṭras Buk̲hārī, "Tamhīd," 9–10.

21. Aḥmad Shāh Paṭras Buk̲hārī, "Tamhīd," 14.

22. See Bernard Cohn, "The Command of Language and the Language of Command," in *Colonialism and Its Forms of Knowledge: The British in India* (Princeton, NJ: Princeton University Press, 1996), 16–57.

23. David Lelyveld, "The Fate of Hindustani: Colonial Knowledge and the Project of a National Language," in *Orientalism and the Postcolonial Predicament: Perspectives on South Asia*, ed. Carol A. Breckenridge and Peter van der Veer (Philadelphia: University of Philadelphia Press, 1993), 208.

24. Carlo Coppola, "The All-India Progressive Writers' Association: The Early Years," in *Marxist Influences and South Asian Literature*, ed. Carlo Coppola (East Lansing: Asian Studies Center, Michigan State University, 1974), 1:5–12.

25. Quoted in Ḳhalīlu'r-raḥmân A'ẓmī, *Urdū meñ taraqqī pasand adabī taḥrīk* (Aligarh: Educational Book House, 1996 [1957]), 43.

26. See, for example, Aḳhtar Ḥusain Rā'epūrī, *Adab aur inqilāb* (Hyderabad, India: Idarah-i ishā'at-i urdū, 1943). In this sense, the progressive critics followed the lead of early twentieth-century North Indian Muslim literary reformers, who also saw the use of Persian forms in Urdu as a product of the tastes of the nobility, as well as foreign and artificial. Muḥammad Ḥusain Āzād, *Āb-e Ḥayāt: Shaping the Canon of Urdu Poetry*, trans. and ed. Frances W. Pritchett with Shamsur Rahman Faruqi (New Delhi: Oxford University Press, 2001), 91–92; Frances W. Pritchett, *Nets of Awareness: Urdu Poetry and Its Critics*.

27. Aamir R. Mufti, "Aura of Authenticity," 93–96.

28. Mufti calls this the "forgetting of the Indianness of Urdu." 'Askarī was in fact a moderate and frequently progressive voice compared to an "Islamic fundamentalism" in Pakistan that was inclined to discard nearly all South Asian cultural expression as un-Islamic. Aamir R. Mufti, "Aura of Authenticity," 95; cf. Kamran Asdar Ali, "Communists in a Muslim Land: Cultural Debates in Pakistan's Early Years," *Modern Asian Studies* 45, no. 3 (2011): 522–26, and Syed Nauman Naqvi, "Mourning Indo-Muslim Modernity: Moments in Post-Colonial Urdu Literary Culture" (PhD dissertation, Columbia University, 2008), 127–88. For criticism of Mufti's "aura of authenticity" as insufficiently sensitive to Benjamin's ideas about aura as a site of historicity, see Talal Asad, interview by Nermeen Shaikh, in Nermeen Shaikh, *The Present as History: Critical Perspectives on Global Power* (New York: Columbia University Press, 2007), 221–22. In my view, Mufti's notion of auratic criticism is useful precisely because it highlights the importance of "authenticity" in Urdu literary debates and cultural criticism, in general.

29. Muḥammad Ḥasan 'Askarī, *Jadīdiyat yā maġhribī gumrāhiyōñ kī tārīḳh kā ḳhākah* (Rawalpindi, Pakistan: 'Iffat Ḥasan, 1979). For more on this aspect of 'Askarī's thought, see Abū'l-kalām Qāsmī, ed., *Mashriq kī bāzyāft: Muḥammad Ḥasan 'Askarī ke ḥavāle se* (Aligarh: Na'ī Nasl Publications, 1982).

30. N. M. Rāshid, "Dībāchah," in *Īrān meñ ajnabī*, 29.

31. In Urdu and Persian poetic genres, a *qiṭ'ah* refers to a series of verses that are to be read as a continuous sequence or, at times, as a complete poem.

32. N. M. Rāshid, "Dībāchah," in *Īrān meñ ajnabī*, 30.

33. N. M. Rāshid, letter to Āġhā 'Abdu'l-ḥamid, Columbo, 30 July 1946, in *N. M. Rāshid: ek muṭāla'ah*, ed. Jamīl Jālibī (Karachi: Maktabah-e uslūb, 1986), 243.

34. N. M. Rāshid, "Ek Muṣāhibah," in *Lā = Insān* (Lahore: al-Miṡāl, 1969), 15.

35. N. M. Rāshid, "Dībāchah," in *Īrān meñ ajnabī*, 30; N. M. Rāshid, "Ek Muṣāhibah," 15.

36. N. M. Rāshid, "Dībāchah," 29.

37. Joan Scott, "The Evidence of Experience," *Critical Inquiry* 17, no. 4 (Summer 1991): 780, 776–77, 782, 793, 797.

38. N. M. Rāshid, "Dībāchah," 28.

39. N. M. Rāshid, "Ḥalqah-e arbāb-e żauq," in *N. M. Rāshid: fikr-o-fan*, ed. Kuñvar Muḥammad Akḥlāq Ḳhāñ Shahryār and Muġhannī Tabassum (Hyderabad, India: Maktabah-e shě'r-o-ḥikmat, 1971), 380.

40. See Aamir R. Mufti, "Aura of Authenticity," 93–95.

41. Alexander D . Knysch, *Ibn 'Arabi in the Later Islamic Tradition: The Making of a Polemical Image in Medieval Islam* (Albany: State University of New York Press, 1999).

42. See, for example, Ja'frī, *Eshiyā jāg uṭhā*, 22–24.

43. David Brandenberger, *National Bolshevism: Stalinist Mass Culture and the Formation of Modern Russian National Identity, 1931–1956* (Cambridge, MA: Harvard University Press, 2002).

44. Dharm Pal, *Campaign in Western Asia* (Calcutta: Combined Inter-Services Historical Section, 1957), 283.

45. "Soviet Scolds Iran For Denying Its Oil," *New York Times*, 30 October 1944, 5.

46. Louise L'Estrange Fawcett, *Iran and the Cold War: The Azerbaijan Crisis of 1946* (Cambridge: Cambridge University Press, 1992).

47. Stephen L. McFarland, "Anatomy of an Iranian Political Crowd: The Tehran Bread Riot of December 1942," *International Journal of Middle East Studies* 17 (February 1985): 52.

48. Farrūḳhī Yazdī, "Musammat-e vaṭanī," in *Dīvān-e Farrūḳhī Yazdī* (Tehran: Bunyād-e naśr-e kitāb, 1984), 186.

49. Ali Gheissari, "The Poetry and Politics of Farrokhi Yazdi," *Iranian Studies* 26, no. 1–2 (Winter-Spring 1993), 35.

50. Aamir R. Mufti, *Enlightenment in the Colony*, 223, 212, 243.

51. N. M. Rashed, "Interview with N. M. Rashed," 9.

52. N. M. Rashed, "Interview with N. M. Rashed," 8.

53. N. M. Rāshid, "Ṭilism-e azal," in *Īrān meñ ajnabī*, 129.

54. Willem Floor, *History of Theater in Iran* (Washington, DC: Mage Publishers, 2005), 265. I am grateful to Willem Floor for this reference.

55. Mīrzādah 'Ishqī, "Rastaḳhīz-e salāṯīn-e īrān," in *Dīvān-e 'Ishqī* (Tehran: Āftāb, 1941), 25–35.

56. William Hanaway, "The Symbolism of the Persian Revolutionary Posters," in *Iran since the Revolution: Internal Dynamics, Regional Conflict, and the Superpowers,* ed. Barry M. Rosen (New York: Columbia University, 1985), 38–39.

57. Mohamad Tavakoli-Targhi, "Refashioning Iran: Language and Culture during the Constitutional Revolution," *Iranian Studies* 23, no. 1 (1990): 77–101.

58. N. M. Rāshid, "Kīmiyāgar," in *Īrān meñ ajnabī*, 54.

CHAPTER THREE

1. N. M. Rāshid, *Gumāñ kā mumkin: jo tū hai maiñ hūñ* (Lahore: Nayā idārah, 1976).

2. N. M. Rāshid, *Lā = Insān* (Lahore: al-Mis̤āl, 1969).

3. Ḳhalīlu'r-raḥmân A'z̤mī, for example, writes, "as is evident from the name of this collection, now the center and axis of his poetry is that global man who has lost the meaning and understanding of his own being. It is as if Rashed now has left the confines of 'the East' and stepped into a more global expanse." "Rāshid kā żahnī irtiqā" in *N. M. Rāshid: fikr-o-fan*, ed. Shahryār and Muġhannī Tabassum (Hyderabad: Maktabah-e shĕʿr-o-ḥikmat, 1971), 28. In an interview, Rashed also explained, "In naming my third collection *Lā = Insān* (X = Human) my point was to make clear that all poetry, not merely my own, is an inquiry into man. And the search for man, if imprisoned within the bounds of any one specific culture, is not possible. Therefore, it is necessary to maintain a view of man and his cultures from an international level." N. M. Rāshid, "N. M. Rāshid se ek muṣāḥibah," interviewed by Saʿadat Saʿīd, in *Maqālāt-e N. M. Rāshid*, ed. Shīmā Majīd (Islamabad: Alhamra Publishing, 2002), 388.

4. Muhammad Iqbal, "Presidential Address Delivered at the Annual Session of the All-India Muslim League, 29 December 1930," *Speeches, Writings and Statements of Iqbal*, ed. Latif Ahmed Sherwani (Lahore: Iqbal Academy Pakistan), 3–25.

5. See, for example, Āftāb Aḥmad, *N. M. Rāshid: shāʿir-o-shaḳhṣ* (Lahore: Māvarā Publishers, 1989), 65.

6. N. M. Rāshid, "N. M. Rāshid se ek muṣāhibah," interview by Nasrīn Anjum Bhaṭṭī, in *Rāshid ba-qalam-e ḳhvud*, ed. Saʿādat Saʿīd and Nasrīn Anjum Bhaṭṭī (Lahore: Department of Urdu, Government College, 2010), 106.

7. On Partition refugees, see Vazira Fazila-Yacoobali, *The Long Partition and the Making of Modern South Asia: Refugees, Boundaries, History* (New York: Columbia University Press, 2007).

8. Fatḥ Muḥammad Malik, *N. M. Rāshid: Siyāsat aur shāʿirī* (Islamabad: Dost Publications, 2010), 30. The verse reads, "yaqīn-e mŏḥkam, ʿaml-e paiham, muḥabbat-e fātiḥ-e ʿālam / jihād-e zindagānī meñ haiñ yih mardōñ kī shamshīreñ." Muḥammad Iqbāl, "Tulūʿ-e islām," in *Bāng-e darā*, in *Kulliyāt-e iqbāl urdū* (Lahore: Iqbal Academy, 1997), 302.

9. N. M. Rāshid, *Īrān meñ ajnabī*, 4th ed. (Lahore: al-Mis̤āl, 1969), 48.

10. N. M. Rāshid, "N. M. Rāshid se ek muṣāhibah," interviewed by Nasrīn Anjum Bhaṭṭī, in *Rāshid ba-qalam-e ḳhvud*, ed. Saʿādat Saʿīd and Nasrīn Anjum Bhaṭṭī (Lahore: Department of Urdu, Government College, 2010), 76.

11. In Urdu, the word "human" *(insān)* is differentiated from the word man *(ādmī)* to mean a more refined human. Rashed does not appear to make that distinction in his poetry.

12. Reynold Nicholson, one of few commentaries on Maʿarrī in English, reads Maʿarrī as a "skeptic" committed to reason rather than a "heretic," who "regards Islam, and positive religion generally, as a *human* institution. As such it is false and rotten to the core. Its founders sought to procure wealth and power for themselves, its dignitaries pursue worldly ends, its defenders rely on spurious documents which they ascribe to divinely inspired apostles, and its adherents accept mechanically

whatever they are told to believe." "The Meditations of Maʿarrí" in *Studies in Islamic Poetry* (Cambridge, UK: University Press, 1921), 173.

13. M. A. R. Habib, "Introduction," in N. M. Rashed, *The Dissident Voice: Poems of N. M.Ráshed*, trans. M. A. R. Habib (Madras: Oxford University Press, 1991), 29.

14. I am grateful to Sara Mirza Bano for this observation.

15. N. M. Rāshid, "Ek Muṣāḥibah," in *Lā = Insān* (Lahore: al-Mis̈āl, 1969), 28.

16. The poem is frequently recited in moments of confrontation with social challenge in Pakistan. A folk-pop version of the song, performed by the band Indian Ocean, also featured in the 2010 Hindi film *Peepli Live.*

17. Tabassum Kāshmīrī, *Lā = Rāshid* (Lahore: Nigārishāt, 1994), 22–23.

18. Tabassum Kāshmīrī, *Urdū meñ ʿalāmat nigārī* (Lahore: Sang-e Meel Publications, 1975), 212; Fatḥ Muḥammad Malik, *N. M. Rāshid: siyāsat aur shāʿirī* (Islamabad: Dost Publications, 2010), 72–80.

19. N. M. Rāshid to Āftāb Aḥmad, New York, 25 June 1963, in Āftāb Aḥmad, *N. M. Rāshid: shāʿir-o-shakhṣ*, 124.

20. See Tabassum Kāshmīrī, *Urdū meñ ʿalāmat nigārī.*

21. See Muḥammad Ḥasan ʿAskarī, "The Use of Adjectives in Literature," trans. Muhammad Umar Memon, *Annual of Urdu Studies* 19 (2004): 287.

22. Muḥammad Ḥusain Āzād, *Nairang-e k̲hayāl* (Lahore: Āzād Book Depot, 1905).

23. Jain names the "masterpieces" of allegory as: Vājhī's *Sab Ras* (1635), *Gulzār-e Surūr* by Rajab ʿAlī Beg Surūr, and Azad's *Nairang-e K̲hayāl.* He also finds some resonances with allegory in Krishan Chandar's satirical short story "Ek gadhe kī sarguzasht." See Gyān Chand Jain, "Urdū meñ tams̈īl nigārī," in *Taḥrīreñ* (Delhi: Idārah-e furoġh-e urdū, 1964), 269–92. Other studies of allegory in Urdu appear to cover the same ground but with no mention of texts after Āzād. See Ġhulām Rasūl Makrānī, *Urdū meñ tams̈īl nigārī* (Gorakhpur: Offset Press, 1988); Manẓar Aʿẓmī, *Urdū meñ tams̈īl nigārī* (New Delhi: Anjuman-e taraqqī-e urdū, 1977).

24. Gyān Chand Jain, "Urdū meñ tams̈īl nigārī," 292.

25. For an accessible overview of the critical history of allegory in European languages, see Jeremy Tambling, *Allegory* (New York: Routledge, 2010).

26. "The resuscitation of allegory in twentieth-century thought," Iftikhar Dadi notes, "was pioneered by Walter Benjamin and has been further explored by Paul de Man, Gayatri Chakravorty Spivak, Fredric Jameson, Aijaz Ahmad, Imre Szeman, Susan Buck-Morss, Craig Owens, Hal Foster, Jenny Sharpe, Rey Chow, and other thinkers influenced by critical theory and poststructuralism" (131, fn. 11). Dadi's article, particularly in its use of Craig Owens's work, has been particularly beneficial to this analysis. See "Shirin Neshat's Photographs as Postcolonial Allegories," *Signs: Journal of Women in Culture and Society* 34.1 (2008): 125–150.

27. Craig Owens, "The Allegorical Impulse: Toward a Theory of Postmodernism," *October* 12 (Spring 1980): 67–86; and "The Allegorical Impulse: Toward a Theory of Postmodernism, Part Two," *October* 13 (Summer 1980): 58–80.

28. Craig Owens, "The Allegorical Impulse," (Spring 1980), 69.

29. Craig Owens, "The Allegorical Impulse," (Spring 1980), 72.

30. Following Benjamin, however, Owen sees this "allegorical reinterpretation" as an attempt to "redeem [the past] for the present"—an aim to which Rashed's poetry, in general, seems perhaps less obviously committed. Craig Owen, "The Allegorical Impulse," (Spring 1980), 69.

31. Mīr writes, "That fearful desert has remained my homeland / hearing of which Khiẓr was afraid to travel" *(vuh dasht-e ḳhauf-nāk rahā hai mirā vaṭan / sun-kar jise ḳhiẓr ne safar se ḥażar kiyā)*, and "Is it a small thing, the terror of the desert of passion / at that place the lions hair stands on end from horror" *(kyā kam hai haul-nākī ṣaḥrā-e ʿāshiqī kī / sheroṅ ko us jagah par hotā hai qashʿarīrā)*. Mīr Tāqī Mīr, *Kulliyāt-e Mīr* (New Delhi: National Council for the Promotion of Urdu, 2003), 211, 436. "Desert of passion" *(saḥrā-e ʿāshiqī)* can also be rendered as the "desert of lover-ship," referring to the state of being an *ʿāshiq* (lover).

32. Mīr, *Kulliyāt-e Mīr*, 374.

33. Mīr, *Kulliyāt-e Mīr*, 205.

34. Shamsuʾr-raḥmân Fārūqī, *Shĕʿr-e shor-angez*, vol. 1 (New Delhi: Taraqqī-e urdū Bureau, 1990), 330.

35. "At one time, this sand-heap of the desert was a caravan / This whirlwind, some desert wanderer" *(thā pushtah-reg-e bādiyah ik vaqt kārvāṅ / yih gird-bād koʾī bayābāṅ-navard thā)*. Mīr, *Kulliyāt-e Mīr*, 230.

36. In another poem from *Lā = Insān*, "Threads of Desire" *(Tammannā ke tār)* for example, Rashed describes the arrival on Earth of some aliens, presumably Martians, who tell the Earthlings to "unravel the twisted threads of desire." To this demand, the Earthlings reply, with "great simplicity," that the aliens, who are probably made of "light" and not matter, presumably do not see the "the colors of twisted arms, / the colors of inebriated looks of love / the colors of sins?" N. M. Rāshid, "Tamannā ke tār," in *Lā = Insān,* 91–93.

37. Said's comments here describe what he calls the first of two visions of the postcolonial world in Conrad's *Heart of Darkness*. This vision "allows the old imperial enterprise full scope to play itself out conventionally, to render the world as official European or Western imperialism saw it, and to consolidate itself after World War Two. Westerners may have physically left their old colonies in Africa and Asia, but they retained them not only as markets but as locales on the ideological map over which they continued to rule morally and intellectually." Against this vision of permanent empire, the second vision, which corresponds strikingly to Rashed's, sees imperialism as temporal. In it, Conrad's narrative is "local to a time and place" and thus recognizes that "European tutelage" would, eventually, end: "like all human effort, like speech itself—it would have its moment, then it would have to pass." *Culture and Imperialism* (New York: Vintage Books, 1993), 25–6.

38. In a published interview with Saʿādat Saʿīd, for example, Rashed states that their "harmony" is an essential goal of the artist. "The artist is responsible to society, not the program of a group. He should protect the freedom of the individual in any form. A harmony *(ham āhaṅg)* between the 'Reality Principle' *(aṣl-e ḥaqīqat)* and the 'Pleasure Principle' *(aṣl-e masarrat)* and a harmony between the body and

soul should be a part of his being so that in his word and meaning *(ḥarf-o-ma'nī)* a harmony can be born." N. M. Rāshid, "Ibtidā-e suḳhan," interview by Sa'ādat Sa'īd, in Sa'ādat Sa'īd, *Rāshid aur s̤iqāfatī muġhā'irāt* (Lahore: Department of Urdu, Government College University, 2010), 7.

39. Annemarie Schimmel, "Sacred Geography in Islam," in *Sacred Places and Profane Spaces: Essays in the Geographies of Judaism, Christianity, and Islam*, ed. Jamie Scott and Paul Simpson-Housley (New York: Greenwood Press, 1991), 166.

40. Muḥammad Iqbāl, *Asrār-e ḳhvudī*, in *Kulliyāt-e Iqbāl fārsī* (Lahore: Shaiḳh Ġhulām 'Alī and Sons, 1973), 39.

41. Muḥammad Iqbāl, "Ḳhiẓr-e rāh," in *Bāng-e darā*, in *Kulliyāt-e Iqbāl urdū*, 286–7.

42. The quotations here are taken from the section titles of Iqbāl's *mas̤navī*. Muḥammad Iqbāl, *Rumūz-e be-ḳhvudī*, in *Kulliyāt-e Iqbāl fārsī*, 85–169.

43. Muḥammad Iqbāl, *Asrār-e ḳhvudī*, in *Kulliyāt-e Iqbāl fārsī*, 20.

44. Muḥammad Iqbāl, *Asrār-e ḳhvudī*, in *Kulliyāt-e Iqbāl fārsī*, 73–86.

45. N. M. Rāshid, "Ek ḳhaṭ (Salīm Aḥmad ke nām)," in *N. M. Rāshid: fikr-o-fan*, ed. Kuñvar Muḥammad Aḳhlāq Ḳhāñ "Shahryār" and Muġhannī Tabassum (Hyderabad, India: Maktabah-e shĕ'r-o-ḥikmat, 1971), 326.

46. Firoozeh Papan-Matin, "The Crisis of Identity in Rumi's 'Tale of the Reed'" (Los Angeles: UC Los Angeles, G. E. von Grunebaum Center for Near Eastern Studies, 2005), http://escholarship.org/uc/item/4qr0x826.

47. See Annemarie Schimmel, *The Feminine in Islam*, trans. Susan H. Ray (New York: Continuum, 2003).

48. See Annemarie Schimmel, *The Triumphal Sun: A Study of the Works of Jalāloddin Rumi* (Albany: State University of New York Press, 1993), 61–74.

49. Annemarie Schimmel, *The Triumphal Sun*, 231.

50. "Tahlīl," in *Encyclopaedia of Islam, Second Edition* (Brill Online, 2012), http://www.brillonline.nl/subscriber/entry?entry=islam_SIM-7312.

51. "You too are in this caravan, Iqbal / that caravan whose chief is Rumi" *(tū bhī hai isī qāfilah meñ iqbāl / jis qāfilah kā sālār hai rūmī)*. Muḥammad Iqbāl, "Yūrap se ek ḳhaṭ," in *Bāl-e jibrīl*, in *Kulliyāt-e Iqbāl urdū*, 479.

CHAPTER FOUR

1. Tehsin Firaqi notes that this phrase reminds the reader of its use in Iqbal's Persian work *Jāved-nāmah*, and that Iqbal in fact took the phrase *mard-e rād* (brave man) from "classical poetry." Taḥsīn Firāqī, *Ḥasan kūzahgar* (Lahore: Department of Urdu, Punjab University and Oriental College, 2010), 29–30. See Muḥammad Iqbāl, *Jāved-nāmah*, in *Kulliyāt-e Iqbāl fārsī* (Lahore: Shaiḳh Ġhulām 'Alī and Sons, 1973), 751.

2. N. M. Rāshid, "N. M. Rāshid se ek muṣāhibah," interview by Nasrīn Anjum Bhaṭṭī, in *Rāshid ba-qalam-e ḳhvud*, ed. Sa'ādat Sa'īd and Nasrīn Anjum Bhaṭṭī

(Lahore: Department of Urdu, Government College, 2010), 106; Āftāb Aḥmad, *N. M Rāshid: shāʿir-o-shaḳhṣ* (Lahore: Māvarā Publishers, 1989), 150.

3. W. H. Auden, "To Christopher Isherwood," in *Poems* (London: Faber and Faber, 1930), 2.

4. W. H. Auden, "September 1, 1939," in *Another Time* (New York: Random House, 1940), 98.

5. W. H. Auden, "September 1, 1939," 99.

6. W. H. Auden, "September 1, 1939," 100.

7. W. H. Auden, "September 1, 1939," 101.

8. Donna Jones, "The Career of Living Things is Continuous: Reflections of Bergson, Iqbal, and Scalia," *Qui Parle* 20, no. 2 (Spring–Summer 2012): 232–33.

9. Muḥammad Iqbāl, "Paiġhām-e bergsān," in *Payām-e mashriq*, in *Kulliyāt-e Iqbāl farsī* (Lahore: Shaiḳh Ġhulām ʿAlī and Sons, 1973), 377.

10. N. M. Rashed, "Social Influences on Urdu Literature," *Asia* 9 (Fall 1967): 35.

11. William A. Graham, *Divine Word and Prophetic Word in Early Islam: A Reconsideration of the Sources, with Special Reference to the Divine Saying or Hadîth Qudsî* (The Hague: Mouton, 1977), 212.

12. Muhammad Iqbal, "Presidential Address Delivered at the Annual Session of the All-India Muslim League, 29th December, 1930," in *Speeches, Writings, and Statements of Iqbal*, ed. Latif Ahmed Sherwani (Lahore: Iqbal Academy, 1977) 3–29.

13. C. M. Naim, "Iqbal, Jinnah and Pakistan: The Vision and the Reality," in *Ambiguities of Heritage: Fictions and Polemics* (Karachi: City Press, 1999), 111–23.

14. Muhammad Iqbal, "Presidential Address Delivered at the Annual Session of the All-India Muslim League, 29th December, 1930," 10. For a defense of this reading, see Rashida Malik, *Iqbal: The Spiritual Father of Pakistan* (Lahore: Sang-e-Meel Publications, 2003).

15. Muḥammad Iqbāl, "Al-vaqt saif," in *Asrār-e ḳhvudī*, in *Kulliyāt-e Iqbāl fārsī* (Lahore: Shaiḳh Ġhulām ʿAli and Sons, 1973), 71–75.

16. Henri Bergson, *Time and Free Will: An Essay on the Immediate Data of Consciousness*, trans. F. L. Pogson. (New York: MacMillan, 1910).

17. Muhammad Iqbal, *Reconstruction of Religious Thought in Islam* (Lahore: Sang-e Meel Publications, 1996), 55.

18. Muhammad Iqbal, *Reconstruction of Religious Thought in Islam*, 55–56.

19. Muhammad Iqbal, *Reconstruction of Religious Thought in Islam*, 55.

20. Muhammad Iqbal, *Reconstruction of Religious Thought in Islam*, 13.

21. Muhammad Iqbal, *Reconstruction of Religious Thought in Islam*, 54.

22. Muhammad Iqbal, *Reconstruction of Religious Thought in Islam*, 141.

23. Muhammad Iqbal, "Presidential Address Delivered at the Annual Session of the All-India Muslim League, 29th December, 1930," 23, 10.

24. Muhammad Iqbal, "Presidential Address Delivered at the Annual Session of the All-India Muslim League, 29th December, 1930," 4–5.

25. Muhammad Iqbal, "Presidential Address Delivered at the Annual Session of the All-India Muslim League, 29th December, 1930," 5, 3.

26. Partha Chatterjee, *The Nation and Its Fragments: Colonial and Postcolonial Histories* (Princeton: Princeton University Press, 1993), 26–27.

27. Benedict Anderson, *Imagined Communities: Reflections on the Origin and Spread of Nationalism*, 2nd ed. (New York: Verso, 1991), 26.

28. Timothy Mitchell, "The Stages of Modernity," in *Questions of Modernity*, ed. Timothy Mitchell (Minneapolis: University of Minnesota, 2000), 14. In "Theses on the Philosophy of History," Walter Benjamin writes, "the concept of the historical progress of mankind cannot be sundered from the concept of its progression through a homogeneous, empty time [eine homogene und leere Zeit]." *Illuminations: Essays and Reflections*, trans. Harry Zohn (New York: Shocken Books, 1968), 261; *Illuminationen* (Frankfurt: Suhrkamp, 1972), 258.

29. Benedict Anderson, *Imagined Communities*, 26.

30. Ayesha Jalal, *The Sole Spokesman: Jinnah, the Muslim League and the Demand for Pakistan* (Cambridge: Cambridge University Press, 1985); Aamir R. Mufti, *Enlightenment in the Colony: The Jewish Question and the Crisis of Postcolonial Culture* (Princeton, NJ: Princeton University Press, 2007).

31. Rashed made this point explicitly in a private letter to Āftāb Aḥmad, who requested in response to a draft of Rashed's poem "I Too Have Some Dreams" *(Mere bhī haiñ kuchh ḳhvāb)* that he give his dreams "the warmth of certainty." Rashed responded that in writing the poem he struggled to determine how "detailed" *(mabsūṭ)* his dreams should be, and to what extent they should remain abstract *(mujarrad)*. He explains that "ideological poets" *(naẓariyyātī shā'ir)* generally express "detailed" dreams in their writing, and that the "detail" of his poem is its weakness, as though he "were speaking as a representative of the almighty." He concludes, "in the end, this is a poem of feeling *(ěḥsās)* alone. It is not a poem of dogma or persuasion. And, if it were to seem so, it would be a completely unsuccessful poem." N. M. Rāshid (New York) to Āftāb Aḥmad, 25 June 1963 in Āftāb Aḥmad, *N. M. Rāshid: shā'ir-o-shaḳhṣ*, 125.

32. Āftāb Aḥmad, *N. M. Rāshid: shā'ir-o-shaḳhṣ*, 146.

33. N. M. Rashed explained the goal as follows: "The Sufi searches for a balance, that is, between the junction of life and death in an eternal union beyond this world. That eternal union would be the end of every type of struggle and, moment by moment, would prove its own being. In different religions, as well, the image of paradise is of a world where there would be life but in a state of complete respite, where there would be time but there would not be movement." N. M. Rāshid, "Ġhālib hamāre zamāne meñ," in *N. M. Rāshid: fikr-o-fan*, 342.

34. According to Saadat Saeed, the figure of the bird here takes on the Sufi metaphor of the soul returning to the divine essence. Sa'ādat Sa'īd, "N. M. Rāshid aur na'e shai'rī ḥavāle," in *Rāshid aur s̤iqāfatī muġhā'irat* (Lahore: Department of Urdu, Government College University, 2010), 26.

35. C. M. Naim, "The Consequences of the Indo-Pakistan War for Urdu Language and Literature: A Parting of the Ways?" *The Journal of Asian Studies* 28.2 (1969): 269–83.

36. See Kamran Asdar Ali, "Communists in a Muslim Land: Cultural Debates in Pakistan's Early Years" *Modern Asian Studies* 45.3 (2011): 501–34.

37. "Idāriyyah," *Nayā Daur* 39–40 (n.d.), 5.

38. "Idāriyyah," 6.

39. N. M. Rāshid, "Ek ḳhaṭ," 1 January 1967, *Nayā daur* 47–48 (n.d.), 424–431. *Naya Daur* published Rashed's letter in a special section titled "*Bunyādī mas'lah*" (Fundamental Problem) that also contained letters in response to his letter by a number of Pakistani critics and intellectuals, all of whom disagreed with him.

40. N. M. Rāshid, "Ek ḳhaṭ," 424.

41. N. M. Rāshid to Jamīl Jālibī, Tehran, 17 February 1968, in *N. M. Rāshid: ek muṭāla'ah*, 295.

42. There is a similar, if veiled, critique in the interview prefacing *Lā = Insān*. In it Rashed states, "Without his own freedom, an individual cannot reach his height and cannot also guarantee society's approach/access *(rasā'ī)*. This perspective in the current age of "planning" *(manṣūbah-bandī)* sounds like a far-off voice, but it is my understanding that no planning can ever be successful unless the people doing the planning are completely free in their thoughts and opinions, that is, until the people are raised in the tradition of complete freedom." N. M. Rāshid, "Ek muṣāhibah," in *Lā = Insān*, 23.

43. A poem entitled "Darvesh" (Dervish), a term for a religious mendicant, similarly addresses a *gadā* outside its narrator's window. N. M. Rāshid, "Darvesh," in *Īrān meñ ajnabī aur dūsarī naẓmeñ* (Lahore: Goshah-e adab, 1957), 75–79.

44. N. M. Rāshid, "Is peṛ pah hai būm kā sāyah," in *Lā = Insān*, 158.

45. "Baro ay zāhid-e ḳhvud-bīn kih z chasm-e man-o-tū / rāz-e īn pardah nihān ast va nihān ḳhvāhad bavad."

46. "añdhere ujāle meñ hai tābnāk / man-o-tū meñ paidā, man-o-tū se pāk." Muḥammad Iqbāl, "Sāqī-nāmah," in *Bāl-e jibrīl*, in *Kulliyāt-e Iqbāl urdū* (Lahore: Iqbal Academy Pakistan, 1997), 454.

47. "miṭā diyā mire sāqī ne 'ālam-e man-o-tū / pilā-ke mujh ko mai-e lā ilâha illā hū." Muḥammad Iqbāl, "Miṭā diyā mire sāqī ne 'ālam-e man-o-tū," in *Bāl-e jibrīl*, in *Kulliyāt-e Iqbāl urdū*, 352.

48. Norman O. Brown, *Life Against Death: The Psychoanalytical Meaning of History* (Middleton, CT: Wesleyan University Press, 1959).

49. For a comprehensive study of Norman O. Brown's work, as well as a comparison of Brown with Marcuse, see David Greenham, *The Resurrection of the Body: The Work of Norman O. Brown* (Lanham, MD: Lexington Books, 2006).

50. This essay was first published out of Lahore in a special issue of Vazīr Aġhā's journal *Aurāq* (June–July 1970): 153–61. It was republished in *N.M. Rāshid: fikr-o-fan*, 331–343. There it is described as originally a radio broadcast (343). Future references will be to the later reprint.

51. For an extended discussion of this essay in relation to two other contemporary treatments of the poet, see A. Sean Pue, "In the Mirror of Ghalib: Postcolonial Reflections on Indo-Muslim Selfhood," *The Indian Economic and Social History Review* 48.4 (2011): 571–592.

52. N. M. Rāshid, "Ġhālib hamāre zamāne meñ," 340–41. Compare Norman O. Brown, *Life Against Death*, 57.

53. Norman O. Brown, *Life Against Death*, 91.

54. Norman O. Brown, *Life Against Death*, 106.

55. Norman O. Brown, *Life Against Death*, 91, 93.

56. Norman O. Brown, *Life Against Death*, 106.

57. Muḥammad Iqbāl, *Jāved-nāmah*, in *Kulliyāt-e Iqbāl fārsī* (Lahore: Shaikḥ Ġhulām ʿAlī and Sons, 1973), 589–796.

CONCLUSION

1. M. A. R. Habib, "Introduction," in N. M. Rashed, *The Dissident Voice: Poems of N. M. Ráshed*, trans. M. A. R. Habīb (Madras: Oxford University Press, 1991), 23–24.

2. These first two lines each consist of four *faʿūlun* (˘ — —) feet, which is the pattern of the meter *mutaqārib mus̈amman sālim*, an acceptable meter for the *ġhazal* and *mas̈navī* genres.

3. "Unravel" in the poem is marked in quotation marks. It most likely is to signal the fact that the phrase is a reference to Iqbal's short poem "Western Man" *(Mard-e farang)* that begins with the declaration, "A thousand times philosophers have unraveled it / but this problem of women remained the same as it was" *(hazār bār ḥakīmoñ ne us ko suljhāyā / magar yih masʾalah-e zan rahā vahīñ kā vahīñ).* Iqbal goes on to declare that the problem in "Western society" is that the "poor simple minded man [there] does not understand women." Muḥammad Iqbāl, "Mard-e farang," in *Ẓarb-e kalīm*, in *Kulliyāt-e Iqbāl urdū*, 604. While Iqbal implies that outside of the West "woman" is better understood, Hasan states that he will never understand a "woman like Jahanzad," and to claim to do so would be to "deceive himself" (lines 26–30).

4. Quoted in N. M. Rashed, *The Dissident Voice*, trans. M. A. R. Habib, 39 n. 1.

5. Muḥammad Iqbāl, "Masjid-e qurṭabah," *Bāl-e jibrīl*, in *Kulliyāt-e Iqbāl urdū* (Lahore: Iqbal Academy, 1997), 419–27.

6. Ḥamīd Nasīm, *Pāñch jadīd urdū shāʿir* (New Delhi: Maktabah Jāmiʿah, 1997), 150.

7. "silsilah-e roz-o-shab, tār-e ḥarīr-e do-rang / jis se banātī hai żāt, apnī qabā-e ṣifāt" (419).

8. Muhammad Iqbal, *Reconstruction of Religious Thought in Islam* (Lahore: Sang-e Meel Publications, 1996), 13, 55.

9. Muhammad Iqbal, *Reconstruction of Religious Thought in Islam*, 13.

10. "hai magar is naqsh meñ rang-e s̈abāt-e davām / jis ko kiyā ho kisī mard-e ḳhudā ne tamām" (420).

11. "ai ḥaram-e qurṭabah! ʿishq se terā vujūd / ʿishq sarāpā davām, jis meñ nahīñ raft-o-būd" (421).

12. "hāth hai al-lâh kā bandah-e momin kā hāth" (424).

13. Muhammad Iqbal, "Presidential Address Delivered at the Annual Session of the All-India Muslim League, 29th December, 1930," in *Speeches, Writings, and Statements of Iqbal*, ed. Latif Ahmed Sherwani (Lahore: Iqbal Academy, 1977) 3–29.

14. Muhammad Iqbal, "Presidential Address Delivered at the Annual Session of the All-India Muslim League, 29th December, 1930," 5.

15. "nuqṯah-e parkār-e ḥaq, mard-e ḳhudā kā yaqīñ / aur yih ʿālam tamām vahm-o-ṯilism-o-majāz" (424).

16. Tabassum Kāshmīrī, *Lā = Rāshid* (Lahore: Nigārishāt, 1994), 9–24.

17. Fatḥ Muḥammad Malik, *N. M. Rāshid: siyāsat aur shāʿirī* (Islamabad: Dost Publications, 2010), 106.

BIBLIOGRAPHY

WORKS IN ENGLISH

Adler, Alfred. *The Science of Living.* New York: Garden City, 1929.

Ahmad, Aijaz. "Jameson's Rhetoric of Otherness and the 'National Allegory.'" *Social Text* 17 (Fall 1987): 3–25.

———. *Lineages of the Present.* New Delhi: Tulika, 1996.

Ahmed, Talat. *Literature and Politics in the Age of Nationalism: The Progressive Writers' Movement in South Asia, 1932–56.* London: Taylor and Francis, 2008.

Ali, Ahmed. "The Progressive Writers' Movement and Creative Writers in Urdu." In *Marxist Influences and South Asian Literature,* edited by Carlo Coppola, 1:34–44. South Asia Series Occasional Papers, no. 23. East Lansing: Asian Studies Center, Michigan State University, 1974.

Ali, Kamran Asdar. "Communists in a Muslim Land: Cultural Debates in Pakistan's Early Years." *Modern Asian Studies* 45, no. 3 (2011): 501–34.

Anderson, Benedict. *Imagined Communities: Reflections on the Origin and Spread of Nationalism.* 2nd ed. New York: Verso, 1991.

Asad, Talal. Interview by Nermeen Shaikh. In Nermeen Shaikh, *The Present as History: Critical Perspectives on Global Power,* 205–24. New York: Columbia University Press, 2007.

'Askarī, Muḥammad Ḥasan. "The Use of Adjectives in Literature." Translated by Muhammad Umar Memon. *Annual of Urdu Studies* 19 (2004): 273–300.

Auden, W. H. "To Christopher Isherwood." In *Poems.* London: Faber and Faber, 1930.

———. "September 1, 1939." In *Another Time,* 98–101. New York: Random House, 1940.

Benjamin, Walter. "Theses on the Philosophy of History." In *Illuminations: Essays and Reflections,* translated by Harry Zohn, 253–64. New York: Shocken Books, 1968.

Bergson, Henri. *Time and Free Will: An Essay on the Immediate Data of Consciousness.* Translated by F. L. Pogson. New York: MacMillan, 1910.

Brandenberger, David. *National Bolshevism: Stalinist Mass Culture and the Formation of Modern Russian National Identity, 1931–1956*. Cambridge, MA: Harvard University Press, 2002.

Brooker, Peter, Andrzej Gasiorek, Deborah Longworth, and Andrew Thacker, eds. *The Oxford Handbook of Modernisms*. New York: Oxford University Press, 2010.

Brown, Norman O. *Life Against Death: The Psychoanalytical Meaning of History*. Middleton, CT: Wesleyan University Press, 1959.

Busch, Allison. *Poetry of Kings: The Classical Hindi Literature of Mughal India*. New York: Oxford University Press, 2011.

Chakrabarty, Dipesh. *Provincializing Europe: Postcolonial Thought and Historical Difference*. Princeton: Princeton University Press, 2000.

Chatterjee, Partha. *The Nation and Its Fragments: Colonial and Postcolonial Histories*. Princeton: Princeton University Press, 1993.

Cohn, Bernard. "The Command of Language and the Language of Command." In *Colonialism and Its Forms of Knowledge: The British in India*, 16–57. Princeton: Princeton University Press, 1996.

Coppola, Carlo. "The All-India Progressive Writers' Association: The Early Years." In *Marxist Influences and South Asian Literature*, edited by Carlo Coppola, 1:1–35. East Lansing: Asian Studies Center, Michigan State University Press, 1974.

———. "Urdu Poetry 1935–1970: The Progressive Episode." PhD diss., University of Chicago, 1975.

Dadi, Iftikhar. *Modernism and the Art of Muslim South Asia*. Chapel Hill, NC: University of North Carolina Press, 2010.

———. "Shirin Neshat's Photographs as Postcolonial Allegories." *Signs: Journal of Women in Culture and Society* 34, no. 1 (2008): 125–50.

Dalmia, Vasudha, ed. *Hindi Modernism*. Delhi: Manohar, 2012.

———. *The Nationalization of Hindu Traditions: Bhāratendu Hariśchandra and Nineteenth-century Banaras*. Delhi: Oxford University Press, 1997.

Doyle, Laura Anne. "Modernist Studies and Inter-Imperiality in the Longue Durée." In *The Oxford Handbook of Global Modernisms*, edited by Mark Wollaeger with Matt Eatough. New York: Oxford University Press, 2012.

Doyle, Laura Anne, and Laura A. Wikiel, eds., *Geomodernisms: Race, Modernism, Modernity*. Bloomington: Indiana University Press, 2005.

Fanon, Frantz. *Black Skins, White Masks*. Translated by Charles Lam Markmann. New York: Grove Press, 1967.

Faruqi, Shamsur Rahman. *Early Urdu Literary Culture and History*. Delhi: Oxford University Press, 2001.

Fawcett, Louise L'Estrange. *Iran and the Cold War: The Azerbaijan Crisis of 1946*. Cambridge: Cambridge University Press, 1992.

Fazila-Yacoobali, Vazira. *The Long Partition and the Making of Modern South Asia: Refugees, Boundaries, History*. New York: Columbia University Press, 2007.

Floor, Willem. *History of Theater in Iran*. Washington, DC: Mage Publishers, 2005.

Freud, Sigmund. *Civilization and Its Discontents*. Translated and edited by James Strachey. New York: W. W. Norton and Company, 1961.

———. "Formulations on the Two Principles of Mental Functioning." In *The Standard Edition of the Complete Psychological Works of Sigmund Freud*, 12:213–26. London: Hogarth Press, 1958.

———. "The Uncanny," in *The Standard Edition of the Complete Psychological Works of Sigmund Freud*, translated and edited by James Strachey, 17:219–55. London: Hogarth Press, 1955.

Gheissari, Ali. "The Poetry and Politics of Farrokhi Yazdi." *Iranian Studies* 26, no. 1-2 (Winter-Spring 1993): 33–50.

Gopal, Priyamvada. *Literary Radicalism in India: Gender, Nation and the Transition to Independence.* New York: Routledge, 2005.

Graham, William A. *Divine Word and Prophetic Word in Early Islam: A Reconsideration of the Sources, with Special Reference to the Divine Saying or Hadîth Qudsî.* The Hague: Mouton, 1977.

Green, Nile. *Sufism: A Global History.* Malden, MA: Wiley-Blackwell, 2012.

Greenham, David. *The Resurrection of the Body: The Work of Norman O. Brown.* Lanham, MD: Lexington Books, 2006.

Habib, M. A. R. "Introduction." In N. M. Rashed, *The Dissident Voice: Poems of N. M. Râshed*, translated by M. A. R. Habib, 1–30. Madras: Oxford University Press, 1991.

Hanaway, Willliam. "The Symbolism of the Persian Revolutionary Posters." In *Iran since the Revolution: Internal Dynamics, Regional Conflict, and the Superpowers,* edited by Barry M. Rosen, 31–50. New York: Columbia University Press, 1985.

Iqbal, Muhammad. "Presidential Address Delivered at the Annual Session of the All-India Muslim League, 29th December, 1930." In *Speeches, Writings, and Statements of Iqbal*, edited by Latif Ahmed Sherwani, 3–25. Lahore: Iqbal Academy, 1977.

———. *Reconstruction of Religious Thought in Islam.* Lahore: Sang-e Meel Publications, 1996.

Jalal, Ayesha. *The Sole Spokesman: Jinnah, the Muslim League and the Demand for Pakistan.* Cambridge: Cambridge University Press, 1985.

Jameson, Frederic. "Third-World Literature in the Era of Multinational Capital." *Social Text* 15 (Fall 1986): 65–88.

Jones, Donna. "The Career of Living Things is Continuous: Reflections of Bergson, Iqbal, and Scalia." *Qui Parle* 20, no. 2 (Spring-Summer 2012): 225–48.

King, Christopher R. *One Language, Two Scripts: The Hindi Movement in Nineteenth Century North India.* New York: Oxford University Press, 1994.

Knysch, Alexander D. *Ibn ʿArabi in the Later Islamic Tradition: The Making of a Polemical Image in Medieval Islam.* Albany: State University of New York Press, 1999.

Lelyveld, David. *Aligarh's First Generation: Muslim Solidarity in British India.* Delhi: Oxford University Press, 1996 [1978].

———. "Colonial Knowledge and the Fate of Hindustani." *Comparative Studies in Society and History* 35, no. 4 (October 1993): 665–82.

———. "The Fate of Hindustani: Colonial Knowledge and the Project of a National Language." In *Orientalism and the Postcolonial Predicament: Perspectives on South Asia*, edited by Carol A. Breckenridge and Peter van der Veer, 189–214. Philadelphia: University of Philadelphia Press, 1993.

Luthra, H. R. *Indian Broadcasting.* New Delhi: Publications Division, Ministry of Information and Broadcasting, Government of India, 1986.

Malik, Iftikhar H. "Regionalism or Personality Cult? Allama Mashriqi and the Tehreek-i-Khaksar in pre-1947 Punjab." In *Region and Partition: Bengal, Punjab and the Partition of the Subcontinent*, edited by Ian Talbot and Gurharpal Singh, 42–94. Karachi: Oxford University Press, 1999.

Malik, Muhammad Aslam. *Allama Inayatullah Mashraqi: A Political Biography.* Karachi: Oxford University Press, 2000.

Malik, Rashida. *Iqbal: The Spiritual Father of Pakistan.* Lahore: Sang-e-Meel Publications, 2003.

Mao, Douglas, and Rebecca L. Walkowitz, eds. *Bad Modernisms.* Durham, NC: Duke University Press, 2006.

———. "The Changing Profession: The New Modernist Studies." *PMLA* 123, no. 3 (2008): 737–48.

McFarland, Stephen L. "Anatomy of an Iranian Political Crowd: The Tehran Bread Riot of December 1942." *International Journal of Middle East Studies* 17 (February 1985): 51–65.

Metcalf, Barbara Daly. *Moral Conduct and Authority: The Place of Adab in South Asian Islam.* Berkeley: University of California Press, 1984.

Mir, Farina. "Imperial Policy, Provincial Practices: Colonial Language Policy in Nineteenth-century India." *Indian Economic and Social History Review* 43, no. 4 (December 2006): 395–427.

———. *The Social Space of Language: Vernacular Culture in British Colonial Punjab.* Berkeley: University of California Press, 2010.

Mitchell, Timothy. "The Stages of Modernity." In *Questions of Modernity*, edited by Timothy Mitchell, 1–34. Minneapolis: University of Minnesota, 2000.

Mufti, Aamir R. "Aura of Authenticity." *Social Text* 18, no. 3 (2000): 87–103.

———. *Enlightenment in the Colony: The Jewish Question and the Crisis of Postcolonial Culture.* Princeton: Princeton University Press, 2007.

Naim, C. M. "The Consequences of the Indo-Pakistan War for Urdu Language and Literature: A Parting of the Ways?" *The Journal of Asian Studies* 28, no. 2 (1969): 269–83.

———. "Iqbal, Jinnah and Pakistan: The Vision and the Reality." In *Ambiguities of Heritage: Fictions and Polemics*, 111–23. Karachi: City Press, 1999.

Naqvi, Syed Nauman. "Mourning Indo-Muslim Modernity: Moments in Post-Colonial Urdu Literary Culture." PhD diss., Columbia University, 2008.

Nicholson, Reynold. "The Meditations of Ma'arrí." In *Studies in Islamic Poetry*, 43–289. Cambridge, UK: Cambridge University Press, 1921.

Orsini, Francesca. *The Hindi Public Sphere, 1910–1940: Language and Literature in the Age of Nationalism.* Delhi: Oxford University Press, 2002.

Owens, Craig. "The Allegorical Impulse: Toward a Theory of Postmodernism." *October* 12 (Spring 1980): 67–86.

———. "The Allegorical Impulse: Toward a Theory of Postmodernism, Part Two." *October* 13 (Summer 1980): 58–80.

Pal, Dharm. *Campaign in Western Asia*. Calcutta: Combined Inter-Services Historical Section, 1957.

Papan-Matin, Firoozeh. "The Crisis of Identity in Rumi's 'Tale of the Reed.'" Los Angeles: UCLA, G. E. von Grunebaum Center for Near Eastern Studies, 2005. http://escholarship.org/uc/item/4qrox826.

Patel, Geeta. *Lyrical Movements, Historical Hauntings: On Gender, Colonialism, and Desire in Mīrājī's Urdu Poetry*. Stanford: Stanford University Press, 2002.

Pritchett, Frances. *Nets of Awareness: Urdu Poetry and Its Critics*. Berkeley: University of California Press, 1994.

Pue, A. Sean. "In the Mirror of Ghalib: Postcolonial Reflections on Indo-Muslim Selfhood." *The Indian Economic and Social History Review* 48, no. 4 (2011): 571–92.

Rai, Alok. *Hindi Nationalism*. New Delhi: Orient Longman, 2000.

———. "Reading Pratik through Agyeya: Reading Agyeya through Pratik." In *Hindi Modernism*, edited by Vasudha Dalmia, 17–29. Delhi: Manohar, 2012.

Rashed, N. M. *The Dissident Voice: Poems of N. M. Ráshed*. Translated by M. A. R. Habib. Madras: Oxford University Press, 1991.

———. "Interview with N. M. Rashed." *Mahfil* 7, no. 1-2 (1971), 1–20.

———. "Social Influences on Urdu Literature." *Asia* 9 (Fall 1967): 34–50.

Robbins, Bruce. "Actually Existing Cosmopolitanism." In *Cosmopolitics*, edited by Pheng Cheah and Bruce Robbins, 1–19. Minneapolis: University of Minnesota Press, 1998.

Rosenstein, Lucy. *New Poetry in Hindi (Nayi Kavita): An Anthology*. New Delhi: Permanent Black, 2002.

Said, Edward. *Culture and Imperialism*. New York: Vintage Books, 1994.

Schimmel, Annemarie. *As Through a Veil: Mystical Poetry in Islam*. New York: Columbia University Press, 1982.

———. *The Feminine in Islam*. Translated by Susan H. Ray. New York: Continuum, 2003.

———. "Sacred Geography in Islam." In *Sacred Places and Profane Spaces: Essays in the Geographies of Judaism, Christianity, and Islam*, edited by Jamie Scott and Paul Simpson-Housley, 163–75. New York: Greenwood Press, 1991.

———. *The Triumphal Sun: A Study of the Works of Jalāloddin Rumi*. Albany: State University of New York Press, 1993.

Schomer, Karine. *Mahadevi Varma and the Chhayavad Age of Modern Hindi Poetry*. Berkeley: University of California Press, 1983.

Scott, Joan W. "The Evidence of Experience." *Critical Inquiry* 17, no. 4 (Summer 1991): 773–97.

"Soviet Scolds Iran For Denying Its Oil." *New York Times*, 30 October 1944.

Spivak, Gayatri Chakravorty. *Death of A Discipline.* New York: Columbia University Press, 2003.
———. *Other Asias.* Malden, MA: Blackwell Publishing, 2008.
———. "Scattered Speculations on the Subaltern and the Popular." *Postcolonial Studies* 8, no. 4 (2005): 475–86.
Stark, Ulrike. *An Empire of Books: The Naval Kishore Press and the Diffusion of the Printed Word in South Asia.* New Delhi: Permanent Black, 2007.
Steele, Laurel. "Ḥālī and His *Muqaddamah*: The Creation of a Literary Attitude in Nineteenth Century India." *Annual of Urdu Studies* 1 (1981): 1–45.
"Tahlīl." In *Encyclopaedia of Islam, Second Edition.* Brill Online, 2012. http://www.brillonline.nl/subscriber/entry?entry=islam_SIM-7312.
Talat, Ahmed. *Literature and Politics in the Age of Nationalism: The Progressive Writers' Movement in South Asia, 1932–56.* New Delhi: Routledge, 2009.
Tambling, Jeremy. *Allegory.* New York: Routledge, 2010.
Tavakoli-Targhi, Mohamad. "Refashioning Iran: Language and Culture during the Constitutional Revolution." *Iranian Studies* 23, no. 1 (1990): 77–101.
Toor, Sadia. "A National Culture for Pakistan: The Political Economy of a Debate." *Inter-Asia Cultural Studies* 6, no. 3 (2005): 318–40.
Viswanathan, Gauri. *Masks of Conquest: Literary Study and British Rule in India.* New York: Columbia University Press, 1989.
Wollaeger, Mark, with Matt Eatough, ed. *The Oxford Handbook of Global Modernisms.* New York: Oxford University Press, 2012.

WORKS IN URDU AND PERSIAN

ʿAbduʾl-ḥamīd, Āġhā. "Rāshid: chand ḳhaṯ, chand yādeñ." In *N. M. Rāshid: ek muṯālaʿah*, edited by Jamīl Jālibī, 38–44. Karachi: Maktabah-e uslūb, 1986.
Āftāb Aḥmad. "N. M. Rāshid." *Adab-e laṯīf* 17-18, no. 6-7 (August-September 1943): 5–13.
———. *N. M Rāshid: shāʿir-o-shaḳhṣ.* Lahore: Māvarā Publishers, 1989.
———. "Rāshid kī yād meñ." *Nayā Daur* 71, no. 2 (1978?): 272.
Aḳhtar Aḥmad Aḳhtar, Sayyid. "Urdū kī rūmānī shāʿirī aur Aḳhtar Shairānī." In Aḳhtar Shairānī, *Ṣubḥ-e bahār*, 17–41. Dehli: Maktabah-e anokhā jāsūs, 1971.
Aḳhtar Ḥusain Rāʾepūrī. *Adab aur inqilāb.* Hyderabad, India: Idārah-e ishāʿat-e urdū, 1943.
Aḳhtar Jaʿfrī, S., ed. *Aḳhtar Shairānī aur us kī shāʿirī.* Lahore: Āʾinah-e adab, 1964.
Aḳhtar Shairānī. *Kulliyāt-e Aḳhtar Shairānī.* Edited by Gopāl Mittal. Delhi: Modern Publishing House, 1997.
———. *Ṣubḥ-e bahār.* Dehli: Maktabah-e anokhā jāsūs, 1971.
ʿĀlam Ḳhūndmīrī. "N. M. Rāshid, insān aur ḳhudā." In *N. M. Rāshid: fikr-o-fan*, edited by Kuñvar Muḥammad Aḳhlāq Ḳhāñ Shahryār and Muġhannī Tabassum, 52–59. Hyderabad, India: Maktabah-e shĕʿr-o-ḥikmat, 1971.

ʿAskarī, Muḥammad Ḥasan. *Jadīdiyat yā maġhribī gumrāhiyōñ kī tārīḵh kā ḵhākah.* Rawalpindi, Pakistan: ʿIffat Ḥasan, 1979.

Āzād, Muḥammad Ḥusain. *Āb-e ḥayāt: Shaping the Canon of Urdu Poetry.* Translated and edited by Frances Pritchett with Shamsur Rahman Faruqi. New Delhi: Oxford University Press, 2001.

———. *Nairang-e ḵhayāl.* Lahore: Āzād Book Depot, 1905.

ʿAzīz Aḥmad. *Taraqqī pasand adab.* New Delhi: Chaman Book Depot, [1945].

Aʿẓmī, Ḵhalīlu'r-raḥmân. "Rāshid kā żahnī irtiqā." In *N. M. Rāshid: fikr-o-fan*, edited by Kuñvar Muḥammad Aḵhlāq Ḵhāñ Shahryār and Muġhannī Tabassum, 16–31. Hyderabad, India: Maktabah-e shĕʿr-o-ḥikmat, 1971.

———. *Urdū meñ taraqqī pasand adabī taḥrīk.* Aligarh: Educational Book House, 1996 [1957].

Ĕʿjāz Ḥusain Baṭālvī. "Āḵhirī majmūʿah, āḵhirī mulāqāt." In the forward to *Gumāñ kā mumkin*, by N. M. Rāshid. Lahore: Nayā idārah, 1976.

Fārūqī, Shamsu'r-raḥmân. *Shĕʿr-e shor-angez.* Vol. 1. New Delhi: Taraqqī-e urdū Bureau, 1990.

Fatḥ Muḥammad Malik. *N. M. Rāshid: siyāsat aur shāʿirī.* Islamabad: Dost Publications, 2010.

Ġhulām Rasūl Makrānī. *Urdū meñ tamšīl nigārī.* Gorakhpur: Offset Press, 1988.

Gyān Chand Jain. "Urdū meñ tamšīl nigārī." In *Taḥrīreñ*, 269–92. Delhi: Idārah-e furoġh-e urdū, 1964.

Ḥālī, Alṭāf Ḥusain. *Muqaddamah-e shĕʿr o shāʿirī.* Lucknow: Uttar Pradesh Urdu Academy, 2002 [1893].

Ḥamīd Nasīm. *Pāñch jadīd urdū shāʿir.* New Delhi: Maktabah Jāmiʿah, 1997.

Ḥanīf Kaifī. *Urdū meñ naẓm-e muʿarrā aur āzād naẓm: ibtidā se 1947 tak.* New Delhi: privately printed, 1982.

———. *Urdū shāʿirī meñ sānit.* New Delhi: privately printed, 1975.

Ḥayātu'l-lâh Anṣārī. *N. M. Rāshid par.* New Delhi: Insha Press, 1945.

"Idāriyyah." *Nayā Daur* 39–40 (n.d.), 5–7.

Iqbāl, Muḥammad. "Al-vaqt saif." In *Asrār-e ḵhvudī*, in *Kulliyāt-e Iqbāl fārsī*, 71–75. Lahore: Shaiḵh Ġhulām ʿAli and Sons, 1973.

———. *Asrār-e ḵhvudī.* In *Kulliyāt-e Iqbāl fārsī*, 1–170. Lahore: Shaiḵh Ġhulām ʿAlī and Sons, 1973.

———. *Jāved-nāmah.* In *Kulliyāt-e Iqbāl fārsī*, 589–796. Lahore: Shaiḵh Ġhulām ʿAlī and Sons, 1973.

———. "Ḵhiẓr-e rāh." In *Bāng-e darā*, in *Kulliyāt-e Iqbāl urdū*, 283–96. Lahore: Iqbal Academy, 1997.

———. *Kulliyāt-e Iqbāl fārsī.* Lahore: Shaiḵh Ġhulām ʿAlī and Sons, 1973.

———. *Kulliyāt-e Iqbāl urdū.* Lahore: Iqbal Academy, 1997.

———. "Miṭā diyā mire sāqī ne ʿālam-e man-o-tū." In *Bāl-e jibrīl*, in *Kulliyāt-e Iqbāl urdū*, 352. Lahore: Iqbal Academy Pakistan, 1997.

———. "Paiġhām-e bergsān." In *Payām-e mashriq*, in *Kulliyāt-e Iqbāl farsī*, 377. Lahore: Shaiḵh Ġhulām ʿAlī and Sons, 1973.

———. *Rumūz-e be-k̲h̲vudī.* In *Kulliyāt-e Iqbāl fārsī*, 85–169. Lahore: Shaik̲h̲ Ġhulām ʿAlī and Sons, 1973.

———. "Sāqī-nāmah." In *Bāl-e jibrīl*, in *Kulliyāt-e Iqbāl urdū*, 450–57. Lahore: Iqbal Academy Pakistan, 1997.

———. "Ṭulūʿ-e islām." In *Bāng-e darā*, in *Kulliyāt-e Iqbāl urdū*, 297–307. Lahore: Iqbal Academy, 1997.

———. "Yūrap se ek k̲h̲aṭ." In *Bāl-e jibrīl*, in *Kulliyāt-e Iqbāl urdū*, 479. Lahore: Iqbal Academy Pakistan, 1997.

ʿIshqī, Mīrzādah. "Rastak̲h̲īz-e salāṭīn-e īrān." In *Dīvān-e ʿIshqī*, 25–35. Tehran: Āftāb, 1941.

Jaʿfrī, ʿAlī Sardār. *Taraqqī pasand adab.* Aligarh: Anjuman-e Taraqqī-e Urdū, 1951.

———. *Eshiyā jāg uṭhā.* Delhi: Maktabah-e Shāhrāh, 1952.

Jamīl Jālibī, ed. *N. M. Rāshid: ek muṭālaʿah.* Karachi: Maktabah-e uslūb, 1986.

Manẓar Aʿẓmī. *Urdū meñ tamsīl nigārī.* New Delhi: Anjuman-e taraqqī-e urdū, 1977.

Mīr, Mīr Tāqī. *Kulliyāt-e Mīr.* New Delhi: National Council for the Promotion of Urdu, 2003.

Mīrājī. "Raqṣ." In *N. M. Rāshid: fikr-o-fan*, edited by Kuñvar Muḥammad Ak̲h̲lāq K̲h̲āñ Shahryār and Muġhannī Tabassum, 235. Hyderabad, India: Maktabah-e shĕʿr-o-ḥikmat, 1971.

Muġhannī Tabassum. "Mujhe vidāʿ kar." In *N. M. Rāshid: fikr-o-fan*, edited by Kuñvar Muḥammad Ak̲h̲lāq K̲h̲āñ Shahryār and Muġhannī Tabassum, 254–66. Hyderabad, India: Maktabah-e shĕʿr-o-ḥikmat, 1971.

———. "N. M. Rāshid: muk̲h̲taṣar ḥālāt-e zindagī." In *N. M. Rāshid: fikr-o-fan*, edited by Kuñvar Muḥammad Ak̲h̲lāq K̲h̲āñ Shahryār and Muġhannī Tabassum, 10–14. Hyderabad, India: Maktabah-e shĕʿr-o-ḥikmat, 1971.

Muḥammad Fak̲h̲ruʾl-ḥaq Nūrī. *Muṭālaʿah-e Rāshid: chand naʾe zāviye.* Faisalabad: Mis̤āl Publishers, 2010.

"N. M. Rāshid kī āk̲h̲irī vaṣiyyat: lāsh ko jalā diyā jāʾe aur merī namāz nah paṛhī jāʾe." *Chaṭān* 28, no. 43 (27 October 1975): 5.

Paṭras Buk̲h̲ārī, Aḥmad Shāh. "Tamhīd." In N. M. Rāshid, *Irān meñ ajnabī aur dūsarī naẓmeñ*, 7–20. Lahore: Goshah-e adab, 1957.

Qāsmī, Abuʾl-kalām, ed. *Mashriq kī bāzyāft: Muḥammad Ḥasan ʿAskarī ke ḥavāle se.* Aligarh: Naʾī Nasl Publications, 1982.

Rāshid, N. M. "Afsānah-e shahr." In *Lā = Insān*, 119–20. Lahore: al-Mis̤āl, 1969.

———. "Āzād shāʿirī." In *Maqālāt-e N. M. Rāshid*, edited by Shīmā Majīd, 8–15. Islamabad: Alhamra, 2002. Originally published in *Ilhām* (May 1941).

———. "Bādal (sāneṭ)." In *Māvarā*, 2nd ed., 47. Lahore: Maktabah-e urdū, [1941].

———. "Chand lamḥe Ak̲h̲tar Shairānī ke sāth." In *Maqālāt-e N. M. Rāshid*, edited by Shīmā Majīd (Islamabad: Alhamra, 2002), 347-366. Originally published in *Ak̲h̲taristān*.

———. "Darvesh." In *Īrān meñ ajnabī*, 75–79. Lahore: Goshah-e adab, 1957.

———. "Dībāchah." In *Māvarā*, 2nd ed., 23–32. Lahore: Maktabah-e urdū, [1941].

———. "Dil, mire ṣaḥrā-navard-e pīr dil." In *Lā = Insān*, 54–63. Lahore: al-Mis̤āl, 1969.

———. "Ek aur shahr." In *Lā = Insān*, 49–50. Lahore: al-Mis̤āl, 1969.
———. "Ek din—lārins bāġh meñ (ek kaifiyat)." In *Māvarā*, 2nd ed., 43–44. Lahore: Maktabah-e urdū, [1941].
———. "Ek ḳhaṭ." 1 January 1967. *Nayā daur* 47-48 (n.d.): 424–431.
———. "Ek ḳhaṭ (Salīm Aḥmad ke nām)." In *N. M. Rāshid: fikr-o-fan*, edited by Kuñvar Muḥammad Aḳhlāq Ḳhāñ Shahryār and Muġhannī Tabassum, 325–30. Hyderabad, India: Maktabah-e shĕʻr-o-ḥikmat, 1971.
———. "Ek muṣāhibah." In *Lā = Insān*, 1–36. Lahore: al-Mis̤āl, 1969.
———. "Ġhālib hamāre zamāne meñ." In *N. M. Rāshid: fikr-o-fan*, edited by Kuñvar Muḥammad Aḳhlāq Ḳhāñ Shahryār and Muġhannī Tabassum, 331–43. Hyderabad, India: Maktabah-e shĕʻr-o-ḥikmat, 1971.
———. *Gumāñ kā mumkin: jo tū hai maiñ hūñ*. Lahore: Nayā idārah, 1976.
———. "Gumāñ kā mumkin—jo tū hai maiñ hūñ!" In *Gumāñ kā mumkin: jo tū hai maiñ hūñ*, 128–34. Lahore: Nayā idārah, 1976.
———. "Gunāh aur muḥabbat." In *Māvarā*, 2nd ed., 90–91. Lahore: Maktabah-e urdū, [1941].
———. "Ḥālāt-o-kavāʼif." In *N. M. Rāshid: ek muṭālaʻah*, edited by Jamīl Jālibī, 7–12. Karachi: Maktabah-e uslūb, 1986.
———. "Ḥalqah-e arbāb-e żauq." In *N. M. Rāshid: fikr-o-fan*, edited by Kuñvar Muḥammad Aḳhlāq Ḳhāñ Shahryār and Muġhannī Tabassum, 376–84. Hyderabad, India: Maktabah-e shĕʻr-o-ḥikmat, 1971.
———. "Hamah ūst." In *Īrān meñ ajnabī*, 59–65. Lahore: Goshah-e adab, 1957.
———. "Ḥasan kūzah-gar." In *Lā = Insān*, 37–42. Lahore: al-Mis̤āl, 1969.
———. "Ḥasan kūzah-gar (2)." In *Gumāñ kā mumkin: jo tū hai maiñ hūñ*, 50–55. Lahore: Nayā idārah, 1976.
———. "Ḥasan kūzah-gar (3)." In *Gumāñ kā mumkin: jo tū hai maiñ hūñ*, 89–94. Lahore: Nayā idārah, 1976.
———. "Ḥasan kūzah-gar (4)." In *Gumāñ kā mumkin: jo tū hai maiñ hūñ*, 135–40. Lahore: Nayā idārah, 1976.
———. "Ḥuzn-e insān (aflāṭūnī ʻishq par ek ṭanz)." In *Māvarā*, 2nd ed., 76–77. Lahore: Maktabah-e urdū, [1941].
———. "Ibtidā-e suḳhan." Interview by Saʻādat Saʻīd. In Saʻādat Saʻīd, *Rāshid aur s̤iqāfatī muġhāʼirāt*, 5–7. Lahore: Department of Urdu, Government College University, 2010.
———. *Īrān meñ ajnabī aur dūsarī naẓmeñ*. Lahore: Goshah-e adab, 1957.
———. *Īrān meñ ajnabī*. 4th ed. Lahore: al-Mis̤āl, 1969.
———. "Is peṛ pah hai būm kā sāyah." In *Lā = Insān*, 157–60. Lahore: al-Mis̤āl, 1969.
———. "Ittifāqāt." In *Māvarā*, 2nd ed., 73–75. Lahore: Maktabah-e urdū, [1941].
———. *Jadid fārsī shāʻirī*. Lahore: Majlis-e taraqqī-e adab, 1987.
———. *Jadīd fārsī shāʻirī: taqrīr az N. M. Rāshid*. Lahore: al-Mis̤āl, 1969.
———. "Kīmiyāgar." In *Īrān meñ ajnabī*, 53–58. Lahore: Goshah-e adab, 1957.
———. *Lā = Insān*. Lahore: al-Mis̤āl, 1969.
———. Letter to Āftāb Aḥmad. New York, 25 June 1963. In Āftāb Aḥmad, *N. M. Rāshid: shāʻir-o-shaḳhṣ*, 124–28. Lahore: Māvarā Publishers, 1989.

———. Letter to Āġhā ʿAbdu'l-ḥamid. Columbo, 30 July 1946. In *N. M. Rāshid: ek muṯālaʿah*, edited by Jamīl Jālibī, 242–43. Karachi: Maktabah-e uslūb, 1986.

———. Letter to Āġhā ʿAbdu'l-ḥamid. Delhi, 1 April 1940. In *N. M. Rāshid: ek muṯālaʿah*, edited by Jamīl Jālibī, 240–41. Karachi: Maktabah-e uslūb, 1986.

———. Letter to Jamīl Jālibī. Tehran, 17 February 1968. In *N. M. Rāshid: ek muṯālaʿah*, edited by Jamīl Jālibī, 295. Karachi: Maktabah-e uslūb, 1986.

———. "Mann-o-salvâ." In *Īrān meñ ajnabī*, 35–40. Lahore: Goshah-e adab, 1957.

———. *Māvarā*. 2nd ed. Lahore: Maktabah-e urdū, [1941].

———. "Mere bhī haiñ kuchh ḳhvāb." In *Lā=Insān*, 68–72. Lahore: al-Mis̤āl, 1969.

———. "Mukāfāt." In *Māvarā*, 2nd ed., 50–52. Lahore: Maktabah-e urdū, [1941].

———. *N. M. Rāshid ke ḳhuṯūṯ, apnī ahiliyah ke nām*. Edited by Nasrīn Rāshid. Islamabad: A. R. Printers, 2010.

———. "N. M. Rāshid se ek muṣāhibah." Interview by Nasrīn Anjum Bhaṭṭī. In *Rāshid ba-qalam-e ḳhvud*, edited by Saʿādat Saʿīd and Nasrīn Anjum Bhaṭṭī, 36–108. Lahore: Department of Urdu, Government College, 2010.

———. "N. M. Rāshid se ek muṣāḥibah." Interview by Saʿādat Saʿīd, 1969. In *Maqālāt-e N. M. Rāshid*, edited by Shīmā Majīd, 385–93. Islamabad: Alhamra Publishing, 2002.

———. "Namrūd kī ḳhudāʾī." In *Īrān meñ ajnabī*, 114–16. Lahore: Goshah-e adab, 1957.

———. *Rāshid: Rāvī meñ*. Edited by Saʿādat Saʿīd and Muḥammad Rafīq. Lahore: Department of Urdu, Government College University, 2010.

———. "Reg-e dīrūz." In *Lā=Insān*, 47–48. Lahore: al-Mis̤āl, 1969.

———. "Shāʿir-e dar-māñdah." In *Māvarā*, 2nd ed., 94–95. Lahore: Maktabah-e urdū, [1941].

———. "Sitāre (sāneṭ)." In *Māvarā*, 2nd ed., 45. Lahore: Maktabah-e urdū, [1941].

———. "Ṯalab ke tale." In *Gumāñ kā mumkin: jo tū hai maiñ hūñ*, 26–28. Lahore: Nayā Idārah, 1976.

———. "Tamannā ke tār." In *Lā=Insān*, 91–93. Lahore: al-Mis̤āl, 1969.

———. "Tamāshā-gah-e lālah-zār." In *Īrān meñ ajnabī*, 97–100. Lahore: Goshah-e adab, 1957.

———. "Tel ke saudāgar." In *Īrān meñ ajnabī*, 84–88. Lahore: Goshah-e adab, 1957.

———. "Ṯilism-e azal." In *Īrān meñ ajnabī*, 127–29. Lahore: Goshah-e adab, 1957.

———. "Vādī-e pinhāñ." In *Māvarā*, 2nd ed., 65–66. Lahore: Maktabah-e urdū, [1941].

———. "Vuh ḥarf-e tanhā (jise tamannā-e vaṣl-e maʿnā)." In *Lā=Insān*, 108–10. Lahore: al-Mis̤āl, 1969.

———. "Yih ḳhalā pur nah huʾā." In *Gumāñ kā mumkin: jo tū hai maiñ hūñ*, 23–25. Lahore: Nayā Idārah, 1976.

———. "Zamānah ḳhudā hai." In *Lā=Insān*, 126–28. Lahore: al-Mis̤āl, 1969.

———. "Zindagī se ḍarte ho?" In *Lā=Insān*, 94–96. Lahore: al-Mis̤āl, 1969.

——— [Rāshid Vaḥīdī, pseud.]. "Bādal." *Humāyūñ* 20, no. 4 (October 1931): 790.

——— [Rāshid Vaḥīdī, pseud.]. "Sitāre." *Humāyūñ* 20, no. 3 (September 1931): 701.

——— [Rāshid Vaḥīdī, pseud.]. "Zindagī." *Humāyūñ* 17, no. 4 (January 1930): 379.
Rāshid, Shahryār. "Mere valid." Translated by Intiẓār Ḥusain. In Āftāb Aḥmad, *N. M. Rāshid: shā'ir-o-shakḥṣ*, 11–22. Lahore: Māvarā Publishers, 1989.
Sa'ādat Sa'īd. *Rāshid aur s̄iqāfatī muġhā'irat*. Lahore: Department of Urdu, Government College University, 2010.
Salīm Aḥmad. *Na'ī naẓm aur pūrā ādmī*. Karachi: Adabī Academy, 1962.
Salīm Akḥtar. "N. M. Rāshid kā matrūk kalām." In *Maqālāt-e ḥalqah-e arbāb-e żauq*, edited by Suhail Aḥmad, 190–217. Lahore: Polimar Publications, 1990.
———. *Nafsiyātī tanqīd*. Lahore: Majlis-e taraqqī-e adab, 1986.
Sāqī Fārūqī. "Ḥasan Kūzahgar." *Nayā daur* 71-2 (1978?): 17–40.
Shahryār, Kuñvar Muḥammad Akḥlāq Ḳhāñ, and Muġhannī Tabassum, ed. *N. M. Rāshid: fikr-o-fan*. Hyderabad, India: Maktabah-e shĕ'r-o-ḥikmat, 1971.
Tabassum Kāshmīrī. *Lā = Rāshid*. Lahore: Nigārishāt, 1994.
———. *Urdū meñ 'alāmat nigārī*. Lahore: Sang-e Meel Publications, 1975.
Tahsīn Firāqī, ed. *Ḥasan Kūzahgar*. Lahore: Department of Urdu, Oriental College, 2010.
Vazīr Āġhā. "N. M. Rāshid." In *N. M. Rāshid: ek mutāla'ah*, edited by Jamīl Jālibī, 182–85. Karachi: Maktabah-e uslūb, 1986.
Yāsmīn Rāshid Ḥasan. "Vaẓāḥat." *Bunyād* 1 (2010): 294–98.
Yazdī, Farrukḥī. *Dīvān-e Farrukḥī Yazdī*. Tehran: Bunyād-e naśr-e kitāb, 1984.
Ẓiyā Jālandharī. "Īrān meñ ajnabī." In *N. M. Rāshid: fikr-o-fan*, edited by Kuñvar Muḥammad Akḥlāq Ḳhāñ Shahryār and Muġhannī Tabassum, 147–51. Hyderabad, India: Maktabah-e shĕ'r-o-ḥikmat, 1971.

INDEX

South Asia Across the Disciplines is a series devoted to publishing first books across a wide range of South Asian studies, including art, history, philology or textual studies, philosophy, religion, and the interpretive social sciences. Series authors all share the goal of opening up new archives and suggesting new methods and approaches, while demonstrating that South Asian scholarship can be at once deep in expertise and broad in appeal.

Extreme Poetry: The South Asian Movement of Simultaneous Narration by Yigal Bronner (Columbia)

The Social Space of Language: Vernacular Culture in British Colonial Punjab by Farina Mir (California)

Unifying Hinduism: Philosophy and Identity in Indian Intellectual History by Andrew J. Nicholson (Columbia)

The Powerful Ephemeral: Everyday Healing in an Ambiguously Islamic Place by Carla Bellamy (California)

Secularizing Islamists? Jamaʿat-e-Islami and Jamaʿat-ud-Daʿwa in Urban Pakistan by Humeira Iqtidar (Chicago)

Islam Translated: Literature, Conversion, and the Arabic Cosmopolis of South and Southeast Asia by Ronit Ricci (Chicago)

Conjugations: Marriage and Form in New Bollywood Cinema by Sangita Gopal (Chicago)

Unfinished Gestures: Devadāsīs, Memory, and Modernity in South India by Davesh Soneji (Chicago)

Document Raj: Writing and Scribes in Early Colonial South India by Bhavani Raman (Chicago)

The Millennial Sovereign: Sacred Kingship and Sainthood in Islam by A. Azfar Moin (Columbia)

Making Sense of Tantric Buddhism: History, Semiology, and Transgression in the Indian Traditions by Christian K. Wedemeyer (Columbia)

The Yogin and the Madman: Reading the Biographical Corpus of Tibet's Great Saint Milarepa by Andrew Quintman (Columbia)

Body of Victim, Body of Warrior: Refugee Families and the Making of Kashmiri Jihadists by Cabeiri deBergh Robinson (California)

Receptacle of the Sacred: Illustrated Manuscripts and the Buddhist Book Cult in South Asia by Jinah Kim (California)

Cut-Pieces: Celluloid Obscenity and Popular Cinema in Bangladesh by Lotte Hoek (Columbia)

From Text to Tradition: The Naisadhīyacarita *and Literary Community in South Asia* by Deven M. Patel (Columbia)

Democracy against Development: Lower Caste Politics and Political Modernity in Postcolonial India by Jeffrey Witsoe (Chicago)

Into the Twilight of Sanskrit Poetry: The Sena Salon of Bengal and Beyond, by Jesse Ross Knutson (California)

Voicing Subjects: Public Intimacy and Mediation in Kathmandu, by Laura Kunreuther (California)

Writing Resistance: The Rhetorical Imagination of Hindi Dalit Literature by Laura R. Brueck (Columbia)

Wombs in Labor: Transnational Commercial Surrogacy in India by Amrita Pande (Columbia)

I Too Have Some Dreams: N. M. Rashed and Modernism in Urdu Poetry by A. Sean Pue (California)

www.ingramcontent.com/pod-product-compliance
Lightning Source LLC
Chambersburg PA
CBHW020936310726
48980CB00007B/792/J

* 9 7 8 0 5 2 0 2 8 3 1 0 7 *